Jews in the Modern World

VOLUME
ONE

Jews
in the
Modern
World

Edited by
JACOB FREID

Twayne Publishers, Inc.   New York

MANUFACTURED IN THE UNITED STATES OF AMERICA BY
UNITED PRINTING SERVICES, INC.
NEW HAVEN, CONN.

TO JANET AND ALLISON

ACKNOWLEDGMENTS

The editor expresses his grateful appreciation to the publishers and authors who granted permission to quote from their material. In addition to the original essays written expressly for this book, the following have been particularly helpful:

The late Samuel M. Levitas and the editors of the *New Leader* for use of their special study of the "Jews in the Soviet Union."

Nathan Belth, for permission to reprint his and Benjamin Epstein's selections from *Barriers*, published by the anti-Defamation League in 1958.

The American Jewish Committee for "The Unequal Treatment of Equals" by John Slawson.

The American Jewish Congress for permission to reprint and update the *Jewish Affairs* pamphlets included here, and the Institute for Jewish Affairs of the World Jewish Congress for access to sources of information.

The American Association for Jewish Education, for permission to include the findings of the Commission for the Study of Jewish Education in the United States in Uriah Z. Engelman's essay "Educating the Jewish Child."

Sam Block, Department of Publications Jewish Agency, for permission to reprint Moshe Sharett's "Jewry between East and West," Robert Gordis' "Judah and Israel," Mordecai M. Kaplan's "The Next Step in Zionism," Nathan Roterstreich's "Judaism in the World of Our Day," David Ben Gurion's "Vision and Redemption," and Salo Baron's "The Dialogue between Israel and Diaspora" from #4 of FORUM, *The Proceedings of the Jerusalem Ideological Conference.*

Cornell University Press for permission to reprint the brief by Alexander Pekelis on "Freedom of the Air" from his book, *Law and Social Action.*

CONTENTS

INTRODUCTION

Arthur Ruppin's book, *Jews in the Modern World*, was published in 1934, with an introduction by Prof. L. B. Namier who arranged for its publication in English.[1] Namier said: "We [the Jews] have a right to demand from anti-Semites, if sane and civilized, that they should honestly try to acquaint themselves with the facts of the problem which seems to exercise their minds." The Eisenhower invitation to Premier Nikita S. Khrushchev of the Soviet Union to visit the United States held out a similar hope—since battered by the summit blow-up—that the premier's first-hand experiences and observations would help overcome misinformation, miscomprehensions and misapprehensions as the prerequisite to easing tensions between Moscow and Washington, and perhaps open the way to a better understanding.

Unfortunately, Namier's demand went unheeded. For Dr. Ruppin, who was Professor of Sociology at the Hebrew University, offered a plenitude of material to friends and foes who wished to be informed. Primarily, however, the book was published for the wide Jewish public in English-speaking countries, who by 1934 were already the single most numerous and most influential body in Jewry. To English-speaking Jewry its information was a helpful guide to its own counsels and actions.

The quarter century since Ruppin's book appeared has been a period of double climacteric for the Jewish people.

The horror of Hitler and the miracle of Israel redeemed and reclaimed in independent statehood were still but a dread and

[1]Arthur Ruppin, *Jews in the Modern World* (New York: Macmillan & Co., 1934). In 1940 he published *Faith and Future* dealing with the same problems.

a hope in 1934. Ruppin's demographic studies estimated some 16,000,000 Jews as its world population, the highest total in Jewish history as registered on the eve of the atavistic Nazi *judenrein* program. Jacob Lestchinsky's "Balance Sheets of Extermination" are a melancholic catalogue of this catastrophe. Following the destruction of the Jewish state in 70 C. E., the Jewish population center shifted. Of some four and one-half million Jews, only one million remained in Palestine. Most of Jewry was scattered from Baghdad to Alexandria. This marked the Oriental period of Jewish history.

In the eleventh century world, Jewry's spiritual and political hub began to shift to Spain. By the year 1492 when Christopher Columbus discovered the New World, Sephardic Jews were, even numerically, the foremost body in Jewry. The Inquisition's persecutions and expulsions rang down the curtain on the Spanish or Iberian stage of Jewish history.

During the next three centuries the Jewish population remained comparatively low. By the time the French Revolution of 1789 ushered in the modern era of Emancipation by according full citizenship to the Jews in France, world Jewry numbered about two and one half millions. By 1800 almost half that number lived in the territory of the late Kingdom of Poland. Study of the birth rate statistics shows that this shift was as much the result of differences in the rate of national increase as of the migrations of the nomadic Jews.

With the growth of Chassidism at the end of the eighteenth and the beginning of the nineteenth century, the age of Yiddish Jewry—brought to life again so evocatively by Menahem Boraisha in "The Story of Yiddish"—began. The democratic-religious movement founded by the Baal Shem Tov sought to better the lowly lot of the common man through religion. It attracted the Jewish population of the Pales of Settlement and gave vital stimulus to the growth of Yiddish. The nineteenth century is the century of the Yiddish-speaking Jew of Eastern Europe and his way of life in his community known as the "Shtetl," and of the intellectual and economic predominance of the German Jew.

The next hundred and thirty-three years until 1933 witnessed

the greatest growth of world Jewry. The estimated population
figures were:

1825	3,250,000	Jews
1850	4,750,000	"
1880	7,500,000	"
1900	10,500,000	"
1925	15,000,000	"
1933 nearly	16,000,000	"
1961 some	12,650,000	"

The numbers and the social, economic and political conditions
of life of the Jewish people may serve as a barometric index
of the degree of world civilization in general and of national
morality and democracy in particular. In the years between
the Treaty of Paris in 1919 and the Fall of Paris in 1940 it
plumbed the depths. The rays of the beacon of the Statue
of Liberty, which shone so brilliantly for the steerage hordes
of Jewish migrants during the late nineteenth and early twentieth centuries, was shrouded by American quota immigration
laws; and Jewish children and grandchildren, who had not
had the biological foresight to be born to parents who had
emigrated before the entrance gates were closed, were caught
in the Hitler death trap.

Since 1933 European Jewry has been reduced to a fraction
of its former numbers. Shtetl life is a wraith of memory, the
subject of books and articles such as *Life is With People* and
The World of Sholom Aleichem by Maurice Samuel. Kasrilevke
is no more. The photo exhibit of its life in the new YIVO building in mid-town New York City in 1959, was a nostalgic, heart-
tugging memorial to a center of Jewish culture and religious
scholarship that invigorated Jewish living everywhere.

Already, in 1934, Namier prophesied that "in Soviet Russia,
Jewry faces dissolution. Religion and occupational segregation
acted in the Diaspora as barriers to social intercourse, assimilation and intermarriage. But in Russia, the Jewish religion is
dying, and the Jewish professions have been destroyed."[2]

[2] *Ibid.*, p. xxiii.

Certainly, today in the Soviet Union the Russian Jewish communities are prevented from living their own way of life. In 1959 Nahum Goldmann pronounced the verdict of post-World War II failure to make a viable Jewish life possible, or else to permit emigration, when he said, "There is no other people in the world suffering more from the cold war than the Jews." The official Soviet policy "is the complete assimilation of the Jewish community within its surroundings," he said. Anti-Semitism is practiced and encouraged in Russia today. Jewish students are discriminated against in admission to universities; military and diplomatic careers are barred to them; the list of the Soviet government elite no longer contains prominent Jewish names; Jewish religious observance and education are severely restricted; Yiddish language and culture have been virtually extirpated. Though Mr. Khrushchev did not meet with the leaders of American Jewry during his visit to the United States in 1959, he reacted testily to a question at the National Press Club in Washington, D.C., concerning the condition of the Jewish minority within the Soviet Union, with the statement that "Jews hold a place of honor," having taken a "foremost part" in the launching of the Soviet rocket to the moon. Apparently this was for Premier Khrushchev sufficient rebuttal to the charges of anti-Semitism.

In the Moslem lands of the Diaspora, Jewish life is in the process of dissolution as its remaining population funnels into Israel in the wake of the success of "Operation Magic Carpet" which marked the end of Galut Yemen by airlift. The situations of "Jews in the Soviet Union" and "Jews in Moslem Lands" are discussed in Part One.

The years since 1933 saw Israel become a state after two millennia. The other center of Jewry is the United States, with its more than five million Jews constituting the most important body in Diaspora Jewry. Today Israel and America are the two great centers of World Jewry.

The argument that Jews are safest where they are fewest, where a small number can fade anonymously into the general population, and being lost as Jews, can rise as individuals without stirring up attention or jealousy, has been refuted by the

more than five million Jews in the United States. Where Jews
are such minute demographic islands, Professor Namier says,
they are engulfed by the surrounding sea of people and "quickly
dissolve and disappear, and reach that supreme security which
for the Jews in the Diaspora lies in non-existence."[3] Writing
on the eve of the Nazi catastrophe in 1934, Namier asked this
question as he pondered the future of "Jews in the Modern
World":[4]

Die out we may through mixed marriages with non-Jews,
or through birth control, and both of these tendencies [as
was shown by Dr. Ruppin] have been on the increase for
some time past. But the question which the Jews must
now ask themselves is whether they can, and should, assume the responsibility for bringing Jewish children into
the world in the Galuth, to face a fate which seems to
become worse each year. It is admitted that parents
shouldn't have children for whom they cannot provide
economically; but is not the moral basis of existence at
least equally important?

The first reaction of some Jews to this contention is that
we are a valuable element and ought not to die out, not
even in the Diaspora. Valuable to whom? And if it is so,
who will lose by our dying out? Not we ourselves. There
is no loss in non-existence. And the world? Looking back
at our history of the last two thousand years we may
perhaps be excused for not worrying as to whether the
world will lose or gain by our disappearance.

Other Jews will cry out against "surrender" to our
enemies. Why pay so much attention to our enemies?
There is no surrender in a determined exit. The people
who will miss us most are the anti-Semites . . . Unless
the half-life of those long centuries can be changed at
last into an integral national existence, had it not better
come to an end?

How valid is this view today, a quarter century later? What
have been the answers of American and world Jewry? We will
attempt to consider them in this book.

[3]*Ibid.*, p. xv.
[4]*Ibid.*, p. xxviii.

The emphasis here is on American Jewry. The great majority of Jews today live in the United States, Latin America, the Soviet Union and Israel. There is a plethora of news concerning Israel in the Anglo-Jewish weeklies, and Israel is a principal subject in the various periodicals and the fiction and nonfiction titles of Jewish interest constantly being published. They are readily available to the interested reader.

The context for the essays which follow is the past quarter century, the most fateful in Jewish history since the destruction of the second Temple and the long centuries of exile and dispersion. The climactic events of the Hitler catastrophe and the creation of the State of Israel have had a vital impact upon all Jewry.

What has happened to Jews and Jewish life in the principal Jewish communities in the world during this past generation? How have they been affected by these events of death and rebirth? What are the significant trends in Jewish existence in this generation and how will they influence the next generation? How was American Jewish youth affected in the decade of the thirties, and what is its situation today? Is creative Jewish living possible in the Diaspora, and particularly in America which has become the new gravitational center of world Jewry in the wake of the destruction of the East European hub of Jewish culture, scholarship and religion?

These essays provide information and insight into these questions for intelligent lay and professional understanding of Jews in the modern world. They examine the cultural, demographic, economic, social and political characteristics of contemporary Jewish life. This is essential knowledge for those concerned with the future of Jews and Judaism, who have the responsibility of making wise provision and community planning for Jewish life in the years to come. The balance sheets of the physical and cultural extermination of European Jewry, the study of Jewish communities in Moslem lands, in the Soviet Union, in Latin America and in the United States, reveal how and why events and trends in Jewry are developing as they are today.

JACOB FREID

PART I

DIASPORA AND GALUT

Only that religion can last "forever" which, while retaining its "eternal" elements, is able to adapt itself to the changing needs and outlooks of man. Judaism has obviously been such a religion. The often-heard question: "Will Judaism survive?" is anything but disquieting to those interested in its survival. . . . It is perhaps one of Spengler's finest insights to have pointed out how "care" (*Sorge*) is fundamental to all historical feeling. And for the Jews, care as well as its opposite, firm hope (*bittahon*) has always played a prominent part. Even the troubled query as to extinction is a symptom of the will to live.

SALO BARON, *A Social and Religious History of the Jews*

CHAPTER ONE

BALANCE SHEET OF EXTERMINATION–I

by JACOB LESTCHINSKY

This is the balance sheet of the campaign to exterminate the Jews of Europe, 1939-1945.*

In a period of six years, more than one-third of the Jewish population of the world was destroyed.

At the end of 1939 there were 9½ million Jews in Europe; 3½ million survived at the close of 1945.

In Lithuania, 90% of the Jews perished; in Austria, 66%; in Holland, 60%; in Poland, 85%; in Czechoslovakia, 82.5%; in Latvia, 89.5%; in Germany, 81%; in Greece, 80%; in Yugoslavia, 73.3%. . . .

In Kielce, Poland, 243 Jews remain out of 17,840. In Kutno 50 remain out of 6,440; in Warsaw, 6,000 out of 352,559; in Leipzig, 15 out of 11,564. . . .

Thus they met their death to a total of six million, in the

* The Eichmann Trial jarred the world's conscience and memory. The retold horror by the eyewitnesses, and their reconstructed lives in Israel and in the decimated Jewish communities of Europe today should be considered from the standpoint of the situation right after liberation. These contemporary post-V-E Day accounts and analyses, by a lifelong student of the demography, culture, and community of the Jews, make it possible to view current circumstances in the sixteen-year perspective of what occurred in Nazi controlled Europe and since World War II. Lestchinsky's revelation of the profound sense of loss and pessimism of the European Jewish scholars who lived, should be compared with the reaction to the recent trial, the condition, hope and new lives of the survivors and their rebuilt families in Israel and Europe, and the Diaspora-Israel dialogue on Jewish survival in Part IV.

17

great cities, the towns and small villages. In all of Hitler's
Europe, from the flood-tide of his armies in Russia to the Atlantic Wall, Jews were sought out and destroyed, singly and in
groups, whole families and entire communities, men, women
and children, the aged and the young, until almost two-thirds
of European Jewry had been wiped out.

* * *

Who perished and what perished with them?

A nation may be bled white by war, be over-run by its
enemies and still preserve its continuity as an organized people
—so long as certain vital roots are left intact. Then time will
heal its wounds, natural increase will make up its losses and
provide incentive for the recreation of its institutions.

One-third of Europe's Jews survive but the roots which nour-
ished the main body of European Jewry are dead. In Great
Britain as well as in the few neutral countries the relatively
small Jewish communities remained intact. France, Belgium,
Romania, Hungary, Bulgaria and Italy were dominated by the
Nazis and their Jewish communities suffered cruelly. But it
was in Poland and the occupied part of the Soviet Union, with
their great Jewish communities, in the Baltic countries, in Yugoslavia, Greece, Czechoslovakia, Holland, Austria and Germany
that the slaughter of the Jews was greatest. The family and
the community, the two most important institutions in the life
of any people, and particularly significant for the landless Jewish people, were almost completely destroyed. Complete family
groups were wiped out—not in isolated instances but in the
hundreds of thousands. In those countries which lost the greatest part of their Jewish populations there are few family groups
that have as many as two surviving members. Thousands of
Jewish communities were literally obliterated; not a trace of
them remains.

Other people lost heavily in the great struggle. Among the
Russians, Poles and Yugoslavs great numbers of those who died
were soldiers who had fought on the field of battle. The civilian
population of these peoples, though depleted, retained intact
the greater part of its family structure, and the threads of

national and communal life were not completely severed even in the case of Yugoslavia. Of the Jews, however, more than 90% of those who perished were civilians. With them, in many countries of Central and Eastern Europe, perished the family, the community—all the complex structure of organized living.

The distinction between the losses of the Jews and those of other peoples goes even deeper. *There are practically no Jewish children left in Europe up to the age of ten.* An entire generation has been lost to the biological balance of the Jewish people. A later analysis will show that the Jews of Europe lost not only six million of their number but also almost any hope of increase of the surviving 3½ million between 1955 and 1985.

With the near-extinction of East European Jewry there is completely lost the vast reservoir of many of the most vital elements of Jewish life. Central and Eastern European Jewry contained within it a considerable element who were biologically the most fruitful and culturally the least assimilated of any of the Jews of Europe. Of this element of European Jewry, more than five million of six and one-half million were annihilated—more than 75%.

For the overwhelming majority of the surviving three and a half million, Europe has become a vast, terror-haunted cemetery. Almost without exception those who remained in countries formerly dominated by the Axis witnessed the torture and slaughter of their people, were themselves looted and herded like cattle from concentration camp to concentration camp, and knew the never-ending nightmare of imminent death. They know there is hardly a people in Europe which fell under Hitler's yoke whose hands are not stained with Jewish blood. What is too frequently overlooked is that not only the Germans committed mass murder but also Poles, Ukrainians, Byelo-Russians, Lithuanians, Latvians, Romanians, Hungarians, Slovaks, Croatians—a whole parade of people lent a hand to the crimes. In France, Belgium, Holland and Norway the local population took practically no part in mass murders. It is significant that Hitler transported hundreds of thousands of Jews from these countries to Poland and other countries in the East for extermination. But this does not mean that in western Europe there were no elements ready to help the Germans to deport the Jews to the gas chambers and crematoriums. Here, too, there were collaborators aplenty, who betrayed their Jewish countrymen without compunction.

Survivors Speak

It is hardly likely that the confidence of Europe's surviving Jews in their neighbors can ever be restored. They lack the will to rehabilitate themselves in the midst of the very people responsible for their ruin.

From Orany, near Vilna, a lone survivor of a family group of 160 persons, writes to his relative, Mrs. A. K. of Pittsburgh:

> We have lost our faith in mankind and in the conscience of the world. . . . We—the handful of survivors—stumble among the fiends who drained us of our blood for three years and who now want to drain from us the last remnants of our strength. . . . All of them, with the rarest exception, young and old, from the common people to the intellectuals—all of them murdered and slaughtered, tortured and looted . . . (*Forward,* July 21, 1945).

From the town of Ostrowiec, in Galicia, a letter to a *landsmanshaft* in New York from one of the few Jews left alive:

> The Jewish town of Ostrowiec is empty and desolated. Can you help us? Can you rebuild the town of our youth? Are you able to bring back to life our fathers, mothers, sisters, brothers and children? Can you recreate a family life out of broken shards and fragments?
>
> We do not want money. We want to be rescued. We want doors opened to us so that we may emigrate. There is no place for us here. We need rescue, not reconstruction. Only death faces us here. Death hovers over the few children who have survived. We are not sure of our lives. (*Forward,* December 4, 1945).

And from Kurow in Poland:

> It was not for nothing that the Germans chose Poland out of all of Europe to be the slaughterhouse for the Jews.

They knew on whom they could rely . . . (*Canadian Eagle*, November 23, 1945).

Symbol of Annihilation

Of all that was destroyed of Jewish life in Eastern and Central Europe, Warsaw stands as perhaps the starkest and most tragic symbol.

In the Jewish district of Warsaw, which covered an area approximately the same size as from 20th Street to 85th Street in New York, there lived before the war more than a quarter of a million Jews. Jews constituted more than 90% of all the residents of the area. The district was the commercial distribution center for the entire country with its 35-million population. On the Sabbath all stores and factories were closed. Jews prayed and studied the Torah in more than a hundred prayer houses and synagogues. Here on Saturday night there would be dozens of meetings and gatherings attended by tens of thousands of people. Yiddish was the prevalent tongue. In this district, five Yiddish daily newspapers were published and more than a score of Jewish weekly periodicals with a cultural influence in Jewish communities the world over. There were dozens of Yiddish and Hebrew schools, secular and parochial, yeshivas and Talmud Torahs. There were Jewish theaters drawing capacity audiences; there were many motion picture houses. The district seethed with traditional and modern Jewish culture—the new literature, political activities, religious and philosophical discussions.

The Nazis' first move was to crowd into this already congested district the more than 100,000 Jews who lived in other sections of Warsaw. It was not long before Jews from the provinces were added to the packed area. At the peak, approximately 600,000 were sealed into this narrow section of the city. In the very first year of the Hitler occupation the number of Jews who died in Warsaw alone was more than 50,000. This was the beginning of the annihilation of Polish Jewry; and step by step the process proceeded until it culminated in the mass deportations to the gas chambers of Maidanek and Oswiecim in the summer of 1942.

The Warsaw Ghetto has disappeared from the face of the earth. Not a single building has been left whole. The area is now a grass-covered desolation—the symbol of the destruction of Polish Jewry. It symbolizes, too, the destruction of all the Jewish communities of Eastern and Central Europe: Vilna and Kaunas, Cracow and Lwow, Iasi and Botosani, Riga and Dvinsk, Vienna and Berlin—and scores of other Jewish communities with tens and hundreds of thousands of members. Destroyed was the firmly-established, deeply-rooted Jewish life, the life that had created centuries-old Jewish cultural and religious values—so thoroughly destroyed that it is inconceivable that a new Jewish seed will ever again be planted in this desolated soil.

The Dead and the Living

Of a total of 9½ million Jews in Europe at the end of 1939, 6 million have since died of starvation or disease or have been slaughtered.

The number of Jews who died during that period is twenty-two times the 273,830 Americans who fell in battle; it is seventeen times greater than the 335,506 British servicemen and civilians who lost their lives.

The relative percentage of Jewish wartime deaths as compared with the losses of other people reveals the crushing extent of the disaster.

We have chosen for this table the most devastated and the least devastated nations. Among the most devastated nations the small Jewish people is at the top of the list. Relatively, Jewish

Jews in Europe	63.0%	(6,000,000 of 9,500,000)
Americans	.12%	(273,830 of 140,000,000)
British	.7%	(335,506 of 45,000,060)
Poles	8.3%	(2,000,000 of 24,000,000)
Yugoslavs	11.0%	(1,760,000 of 15,000,000)
Germans	9.0%	(7,000,000 of 78,000,000)
(Including Austrians and Sudetens)		
Russians	11.4%	(20,000,000 of 175,000,000)

(Jewish losses are of European Jewry only. Jews who died in the Allied armies are included in the total of their respective countries.)

losses were more than five times that of the Yugoslavs, almost a ninth of whose people perished. The percentage of Jewish losses is almost six times greater than the losses of the Russians, and almost eight times the losses of the Polish people, although the Poles, Yugoslavs and the Russians are generally regarded as the greatest sufferers of the war. Jewish losses in comparison with those of the British were ninety times greater; they were 525 times greater than the losses of the United States.

The losses among German and Austrian Jewry are in the higher brackets because these percentages are based on the population figures of 1939. If, however, the year 1933 is taken as the basis for computing the losses of German Jewry, and the year 1938 for the losses of Austrian Jewry, the percentage of loss will be much smaller, since the Jews in these countries

Jewish Losses in Nazi-Occupied Countries of Europe

Country*	Jewish Population September 1939	Number of Jews Lost‡	Percentage of Jews Lost
Poland	3,300,000	2,800,000	85.0
Soviet Union (Occupied area)	2,100,000	1,500,000	71.4
Romania	850,000	425,000	50.0
Hungary	404,000	200,000	49.5
Czechoslovakia	315,000	260,000	82.5
France†	300,000	90,000	30.0
Germany	210,000	170,000	81.0
Austria	60,000	40,000	66.6
Lithuania	150,000	135,000	90.0
Holland†	150,000	90,000	60.0
Latvia	95,000	85,000	89.5
Belgium†	90,000	40,000	44.4
Yugoslavia	75,000	55,000	73.3
Greece	75,000	60,000	80.0
Italy†	57,000	15,000	26.3
Bulgaria	50,000	7,000	14.0
Miscellaneous§	20,000	6,000	30.0
Totals	8,301,000	5,978,000	72.0

‡ Jews who survived annihilation have not always remained in their country of origin.

* Considered with pre-war borders.

† Figures for Holland, France, Belgium and Italy include refugees.

§ Denmark, Estonia, Luxembourg, Norway, Danzig.

managed to emigrate in large numbers in the "favorable" years
before the war, when the Nazis sought to ruin the Jews economically rather than to exterminate them.

Dead—A Generation of Children

There were practically no Jewish children up to the age
of ten left in liberated Europe in 1946. This means that between
1955 and 1975 the marriage rate between young couples will
have dwindled to negligible proportions. These decades will
witness the almost complete absence of marriages, and con-
sequent issue, of couples between the ages of 20 and 40, the
most fruitful ages for reproduction. Among survivors in the
liberated areas, there are many between the ages of 20 and 40,
but they are now, and will for a long time remain, in such
physical, psychological and economic condition as to make the
establishment of normal family life for most of them highly
improbable.

A comparison of the percentages of children up to the age of
fourteen in various Jewish communities before the war enables
us to estimate more sharply the loss to world Jewry of the Jews
of Eastern Europe. For it was among them that there was the
largest percentage of children.

Among the more than three million Polish Jews there were
approximately as many children up to the age of fourteen as
among the five million Jews in the United States. The largest
percentage of children in all Jewish communities was among
the orthodox Jewry of Carpatho-Russia. The few adults who
survived—at the most 10,000 out of 100,000—are in such cir-

Country	Children Up to 14 Years (*Percentage of Jewish Population*)
Carpatho-Russian (1930)	36.6
Palestine (1931)	32.6
Poland (1931)	29.6
Lithuania (1923)	29.4
Slovakia (1930)	23.9
United States (10 largest cities 1935-1938)	20.6
Hungary (1930)	17.6
Prussia (1933)	15.8

cumstances that it will take many years before they are able
to restore a normal family existence. Among these survivors
hardly any are children. In this region the Ukrainians surpassed
even their German masters in barbarity and cold-blooded slaughter. In Poland, too, hardly any Jewish children remain. Out of
80,000 surviving Jews accounted for in August, 1945, there were
only 5,000 children—approximately 6%. In the displaced persons
camps the percentage of children of this age group is even
smaller. The Nazis worked scientifically; they cut at the roots.

Material Damage to the Jews in Nazi-Occupied Countries

According to the most conservative and careful estimate,
the material loss suffered by the Jewish people in the Nazi-
occupied countries amounted to approximately eight-and-one-
half billion dollars. This is practically one-half of the pre-war
wealth of Poland and approximately two million dollars more
than the farm income of the United States in the year 1941
or twice the farm income of the United States in 1938. In less
than a decade nearly all the fruits of toil and planning by
individuals and organizations over many generations were expropriated or destroyed. European Jewry was stripped of its
possessions, private and communal. Of those who survive all
but a few are economically and materially ruined.

The wealth destroyed does not represent the holdings of a
wealthy class of coupon clippers. There was such a class among
the Jews of Eastern Europe, but they amounted to barely 2
percent of the total Jewish population. It represents the toil of
hundreds of thousands of small businessmen, craftsmen, workers and tens of thousands of doctors and dentists, lawyers and
engineers, writers and teachers, and many other professional
and intellectual callings. All of these were social groups which
had worked diligently for their livelihoods and for their economic status. The investment in the hundreds of thousands of
stores and shops, factories, workrooms and offices represented
not only capital but toil and sweat; and this not only by one
or two generations but over centuries.

On the basis of a comprehensive analysis of official census
data, we find that the Jews in Hitler-occupied Europe (exclud-

ing Russia) lost about one million business, professional and industrial establishments.

Destruction of Communal Institutions

The loss to private owners, however, does not exhaust the toll of Jewish losses. The destruction of Jewish institutions, which could be counted in the thousands and which were the most vital symbols of Jewish communal life, is no less important. The surviving Jews who crept out of their caves and hiding places and left the forest thickness to return to their homes, report that an overwhelming feeling of lonesomeness and desolation enveloped them. That sense of desolation is due not only to the pitifully small number of Jewish survivors but also to the complete disappearance of the Jewish institutions to which the Jew has been accustomed for ages to repair at the time of his deepest distress.

The *Kehillah* (organized Jewish community) occupied the central place in Jewish communal life. It was the Kehillah which united Jews of all nations. To be excluded from the Kehillah meant, in many European countries, to be excluded from Jewish life itself. In many countries, such as Poland, Germany, Austria and Czechoslovakia, the Kehillah was legally recognized and had the right to impose taxes. In Poland, for example, there were approximately 900 Jewish communities; in Germany in 1931 there were 960 Kehillot; in Czechoslovakia 505.

Among Polish Jewry, with its numerous ideological divisions, private societies and institutions supplemented the Kehillot activities in various fields. In national education and culture, private institutions expended annually almost as much as the Kehillah itself. In other fields such institutions as Tomchei Aniim (Support of the Poor), Linat Tsedek (Sick Benefit Society), Hachnasat Kalah (Dowries for Indigent Brides) and the private health societies—Toz, Marpah, Briut—had reached a high stage of development.

Some idea of the intensive cultural activity of the Jews in Europe can be obtained even from the inadequate information available concerning schools and published material. In Poland in 1935 there were 1,465 private schools with more than 180,000 pupils. Together with the trade schools of the ORT and ICA, the Kehillot and the teachers' seminaries, there was a total of some 200,000 students in Jewish-supported schools in Poland. In Lithuania there were 13,607 students in 108 elementary schools and several thousand students in Jewish secondary schools.

European Jewry also published 43 daily newspapers (38 of them in Yiddish), 171 weekly periodicals (130 in Yiddish or Hebrew) and 164 bi-weekly and monthly publications (105 in Yiddish or Hebrew). The largest number of these periodicals were published in Poland, mostly in Yiddish or Hebrew. Germany occupied second place, with German-language periodicals predominating.

This characteristically Jewish tradition of self-help, education and charity had achieved for Europe's Jewish communities, over many generations, considerable communal wealth—build-

The Jews of Europe at the End of World War II and Today

Country	Number of Jews After Liberation	1961
Poland	60,000– 70,000	11,000
Romania	300,000–320,000	220,000
Germany	6,000	30,000
Hungary	200,000	100,000
Czechoslovakia	30,000 35,000	18,000
France	170,000–180,000	350,000
Austria	5,000	10,500
Holland	25,000	26,000
Yugoslavia	9,000	7,000
Greece	16,000	6,500
Belgium	30,000– 35,000	35,000
Italy	35,000	32,000
Bulgaria	40,000	7,000
Denmark	5,000– 6,000	6,500
Luxembourg	500	1,000
Norway	700	1,000
Lithuania	2,000– 3,000	—
Latvia	1,000	—
Estonia	500	—
Soviet Union (all)	1,800,000	2,260,000

Figures for Germany, Austria, Italy and Czechoslovakia do not include Jews who were in displaced persons camps located within their borders.

ings, hospitals, homes for the aged, orphanages, synagogues, libraries, schools, museums, etc.—valued conservatively at $250,000,000.

This computation does not take into account those institutions which had the character of mutual help organizations, such as the cooperatives. Of such cooperatives there were in Europe in the 1930's some 1,120, taking in approximately 300,000 members (together with their families about 1,200,000 persons), with a capital of more than $5,000,000, with deposits of over $15,000,000, and with outstanding loans of more than $20,000,000. To these must be added the free loan institutions, of which there were 826 in Poland alone in 1938, with a capital of over $2,000,000.

A representative sampling of post-war Jewish populations in the various cities of Poland and Germany with corresponding populations before the war, provide a clear indication of what is left of pre-war Jewish communities.

Germany	1933	1945
Berlin	160,564	6,000
Vienna	178,039	5,000
Frankfort	20,202	450
Cologne	14,816	100
Leipzig	11,564	15
Munich	9,006	600
Total	394,191	12,165

Poland	1931	1945
Warsaw	352,559	6,000
Lodz	202,497	19,882
Radom	25,159	959
Kielce	18,083	243
Petrikow	11,400	372
Kalisz	19,248	360
Krakow	56,515	4,552
Katowice	5,716	2,152
Czectochowa	25,588	2,462
Lublin	38,937	2,342
Przemyszl	17,326	1,231
Bendzyn	21,625	1,501
Kutno	6,440	50
Tarnow	19,330	370
Ostrowiec	9,934	187
Total	830,357	42,663

It can be assumed that those Jews who had managed to find refuge within Poland and Germany during the war years have already managed to find their way back to their native cities. Certainly those who had family or possessions in their native cities have already returned there. There is thus no reason to assume that the Jewish population of these cities will be substantially increased. In Poland after the war there were many accounts in the newspapers of the flight of hundreds of refugees from Poland to Berlin to escape the violent anti-Semitism of the Nazi-indoctrinated Poles.

Passing from the Eastern European scene to the countries of Western Europe, particularly to France, Belgium and Holland, the situation becomes somewhat more favorable, although not to any substantial extent. In France especially, any attempt by the surviving Jews to recover not only their business enterprises, but even their homes, is fraught with extreme difficulty. In the first months after the liberation of France, the local anti-Semites made open and unashamed efforts to prevent the return of Jewish properties to their original owners. Eventually the French government banned the existence of anti-Semitic organizations.

The few survivors in Eastern and Central Europe show no desire to remain in their native cities. Only a few of them have managed to find work, of whatever nature; the majority are overwhelmed by a feeling of such homelessness and desolation that the only dream left to them is the hope of leaving the soil where every step they take confronts them with the murderers of their families and looters of their possessions.

The miserable plight of the 100,000 Jewish survivors in the displaced persons' camps has been extensively reported in the press. Almost without exception those who have visited the camps agree that all but a small percentage of the Jews in the camps are thinking of only one thing—to establish themselves permanently, and at long last, in the national homeland of their people, Palestine.*

---

* This is what happened in significant numbers with the independence of Israel in 1948, when the British bars to Jewish immigration were removed.

CHAPTER TWO

BALANCE SHEET OF EXTERMINATION–II

by JACOB LESTCHINSKY

The annihilation of six million European Jews had a twofold effect: It reduced European Jewry to less than a third of its former numbers and swung the statistical balance of Jewry, for the first time in more than a thousand years, outside the continent of Europe. In 1938, Europe held 56 percent of the world's Jews. In 1946, the greatest number of Jews lived in the United States—48.2 percent—while only 26 percent remained in Europe.

The annihilation of two-thirds of Europe's Jews also involved the physical destruction of the institutions which concretely embodied the experience and values of Jewish cultural and communal life.

A balance sheet of what was destroyed has an immediate and a long-range importance. We must know what was destroyed and what role it played in European Jewish life in order to estimate the needs of those who have survived and will continue, through choice or absence of alternatives, to live in Europe. For Jewry in general a balance sheet of destruction is a necessary first step toward fulfilling the historic obligation of preserving the Jewish heritage. What was lost represented the fruits of centuries of the best in Jewish learning and communal experience. The balance sheet of destruction will indicate what we must recover and transplant in other Jewish communities.

European Jewry

European Jewry was more than a geographical concept. Despite the fact that as a people the Jews were widely dispersed over the face of Europe, split off and enclosed within many different national groups, they were able to keep alive a certain unity. During the last three hundred years, there was an unceasing movement of Jews from Eastern Europe to Central and Western Europe. By 1920 approximately half of the Jews in Vienna consisted of new settlers from Galicia, and the "ghettos" of Paris, London, Brussels and Antwerp were made up almost entirely of newly arrived Eastern European Jews. By 1900, Eastern European Jews constituted more than two-thirds of all World Jewry and 80% of European Jewry. They had impressed the peculiar pattern of Jewish life in Eastern Europe on every Jewish community in which they settled. Coming from the large, highly integrated Jewish communities of Russia and the bordering states, these migrants held firmly to their language and their religious and cultural traditions. They were even able to impress many of their folkways and values on those sections of Western Jewry which had been drifting heavily toward assimilation.

Yiddish, the language of Eastern European Jews, came to be spoken wherever Jews were found. For example, according to the Polish census of 1931, 87.8% of the Jewish population spoke Yiddish or Hebrew. In the 1926 census in Soviet Russia 73% of the Jews gave Yiddish as their mother tongue; and in White Russia the figure was as high as 90%. According to the 1930 census taken in Bessarabia and Bukovinia, more than 90% of the Jews used Yiddish as their daily language. And it can be safely assumed that not less than 50% of British Jewry and not less than two-thirds of French and Belgian Jewry had an adequate understanding of Yiddish and were able to express themselves in the mother tongue. In general, it can be assumed that out of 9½ million Jews in Europe in 1939, 8 million understood Yiddish well, and more than 6 million Jews utilized the language in their family life.

The insecure position of the Jews in the countries of exile throughout the 19th century; the frequent annihilation of entire

communities; the repeated pogroms and the ruin of Jewish settlements; the thousand and one discriminations in relation to all
civil rights—these served to intensify in the Jewish people the
feeling of their common interests as Jews and the necessity for
developing their capacity for mutual help and support. Above
all, there was the traditional unifying factor of religion. The
frankly social character of biblical teaching, with its emphasis
on the protection of the weak from the appetites of the strong,
and the prophetic concept of social and economic justice were
absorbed by the Jewish child from his earliest years. They
intensified the social consciousness of the Jew and made him
more responsive to the needs of his brethren.

Two Currents

The breakdown of the barriers that for centuries kept the Jew
an outcast came earlier in the Western and Central European
nations than it did in Russia and other countries of Eastern
Europe where the greatest number of Jews lived. In the former
countries the tendency toward cultural assimilation was sharp.
But in Eastern Europe, where emancipation was slow in coming, large and tightly knit masses of Jews continued to live in
conformity with their traditions and assimilation captured only
a fraction of the intelligentsia and the upper middle class.

Because the Western Jewish communities viewed their "Jewishness" as primarily a matter of religion, their communal activities were of a different character from those developed by the
Jewish communities of Eastern Europe. Philanthropic institutions expressed their major interests. In Eastern Europe, however, the activities of Jewish communities assumed far more
complex forms.

Communal Organization—The Kehillah

The Kehillah was the basic form of community organization
for the European Jew. While local political and social conditions determined the character of the Kehillah, in each case the
Kehillah was an expression in varying degrees of the Jewish desire for autonomy. In those countries where emancipation had

come early and assimilation was marked, the influence and per-
vasiveness of the Kehillah was relatively less than in Eastern
Europe. But there was no country in Europe without some
form of Jewish communal organization.

In Eastern Europe where the Kehillah was tightly knit and
gave expression to almost every aspect of the interests of its members, it came to be regarded as the official voice of the Jews in
their relation with the non-Jewish world.

When, for example, Jews were driven out of small villages in
Czarist Russia, the Kehillah not only provided for the refugees
but acted as their spokesman in defending their dwelling rights
before the government authorities. When Poland became independent and the Polish government renounced its support of
Jewish schools, it was the Kehillah which fought politically for the
right to receive official subventions from the treasuries of the
central or local governments.

The poor Jew looked to the Kehillah for medical aid when he
was ill, for fuel when he was cold, for assistance when he was
in financial straits. It was the Kehillah which set up a network
of schools so that his child might be educated. Until the 19th
century its competence, especially in Poland, even extended to
many aspects of economic life, such as the regulation of trade
between its members and merchants of other Kehillot.

Sources of Revenue

In order to finance its broad functions, the Jewish community
organization was authorized by the state to collect taxes from its
members and to determine the amount of the taxes.

Some idea of the scale of Kehillah expenditures in the twenty
countries which were subsequently occupied or controlled by
Hitler can be gained from the comparative tables which appear
on the following pages.

The 3,000 Jewish community organizations of these twenty
countries met their annual expenditures of over $22,000,000
through the full participation of every Jew in the giant communal undertakings, the per capita tax averaging $3.24 annually.
The taxes were both direct and indirect. In countries with a

Kehillah Budget in Various Countries (1930-1938)

Country	Year	Number of Jews	Total Budget (in Dollars)	Per Capita
Germany	1931	535,000	7,583,000	14.2
Austria	1934	192,000	1,211,000	6.31
Italy	1935	47,500	350,000	7.31
Holland	1935	112,000	527,000	4.71
France	1935	260,000	1,225,000	4.71
Belgium	1935	75,000	353,000	4.71
Denmark	1935	6,000	28,000	4.71
Norway	1935	1,700	8,000	4.71
Luxembourg	1935	3,400	16,000	4.71
Hungary	1930	444,000	1,990,000	4.48
Lithuania	1930	155,000	694,000	4.48
Latvia	1930	93,000	417,000	4.48
Esthonia	1930	5,000	22,000	4.48
Yugoslavia	1930	75,000	336,000	4.48
Bulgaria	1930	50,000	224,000	4.48
Danzig	1930	10,000	45,000	4.48
Czechoslovakia	1937	353,000	1,333,000	3.77
Poland	1938	3,250,000	4,500,000	1.40
Romania	1938	850,000	1,190,000	1.40
Greece	1938	78,000	109,000	1.40
Total		6,595,600	22,161,000	3.36

poor Jewish population the indirect taxes yielded the greater sum. Usually these indirect taxes were in the form of ritual slaughter and cemetery fees. Fees collected in Poland in 1929 for ritual slaughter (*shechitah*) amounted to 6,297,000 zlotys. Cemetery fees yielded 1,771,078 zlotys in the same year. The income from these two sources covered more than 29% of all expenses. But this is typical only of countries with Eastern European Jewish populations; in the wealthier Western European countries cemetery fees constituted a substantial percentage, but income received from direct taxes was much higher than in Eastern Europe.

The table offers a fairly reliable indication of the general economic situation of Jews in various countries, although we must bear in mind that the Kehillah budgets were dependent not only on the economic circumstances of the Jewish population, but on the extent of the functions which the Kehillot embraced. German Jewry, for example, had the largest Kehillah budgets;

ten times greater per capita than those of Polish Jewry. It would be a mistake to conclude, however, that this was only a result of a higher economic standard. A second factor operated here— Polish Jewry was more widely differentiated ideologically and the Kehillot had therefore not been able to take as many functions into their competency. Polish Jewry, as a result, expended more money on institutions and organizations that were privately controlled.

In general, however, the table reflects the great differences in the conditions of the Jews in various countries. The highest standard was found in Germany, Austria and Italy. In these three countries the Kehillot were strongest organizationally and enjoyed the most secure official status. The per capita figure for Holland is only a third of the German figure. For, although Holland Jewry had a class of Jews who were as rich as the German upper bourgeoisie, its proletariat constituted a far larger percentage than among the German Jews.

France, Belgium, Denmark and Luxembourg had the same per capita figure as Holland. In these countries the long-settled Jewish population was extremely rich but there was a larger percentage of Eastern European Jews of the first and second generations who still belonged to the extremely low income groups. In Hungary, Lithuania and Latvia, economic conditions were better than in Poland or Romania, but not as good as in Italy. At the end of the table are countries with the lowest standards of living and with the most widely differentiated Jewish populations. Here private organizations played as great a role as the Kehillot—if not greater.

The extent of the development of the Jewish Kehillot in the years before the war can be seen from the following facts: In Warsaw the budget of the Jewish community organization in 1929 amounted to $436,400; by 1938 it had grown to $617,300, an increase of more than 41%. The budget of the Prague Kehillah was increased about 60% from 1924 to 1938.

Typical of the expenditures made by the Kehillot of the Western European countries is that of the German Kehillot, as indicated in the following breakdown (in percentage figures) of the money spent in different fields in 1931:

Religious affairs 28.0
Charity expenditures 30.0
Education 11.4
Administration 18.1
Miscellaneous 12.5

    Total 100.0

The expenditures of the Kehillot in Poland in 1929 were:

Religious purposes 40.3
Social purposes 13.7
Educational affairs 7.3
Health 3.7
Administration 11.0
Miscellaneous 24.0

    Total 100.0

There is a marked difference in the types of allocation made by the German and Polish Kehillot which is not apparent in the foregoing tables. For example, the expenditures of the German Kehillot on health matters are included under the heading of "charity expenditures," while in the case of the Polish Kehillot this category is listed separately. But in general it can be assumed that in the Kehillot of Eastern Europe more money was expended on religious matters, and in the Western European countries more in the field of charity.

Eastern European Kehillot

What were the major achievements of the Kehillot in Eastern Europe? In keeping with the deep desire for autonomy of the Jewish masses, these Jewish community organizations had woven into their broad framework many institutions designed to give expression to the very richest traditions of the Jewish people. Educational systems had been evolved by the Kehillot (though there were many non-Kehillah educational institutions as well), which came to be the great pride of the Jewish masses. In Poland, for example, an extensive network of schools included: folk-schools, *chederim,* and *talmud torahs,* up to high schools and *yeshivot.* These schools were one of the main reasons for the primary position in Jewish life of Polish-Lithuanian Jewry. No Jewish community fought so stubbornly for its own educational system. It saw clearly the central role played by education in preserving the national identity of the Jewish people.

So firmly established had the Kehillah become in Eastern Europe that in the 18th century when the former Polish empire was partitioned by the Russians and the recognition formerly given the Kehillot in the Lithuanian, White Russian and Ukranian territories was annulled—the Kehillot continued to exist, masquerading under different names.

The tendency of the Jewish Kehillot to widen their functions and to extend their influence over Jewish life came up against obstacles and hindrances on the part of the governments. This was especially the case in Poland and Lithuania, where the policy of the government operated, on the one hand, to isolate the Jewish population and to drive them toward emigration and, on the other, sought to compel the Jewish population to abandon its national individuality and adopt the language and culture of the majority.

Regardless of the civil status of the Jewish Kehillot in any particular country, the general tendency throughout Europe was to create new institutions and improve the old, to democratize the leadership and create administrative centers. The growth of such institutions as teachers' seminaries, libraries, archives and museums was intense.

Unfortunately there is no complete list of Jewish institutions and organizations in Poland prior to the Hitler invasion. But the few figures available concerning individual Kehillot indicate the vast scale of communal activity. The holdings of the Warsaw Kehillah, valued at $8,750,000, consisted of the following immovable properties: four apartment houses, a convalescent home for children, a dormitory for students, two farms near Warsaw, two homes for the aged, two houses for Jewish employees, a youth home, three hospitals, the community house, an orphan home, two bath houses, seven school buildings and twelve synagogues and prayer houses.

The smaller and much poorer Kehillah of Vilna owned the following properties valued at $2,950,000: thirty buildings, two large buildings housing the Jewish Cooperative Bank, a home for the aged, two orphanages, two buildings housing communal

kitchens, a communal bath house, ten schools, one hundred
and five synagogues and prayer houses (among them many of
historic importance, such as the Vilna Gaon's prayer house, the
"Great Synagogue" and others) and a theatre auditorium.

These holdings were typical of large and middle-sized Jewish
communities in Poland. While the scale of communal activity
in the smaller towns was not as extensive, nevertheless many of
them possessed substantial properties. The Lomza Kehillah, for
example, with a population of 10,000 Jews, owned a home for
the aged, two orphanages, a communal bath, eleven synagogues
and prayer houses, and two school buildings. This communal
property was estimated at $125,000. The Kehillah of Krynki, with
a population of only 3,000 Jews, owned four prayer houses,
three school buildings, a communal bath and a cooperative
bank building—property valued at $230,000.

Prior to the German invasion of Poland, it was estimated that
the combined properties of all the Polish Jewish Kehillot
amounted to at least a quarter billion zlotys, or approximately $50,000,000.

Central and Western Europe

Even in the Western and Central European countries where,
at the beginning of the period of Emancipation, the old Kehillot
declined rapidly, Kehillah activity greatly increased and was
strengthened by the fresh energies brought into Jewish life by
Zionism. In Germany this expressed itself, in the early part
of the 20th century, in a great increase in philanthropic institutions. By 1929, over 311 institutions were operated by the
Kehillot to serve the needs of the community:

Homes for the aged	43
Hospitals	20
Institutions for the Blind, Deaf and Dumb	7
Convalescent homes	53
Nursing homes	19
Orphan homes	41
Girls' homes and kindergartens	89
Trade schools	5
Cheap or free kitchens	27
Homes for expectant mothers	4
Homes for migrants	3

A comparison of the budgets of the Jewish Kehillot in Germany over a quarter of a century illustrates the striking growth of Jewish communal activity:

	(In marks)	(Per capita)
1907	8,906,000	14.6
1926	22,108,000	39.2
1931	31,850,000	59.5

It is difficult to estimate the material worth of all the institutions owned by the Jewish communities in Germany but it was undoubtedly enormous. Some idea of the value is given by the following figures: The administration of the funds of the Jewish Kehillot amounted to 2,914,000 marks ($694,000) in 1931. If we assume the administration costs came to about 1½%, we may infer that the total amount of the funds was about $52,000,000.

A short list of some of the institutions of the Berlin Jewish community in 1937 (population 140,000) will give us a more concrete picture not only of the extent of communal activity, but also of its variety.

The Berlin Jewish community gave employment to about 1,300 rabbis, teachers, social workers, etc. The community owned six folk schools, two high schools, one trade school, one domestic science school, a school for Hebrew. It had forty youth camps, three sports arenas, seven playgrounds, ten gymnasiums, four vocational training establishments, eight homes for the aged, two orphanages. And this list does not include non-communal institutions devoted to health, medicine and education.

National and International Organizations

In Tsarist Russia, where approximately half the Jews of the world lived, national organizations began to spring up during the latter part of the nineteenth century. The *Cheverath M'fitsei Haskala* (Society for the Promotion of Secular Education) was established in the '60's and ORT appeared in the '80's.

The greatest increase in organizations took place in the 20th century when a number of national organizations such as the

Yiddishe Literarische Gezellschaft (Jewish Literary Society) with over a hundred affiliates, the new credit cooperatives, the *Yiddishe Musikalische Gezellschaft* (Jewish Musical Society), the Historical-Ethnographical Society and many others appeared on the scene.

However, all these organizations were limited in scope. The 19th century had brought with it new and more complex problems for European Jewry that could not be dealt with by single communities or even national organizations.

One of the essential problems that had to be faced was the defense of Jewish rights in those countries where the Emancipation remained unrealized. An international body was needed to deal with the gigantic task of aiding the impoverished East European Jewish masses to establish their economic life on a sounder basis. Problems arising out of emigration also had to be met, and mass colonization needed the support that only a strong international organization would be able to give.

In 1860 there appeared the *Alliance Israelite Universelle* which had the specific purpose of defending Jewish rights. The need for such an international organization to fight for the political rights of Jews, wherever they might be, had been dramatically illustrated by the blood libel incident in Damascus in the '40's, and in the forced conversions which were increasingly taking place in Tsarist Russia under Nicholas I.

Special local committees to defend Jewish rights began to arise in all of the democratic countries of the world: The Committee for Foreign Affairs in the Board of Deputies in London, the *Hilfsverein der Deutschen Juden* in Germany, the American Jewish Committee in the United States.

However, it was only with the creation of the League of Nations that there developed the idea of a democratically elected international political body which would fight for the rights of Jews in all countries. It was this idea which was eventually embodied in the World Jewish Congress, formed in 1936.

The ICO (Jewish Colonization Association), established at the end of the 19th century, at first directed all of its activities toward colonization in Argentina. Later it also became one of

the chief agencies for granting cheap credit to Jews in various
countries, extending help to emigrants, making resettlement possible and providing facilities for vocational training.

ORT and OSE (Jewish health organization), were both originally set up by and for Russian Jews. Both became international in scope after World War I, carrying on activities not
only in the countries of the recipients, but also in the countries
of the donors. The World Jewish Congress, although at its in-
ception established for the purpose of supporting the interests
of Jews in Eastern European and Moslem countries, eventually
found it necessary to extend its activities to many countries of
the Western Hemisphere. The Joint Distribution Committee in
the United States, created as a result of the persecution of the
Jews in Russia during World War I, found itself transformed
into an organization to supply permanent help for Jews in
various countries, and in periods of relative peace, when the
world was not wracked by persecution and pogrom, the JDC
widened its activities even further to include all field of Jewish
relief.

In the cultural field, the establishment of the Jewish Scientific Institute (YIVO) in 1925 marked the peak of organized
Jewish life in Europe. YIVO sought to conduct scientific research into the conditions which the previously mentioned organizations were seeking to ameliorate and improve. This, however, was only one of its principal goals; the *raison d'etre* of
the institute consisted in its conviction that the seven million
East European Jews, with their folk language and folk culture,
represented such a deeply integrated branch of the Jewish people, possessed such rich spiritual treasures, and had so firm a
will for national existence, that the center of gravity of world
Jewry would always remain in the same historic framework
regardless of the changes that might take place in the political
boundaries of Eastern Europe.

These national and international Jewish organizations possessed hundreds of institutions in the occupied countries of
Europe, including among them, credit cooperatives, trade schools
and training farms. Materially, these institutions were worth

millions of dollars; of even greater worth were their spiritual and cultural values.

Outside the Kehillah Framework

We have thus far discussed only the institutions which existed within the Kehillah's framework. However, a great volume of Jewish activity was carried on by institutions not directly subject to the jurisdiction of the Kehillah. This was especially true in regard to the countries of Eastern Europe, particularly Poland, the largest and most fertile Jewish *yishuv* of all.

Outside the Kehillah's domain were many educational institutions, especially in the field of modern Yiddish and Hebrew education, as well as secular cultural institutions such as libraries and publishing enterprises, sport unions, cooperatives and various professional unions.

Education

Up to the Emancipation period, Jewish children were always educated in Jewish institutions; among orthodox Jews this practice was sacrosanct no matter what the country, no matter what the political system. But with the decline of orthodoxy, even in the Eastern European countries, the task of keeping alive the Yiddish and Hebrew languages and Jewish traditions was taken up by almost all of the Jewish national parties including the anti-religious Social Democratic Bund. A national school system with Yiddish or Hebrew as the language of instruction, but also including the language and literature, geography and history of the dominant nationality, was the high point in the program of all the Jewish movements in Tsarist Russia. In Galicia, and in Romania and Hungary, this urge was not as strong. The Jews in these countries contented themselves with national schools, which although almost exclusively conducted in the official language, at least provided for instruction in Jewish history and culture.

The strongest fight for education in Yiddish or Hebrew took place among those sections of Russian Jewry which were later to be included in the new Poland and in the independent states of Lithuania and Latvia.

Poland

In this indescribably poor country there existed a vast chain of schools with instruction in Yiddish or Hebrew, supported almost entirely by the impoverished Jewish masses. The table below indicates the strength of these schools, which existed outside of the Kehillah. Jewish schools where the instruction was in Polish have not been included.

About 5,000 children attended Jewish schools where instruction was in Polish. These were exclusively high schools, united in an association led by Zionists. Their joint budget amounted to approximately 5,000,000 zlotys. The budget for all the Jewish schools in Poland was about 25,000,000 zlotys. State subsidies and collections in foreign countries covered only about 10% of the total budget.

Approximately 12,000 pupils attended the trade schools and more advanced educational institutions such as the Judaica Institute in Warsaw, and the teachers' seminary of the Agudath in Cracow. Together, a total of 200,000 pupils attended the special Jewish educational institutions in Poland.

Type of School	Number of Schools	Number of Pupils	Budget (In Zlotys)
Tarbut	269	44,780	3,041,049
Cysho (Yiddishist)	169	16,486	1,911,308
Shul-kult (Poale-Zion)	16	2,343	115,692
Yabneh (Mizrachi)	229	15,923	3,323,800
Horeb (aguda)	177	49,123	3,347,712
Yeshivot	167	15,941	3,311,120
Bet Yakov (aguda) (girls)	248	35,586	1,264,522
Total	1,275	180,182	16,315,203

Lithuania and Latvia

In 1936, Lithuania had 13,607 students enrolled in 108 Jewish elementary schools. In addition, there were 14 Hebrew and Jewish high schools with approximately 4,000 pupils. Latvia had 10,787 students going to its Jewish elementary schools in 1935 and several thousands attended the high schools. Altogether in these two countries there were approximately 30,000 pupils in Jewish schools—about 80% of all Jewish children of school age.

Germany

There were 124 Jewish elementary schools in Germany in 1927-1928. Unfortunately, there is no computation of the actual number of pupils attending these schools. But we can gain some idea of the attendance by studying some enrollment figures for Jewish high schools in typical German-Jewish communities. In Hamburg, with a Jewish population of 20,000, there were the following Jewish schools in 1930: the *Talmud Torah* (*Oberrealshule*) with 220 pupils; the Community Girl's School, with 334 pupils; and the Girl's *Realshule*, with 190 pupils—a total of 744 pupils. This constituted from 25% to 30% of all Jewish children of school age.

Cologne, with a Jewish population of 14,000, had five Jewish high schools in 1934. It is estimated that not less than 50% of the Jewish children of school age living in Cologne attended Jewish schools.

Bulgaria, Hungary and Rumania

The Jews of Bulgaria had religious autonomy, including the right to maintain their own educational system. In 1927 there were 19 kindergartens, 18 four-class elementary schools, and six pre-gymnasia. The state subsidies amounted to barely 13% of the expenditures.

In spite of the veritable plague of conversions and mixed marriages among Hungarian Jews, the Jewish community in that country had a substantial number of high schools and elementary schools. They also had several *Yeshivot* and *Talmud Torahs*. Among the more modern schools were the Israel Gymnasium, 625 pupils; Israel Girls Gymnasium, 699 pupils; Israelite Teachers' Seminary, 121 pupils; Rabbiner Seminar, 67 students; trade high schools in Nanekanisha, 246 pupils; Debretchin Real Gymnasium, 400 pupils; the Miskoltz Seminar, 38 pupils.

Rumania also developed a network of schools. In Bessarabia and Bukovina, there were both Yiddish and Hebrew schools. In more recent years Rumanian was also used as a language of instruction, but the curriculum was devoted to traditional Jewish subjects.

Among the many higher institutions of learning in Eastern
Europe were the Judaica Institute, the Teachers' Seminary of
Agudath, and the Scientific Institute. The Yeshivah Chachmei
of Lublin, founded in 1924, was the great pride of orthodox
Jewry all over the world.

Poland had more than 700 Jewish libraries. Priceless collections of volumes, including many rare manuscripts, were available to the Jewish scholar. The YIVO library with approximately
50,000 volumes; the Strashum Library, with its collections of ancient rabbinical manuscripts; the large library of the Warsaw Jewish community with more than 40,000 volumes; the Bialystock
Sholem Aleichem Library containing 35,000 volumes, the hundreds of small libraries—made Poland the great treasure house
of Jewish learning.

Included among other great Jewish libraries in Europe were
the Library of the Berlin Jewish Community, the Library of
the *Alliance Israelite Universelle* in Paris and the Library of
the Vienna Jewish Community.

Press and Publications

Over 400 Jewish periodicals were published in Europe. Of
44 Jewish dailies printed in Europe, 39 were in Yiddish. Jewish
dailies were published not only in Eastern Europe but also in
London, Paris and Antwerp. Approximately 200 weeklies dealt
with Jewish affairs; 135 were printed in Yiddish or Hebrew.
Of the 175 bi-weeklies and monthlies concerning themselves
with Jewish affairs, 110 were issued in Yiddish or Hebrew. Even
in those periodicals which were printed in the language of the
country where they were published, there often appeared
translations from Hebrew and Yiddish literature.

There were also publishing firms which issued Yiddish and
Hebrew books as well as books in all European languages. Poland, Lithuania, Latvia, Soviet Russia, Rumania and Hungary
produced a steady stream of books for an eager Jewish public.
In addition, there were many books on Jewish themes published
in the various European languages. German Jewry was particularly productive in this field, producing books in German dealing with Jewish antiquity, Jewish history in the Middle Ages

and with contemporary themes. In 1931 and 1932, for example, four large works were issued on the economic history of the German Jews.

Self Help

It is impossible to discuss the hundreds of Jewish organizations, such as *Talmud Torahs,* invalid homes, homes for the aged, athletic associations, homes for the poor, cultural societies, etc., which enriched the texture of Jewish communal life in Europe. Such organizations were numerous in all countries with substantial Jewish populations.

TOZ, the Polish Section of OSE, an international Jewish health organization, affords a good example of the ambitious scale on which some of these organizations operated.

TOZ, in partnership with Jewish schools and other organizations, set up summer camps for sick and poor children. By 1930 there were 145 such camps, providing vacations for 17,066 children. In 1937 there were 386 camps which catered to more than 57,500 children.

TOZ also organized a system of school hygiene for the community schools. In 1936, 131,208 children received health examinations; of this number, 41,705 were given special medical treatment. It also made itself responsible for the feeding of school children and in 1937 provided daily meals for 37,550 young boys and girls.

In 1922, TOZ was organized into 15 departments with 26 institutions. By 1936 it had 52 departments and 209 institutions. Its budget was approximately $100,000 a year. TOZ, however, did not represent all the communal activity in this field. Under the leadership of two organizations, Briuth and Marpe, an intense campaign was waged against tuberculosis. Briuth had one of the best sanitariums in Poland at its disposal.

This concern with the health of the young was not unique with Polish Jews. In Latvia and in Lithuania, the OSE was extremely active.

Large organizations also existed for the care of orphans. In Poland, where such activity reached its highest peak, 27,536 orphans were provided for by *Centos* in 1935. Of these 7,332 were in special orphanages; 16,536 in camps and sanitariums. The balance was maintained in private homes. More than 6,000 of these orphans attended schools. More than 2,000 were taught trades in shops and trade schools.

This type of activity was also widely developed in other Jewish communities. Each community felt itself deeply concerned with the care of orphans and there were hundreds of orphanages throughout Europe.

A typical example of the profusion of organizations within a single community is found in the twenty page list of Jewish organizations and institutions in Cologne. These include both traditional and modern groups—all societies, psychiatric institutes, travel societies, etc. The same abundance was also evident in every city with a large Jewish population in Poland, Lithuania, Hungary, Belgium and Holland.

In Poland, for example, there were 768 associations of small merchants and traders, 594 associations of Jewish artisans, 700 Jewish credit cooperatives and 826 *Gmilis Chasodim* (non-interest taking credit organizations). In addition, there were trade unions of workers and employees, associations of physicians, lawyers, engineers, chemists, teachers, and many others.

The various party organizations, which attracted large masses, have not been touched upon, but each had its own institutions such as libraries, schools, athletic associations, etc.

Although there are no detailed itemized budgets available for a great majority of these private organizations, it is reasonable to conclude that their yearly budget certainly was no smaller than that of the Kehillot.

Conclusion

This then, in brief, is a description of what European Jewry had achieved in various fields of endeavor. It is not the whole story and omits entirely the vibrant intellectual and political currents which informed their institutional life and gave it unique vitality and stature.

In Eastern Europe, where solidarity with the past provided the form and substance of Jewish existence, the rich pattern of their communal life is perhaps less important than the deep creative sources of which it was the expression. Until the close of the nineteenth century, East European Jewry had, for more than four hundred years, exercised a cultural and spiritual hegemony in Jewish life that left its impression on every Jewish community in the western world. Never, perhaps, in all the thousands of years of Exile was there a Jewry as self-contained, as single-mindedly devoted to the cultivation of what was indigenous to Jewish life. Perhaps their greatest achievement was the classical elaboration of orthodoxy in life and literature which formed a bulwark against the dissolution of Jewish identity and formed the matrix for later expressions of Jewish nationalism. From Eastern Europe flowed most of the currents that converged to shape the modern Jew—the Haskalah movement, the development of Yiddish and the revival of the Hebrew language, Zionism and Jewish socialism.

Physically, the destruction of organized life in Europe is almost complete, but the real roots of Jewish life in the Diaspora have never been dependent on any fixed geographical anchorage. They have found their nourishment in the minds and hearts of Jewish men and women regardless of political or geographical clime, and whatever is cherished in the historical memory of Jewish people can be made to grow again. It is significant that no sooner had the concentration camps been delivered by the Allies, than the survivors, emaciated and without material resources, set themselves with incredible energy to reviving their cultural and religious life.

The relatively few Jews who will remain in Europe, through choice or necessity, have thus already begun, with the limited means now available to them, to rebuild their institutional life. To assist them in their task is an essential obligation of world, and particularly American, Jewry.

However, most of what was destroyed with the six million dead can never reappear again on European soil. The simple fact of numbers, the density of the Jewish population in Eastern Europe, had been one of the chief factors in enabling the Jewish masses to develop and enrich their own homogeneity and to resist so successfully the forces of assimilation. Jewry in other lands, and particularly in the United States, which now has the largest Jewish population in the world, must learn what has been lost and, wherever possible, add what has been lost to their own experience so that the continuity of the Jewish heritage will remain unbroken.

Both Eastern European and German Jews, who composed the two major streams of Jewish immigration to this country, established institutions and folkways in the United States which were patterned after those in their native countries. The German Jews established many of the great Jewish charitable institutions—orphanages, hospitals, and national federations for the relief of the poor. The German Jews tended to consider themselves as primarily a religious group and such secular expressions as lodges and philanthropies had only the faintest national coloration. The Russian Jews, who were far more numerous than the German Jews, brought with them the experience of a highly integrated group life that encompassed almost every aspect of their daily needs and interests. They were the source of Zionism and Jewish nationalism and a wealth of economic and cultural organizations. They set up their own newspapers in Yiddish and Hebrew, theatres, labor unions, literary societies, and a multitude of small synagogues and community centers. Their secularism, unlike that of the early German Jewish settlers, was in all essential respects a Jewish secularism.

But it must be remembered that those who established the first great patterns of Jewish life in this country were immigrants whose intellectual and cultural roots were still in the old country. That generation is passing from the scene and the present generation of American-born Jews, subjected to much more intense assimilationist forces, on the whole possesses neither the knowledge nor the inspiration to keep those institutions vital, much less to assure their continued development.

Fortunately, there are some in this country and in Europe who are still in possession of the keys to the great cultural and spiritual treasures which came to us from Europe. As Dr. Abraham Heschel warned at the Annual Conference of the Yivo in 1945, "If we do not uncover the treasures, the key will go down to the grave with us, and the storehouse of the generations will remain locked forever."

CHAPTER THREE

JEWS IN MOSLEM LANDS

by NEHEMIAH ROBINSON

INTRODUCTION

In 1933, the Jews of the Moslem lands lived, on the whole, in stable, though not necessarily thriving conditions. The political changes which took place in some parts of that region, following upon and in consequence of World War I, had led to the strengthening of Arab nationalism. It contributed, in some areas, to the growth of the inbred animosity toward the local Jews as the result of the Arabs' antagonism to the Jewish colonization in Palestine, but—with few exceptions—these anti-Jewish feelings had not yet led to official anti-Jewish measures or the corrosion of the basic structure of the local Jewish community and its way of life. Although Yemen, Afghanistan, Turkey, Egypt, and Iran were independent nations, other parts of that region were at that time still under the political influence—as mandates or protectorates—or, as colonies, under the sovereignty of Western powers. Iraq's independence was only one year old and she had to make, before the League of Nations, a declaration guaranteeing certain rights to her minorities. With the exception of Egypt, which had been in lively intercourse with foreign countries for decades, and Turkey, the rest of that region had not yet developed extensive contacts with the outside world and the Jews led for the most part, despite some penetration of Alliance Schools, almost the same traditional and secluded life as decades before. In Syria, for instance, very few foreign papers were received.

The inferior status of Jews as infidels was at that time already eliminated in the areas which before 1914 belonged to Turkey (in addition to Turkey, the present Iraq, Syria and Lebanon, Libya) and in Tunisia, although it persisted in all its severity in Yemen and Afghanistan, was much in evidence in Morocco, and continued less by law than by custom, in Iran.

The accession of the Nazi party to power in Germany had dire consequences for the status of the Jews in the Moslem lands. They became immediately evident in Iraq, where the Axis propaganda affected the army and students. The anti-Jewish sentiments were intensified there and in Syria with the arrival in Iraq in 1936 of the Jerusalem ex-Mufti, an ally of the Axis, who inflamed the population with his anti-Jewish sermons. With the start of the war and the accession to power in Iraq of a pro-Axis government, pogroms took place which ended only when British forces occupied the country.

Although the same clear-cut connection between Nazi propaganda and the deterioration of the Jewish position was not evident elsewhere, the influence of the Nazis and their allies, particularly through their agents, on the situation of the Jews in that region could hardly be overestimated. Direct impact was made by the pro-Vichy French administration in Syria and Lebanon, Tunisia and Morocco, and by Fascist Italy in Libya. The waves of anti-Jewish terror in consequence of the Israel war of independence and the establishment of Israel, swept away the last barriers to Jewish disfranchisement and elimination in Iraq and Syria, and contributed to the exodus from Yemen, Libya, and Egypt. The general situation in the country and the call of the reborn Jewish State caused large-scale emigration from Iran, Turkey, Morocco, and Tunisia. The continued tension between the Arab States and Israel and the Suez Canal intervention in 1956 signaled the practical end of the Jewish community in Egypt. In consequence, this area has in the last 25 years become, to a large extent, the graveyard of small groups of mostly elderly Jews who have chosen or are forced to remain in their respective homelands, in isolation from both the local population and the outside world, in Iraq, Syria, Libya, and Egypt. In other countries (Iran, Turkey, Tunisia, Morocco) substantial, although considerably reduced in size, Jewish communities are still in existence, struggling to maintain their institutions and identity. In some instances at least, the larger size is the result of restricted or prohibited emigration. The only country which has not practiced considerable discrimination is Lebanon. Unless radical changes occur, the Jewish groups which, in most of the areas, have lived for many centuries if not millenia, may in time totally disappear.

The countries of the Moslem world were, at the start of the period under consideration, quite different in the state of their development and organization. Turkey and Egypt were, in 1933, well advanced culturally and politically, while Yemen and Afghanistan were practically as backward as a century earlier. The common characteristic of all of them was the Moslem religion. Since, in essence, a Moslem state is a theocratic society, non-Moslems cannot be part of it; they may only be tolerated, the degree of tolerance depending on the particular characteristics of the non-Moslem group and the evolution of the state. Mohammedanism regards Jews substantially as a "protected people." Strictly speaking, Jews cannot be the equals of the Moslem; they have to pay a special tax, are not allowed to bear arms, to give evidence against a Moslem in a court of law, or to marry a Moslem woman. While these were mandatory disabilities, another set of handicaps also existed in Moslem society: the obligation to wear distinctive clothing or a distinguishing mark, not to build homes taller than those of the Moslems, not to read the Holy Scriptures in a loud voice, not to drink wine in public, to mourn the dead in silence, and never to ride horseback. In 1933 these disabilities were not imposed by law in countries which had introduced modern codes or constitutions, but the cult of Jewish "inferiority" continued to exist there as part of the mores of the masses—something which came to the fore whenever law broke down.

The negative aspect of the attitude of the Moslem religion toward the Jews had its counterpart in the so-called Millet system, which allowed the Jews to manage their own communal affairs on the basis of a certain autonomy. The communities had their own councils comprising religious and lay leaders. Their competence embraced religious affairs, education, family status, and sometimes testamentary dispositions. The communities had their own courts whose sentences were executed on their behalf by the state. This system, contrary to this negative aspect, did not exist in Iran or Lebanon and was disappearing in Egypt.

In all these regions the Jews were a small and helpless minority serving as ready targets for mob violence and discriminatory treatment by the authorities, who could at will make them the scapegoats for whatever failure or misfortune befell the country.

Despite the general trends of deterioration, the development in the last twenty-five years was not uniform in the countries involved. Generally speaking, the countries could be divided into three groups: (a) those where overt persecution became ever more menacing (Iraq, Syria, Egypt, Afghanistan, and Libya); (b) where the centuries-old discrimination became intolerable in view of the creation of Israel (Yemen and, in part, Iran); and (c) those where the rise and growth of a native, non-Jewish middle class and the changes in the political and economic situation were mostly responsible for the deterioration (Tunisia, Morocco, Turkey).

It must be remembered, while viewing the situation country by country, that there is a unity in the fate of all these individual Jewish communities.

The reports on the Jewish communities in eleven Moslem countries tell a sad story of elimination or, at least considerable reduction, of well-established Jewish communities, almost all of them among the oldest in the world.

To complete the survey of the fate of Jews in Moslem countries, the following few lines may be added:

(1) Pakistan numbered before the partition of India about 2,500 Jews. Now only about 400 remain.

(2) Aden (although a British colony—the city—or protectorate—the hinterland), with a Moslem majority, had a Jewish population of over 7,000 in 1946. At present only about 700 remain.

IRAQ

The Situation in 1933

In 1933, over 110,000 Iraqi Jews lived in a country which had just (1932) become independent. As a condition of admission to the League of Nations, Iraq had made a declaration before the Council of the League guaranteeing her minorities equality and certain rights of autonomy. A General Council administered the four main Jewish communities of Baghdad, Mosul, Basra, and Kirkuk. The Council consisted of fifty-three lay and seven religious members elected for four years by public suffrage. It was authorized to impose certain taxes and to allocate funds for various communal activities. Religious courts were run by a religious council of seven rabbis under the chairmanship of the Chief Rabbi. These courts had jurisdiction over matrimonial and other family and religious affairs.

The Jews were represented in the Lower House of Parliament by five members—two from Baghdad and one each from the other three communities—and in the Senate by one. Many Jews were in civil service. They were manufacturers, merchants, financiers, professional men, officials, agents, craftsmen, and domestic servants. The Kurdish Jews, who lived in the North, were small traders and craftsmen and also engaged in agriculture. The Jewish communities had the best schools in the country, with an attendance of 10,000 in Baghdad and some 6,000 in the provinces.

The Period of 1933-1949

With the accession of the Nazis to power in Germany, Axis propaganda made a full effort in Iraq. It scored most heavily with the army and the students. Already by 1935, Jews began to experience difficulties in entering the civil service, a number of Jewish civil servants were dismissed, and an unwritten *numerus clausus* in governmental educational institutions was introduced. Jewish schools were put under governmental supervision and the teaching of Hebrew, except for purely religious instruction, was prohibited. With the arrival in Iraq of the former Grand Mufti of Jerusalem and his followers in 1936, anti-Jewish propaganda was intensified. In July, 1937, anti-Jewish demonstrations took place in Baghdad resulting in two fatalities. In 1938, terrorist acts occurred, with nitric acid being thrown at Jewish passers-by.

The hostility toward the Jews, fanned by traditional religious hatred and the alleged "economic power" of the Jewish population, manifested itself most violently in the 1941 pogroms in Baghdad, Basra, Mosul, and smaller towns, in the last days of the pro-Axis government of Rashid Ali Gailani. According to official figures, the Baghdad pogrom cost 110 Jewish lives; 240 Jews were wounded, 86 Jewish enterprises looted, and 911 houses destroyed. Unofficial accounts put the number of the killed at 150 and of the wounded at over 700, with the material damage estimated at 750,000 dinars. These riots and pogroms produced a pervasive sense of insecurity and a considerable emigration to Palestine and America, in search of greater security and opportunity.

The following years were a period of growing hostility toward the Jews, marked by discrimination and persecution. Resurrected from Medieval Christianity were accusations of poisoning wells and Arab children. Restrictions on the freedom of movement of Jews (especially abroad), which started in 1947, were the forerunners of the overt anti-Jewish measures introduced after the proclamation of the State of Emergency on May 15, 1948, when Israel declared her independence. This was followed by the branding of "Zionism" as a crime punishable by no less than seven years imprisonment in July, 1948. After the establishment of Israel, all Jews began to be regarded as enemy aliens and potential spies. Jewish public institutions were requisitioned to shelter Arab refugees. Wholesale dismissals from public services—except for the most indispensable officials—took place. Jews residing abroad were required to return at once, otherwise their property would be confiscated by the state. There were dismissals from private employment, closing of businesses, and police searches followed by brutal acts against the Jews. These acts, plus blackmail on a grand scale, financial extortions by the government estimated at well over ten million Iraqi dinars (under the guise of confiscation of property for crimes not committed), and especially the arrests and large number of trials by court martial on various pretexts without a possibility of finding justice, and resulting in stiff prison terms and fines—all became the order of the day. The most notorious of the trials was that of the Jewish millionaire Shafiq Ades, who was sentenced to death by a military court on charges of assistance to Zionism: after his execution all his property, valued at five million dinars, was confiscated by the Iraqi Treasury. Another Jew, Salem Simeaon, was tried by a military court for alleged contact with "Israeli bands" and responsibility for the economic debacle of Iraq. He was found guilty of the charges and his property, valued at one million dinars, was confiscated.

In October, 1948, the number of arrests and other anti-Jewish acts began to diminish, a few dismissed civil servants were rehired, and some Jewish businessmen were encouraged to resume operation. Two months later, however, arrests were resumed and continued throughout the greater part of 1949.

The Exodus

The situation improved somewhat in the second half of 1949, and on March 3, 1950, Law No. 1 (1950) was promulgated, permitting Jews to leave the country on condition that the registrants forfeit their Iraqi citizenship. The time limit was one year, but upon its expiration it was tacitly extended for several months. Before legal emigration was authorized, 15,000 Jews had left the country clandestinely, mostly through Iran, in 1949 and the first two months in 1950, despite official prohibition and heavy sentences if caught.

Apparently, in order not to impede the exodus, the government refrained for some time from interfering with the disposal of the assets of the emigrants or the denaturalized, on condition that they be sold to Iraqi citizens. Nor was there, during this time, any violence against the Jews, whether or not they were leaving or remaining.

As of August, 1951, nearly 110,000 Jews emigrated from Iraq since the establishment of the state. By 1955 the total was 126,000.

The registration and emigration of Iraqi Jews may be divided into two distinct periods: During the first period, registration and emigration proceeded on a considerable scale but without undue haste or panic; in the last eight months of 1950, about 60,000 had registered for emigration and some 23,000 had arrived in Israel. Registration and emigration increased in January, 1951, when new outrages against Jews commenced: on January 14, 1951, a bomb was thrown into the Masouda Shemtob Synagogue in Baghdad, resulting in the death of several and the wounding of several scores of Jews. About the same time, bombs were hurled into two Jewish-owned automobile showrooms and a coffee shop, and some time later the economic center of Baghdad Jewry, the Sayyard Bazar, was occupied by troops. These acts undoubtedly were intended to lead, and actually contributed, to a more intensive registration and emigration: while, as stated, in the last 8 months of 1950, less than 8,000 a month registered, 40,000 registrations took place between January 14 and March 10, 1951 (or over 20,000 a month).

After the expiration of the deadline for emigration on March 1, 1951, special laws were enacted to deal with the property of the denaturalized Jews; they were used not only to deprive the emigrants of their property but also to send hundreds of would-be emigrants to prison on charges of trying to dispose of their assets. In addition, mobs swarmed through Baghdad looting Jewish shops and attacking Jewish pedestrians, without police interference.

By the end of March, 1951, the wave of terror and lawlessness sweeping Iraq had gained momentum, making the position of the 65,000 Jews still left in the country extremely precarious. Deprived of their assets and prevented from working, many Jews were completely destitute; they were unable to buy food and pay their rent. Police, armed with revolvers and truncheons, as well as bands of professional criminals, roamed the streets of the main Jewish centers, waylaying Jews and robbing them of whatever meager possessions they still had. They also invaded Jewish homes and stole money and movable property. Many Jews were robbed and then denounced to the police as "smugglers." In Basra, police cars patrolled the Jewish district to "insure" that Jews did not smuggle their property across the nearby Persian border. The situation became so dangerous that the government found it necessary to publish a statement warning against attacks upon Jews and requesting those assaulted and beaten to report to the police. After this warning the number of attacks upon Jews declined.

Until the law freezing Jewish property was introduced, every adult emigrant was permitted to take with him fifty dinars and minors thirty dinars in checks on the Ottoman Bank, in addition to sixty pounds of luggage per person. Thereafter, no transfer of money was possible and severe restrictions were put on the amount of household goods to be exported.

On March 10, 1951, at a secret meeting, both chambers of Parliament adopted Law No. 5 (1951) under which the property of persons who had lost their nationality was frozen. It could not be disposed of in any way, except in accordance with the law and its implementary regulation. To deal with this property a custodian general with a large staff was appointed. The regulations issued under Law No. 5 authorized the Custodian General also to dispose of and liquidate Jewish property, including businesses and commercial premises. In general, the Custodian was in full charge of the property.

The regulations also imposed on all persons, banking and public bodies the obligation to report to the Custodian General real property belonging to a denaturalized person. Movables (including currency, bills, stocks) had to be handed over to the Custodian. The only property exempt was household furniture and effects, food and personal clothing, insofar as they did not exceed the needs of the person involved.

By these regulations the registrants were suddenly prevented from disposing of their property and all other Jews were placed under suspicion of possessing property to be frozen, or of assisting emigrating Jews in exporting something from Iraq. Since nobody knew who among the Jews had registered or not, the whole Jewish community became *a priori* subject to new legal disabilities.

Although the anti-Jewish measures paralyzed the economic life of the country, resulting in a loss in business turnover and a decline in the amount of available capital, these consequences did not induce the government to relent. On the contrary, on March 22, 1951, another law was enacted to deal with Jews who had left the country otherwise than on the basis of Law No. 1 (1950). It provided for the freezing of the assets of all Jews who left Iraq with a passport on or after the first of January, 1948. The provisions of Law No. 5 (1951) were also to be applied to such property. Every Jew to whom this law applied had to return to Iraq within two months from the day of posting a relevant public notice by the Iraqi diplomatic or consular services. Returnees were to be reinstated in their property rights; the others were considered to have lost their Iraqi nationality and their property was to be sequestered.

The Minister of the Interior was given authority to order the expulsion of all Jews who lost their nationality under this law, except when their stay was considered to be in the interests of Iraq. According to reports, 4,000 Jews were deported against their will, apparently on the basis of this order.

The Post-Exodus Period

On March 22, 1951, the Iraqi government assured the Jews who retained their citizenship that they would be treated on an equal footing with all other citizens and would be granted all rights and the just treatment guaranteed by the Iraqi constitution.

Despite this statement, the freezing order was also applied for some time to the deposits of Jews of Iraq who had not registered for emigration. When the blocking of the property was lifted, the Jews were permitted to reopen their businesses, but all remaining Jews were ordered to sign a declaration swearing that they were not in possession of goods or articles which formerly belonged to emigrants. Permission to travel abroad was to be granted for medical treatment, business, study, and a short vacation only. No import licenses were granted.

In the following years arrests of Jews on various spurious grounds took place from time to time. In June, 1951, a number of Jews were arrested on charges of having stored ammunition in a Baghdad synagogue. Other Jews were detained in a concentration camp for alleged Communist activities. At the end of 1953, military equipment and explosives, as well as Israeli flags, were "discovered" in a Basra synagogue. Even as late as 1955, a few Jews were sentenced to fifteen years imprisonment for alleged Zionist activities. Denaturalization of non-returnees and expulsion of Jews who had served their sentences continued.

At present the 4,000 to 5,000 Jews remaining in Iraq, mostly concentrated in Baghdad, live and conduct their affairs practically unmolested. They are even granted passports for a prolonged stay abroad. However, the communal elections and activities in Baghdad (the only organized community left), are strictly supervised by the government, and most of the communal property is under control of governmental custodians. Of the former twenty communal schools, only two are still functioning; of Jewish affairs only religion is taught.

The new revolutionary Abdul Karim Kassim regime has proclaimed that Jews, Iraqi citizens, who have no connection with Israel or Zionism, will suffer no harm. However, expulsion of Jews who have served their sentences and the sale of sequestered Jewish property at auction continues. It is noteworthy that the Minister of Culture, Gaber Omar, was one of the prime movers of the abortive 1941 pro-Axis *putsch*. He fled to Berlin, where he made Nazi broadcasts to the Middle East and wrote anti-Jewish articles in the Nazi papers.

EGYPT

The Jewish Position before 1945

In 1933 the more than 70,000 Jews of Egypt lived in conditions that were comparatively normal politically, and stable socially and economically. In some instances they might even be termed favorable conditions, despite the growing xenophobia in Egypt which also affected the Jews, the majority of whom were either foreigners or stateless persons. Occasional outbursts against foreigners and Jews occurred in the twentieth century, in the post World War I years 1919, 1921, and 1924.

Of all Middle Eastern countries, Egypt had the broadest stratum of wealthy Jews who occupied an important position in the economic life of the country. The Jews were financiers, merchants, members of the liberal professions, clerks, artisans. Among them were old established, great Egyptian families which had important banking interests, owned department stores, were prominent in the cotton trade, on the stock exchange in foreign trade, and in the non-Arabic press. Jews had contributed largely to the economic prosperity of Egypt by establishing and directing many enterprises, including mortgage banks and sugar refineries; even the establishment and expansion of the National Bank of Egypt was due to Jewish efforts. Jews also occupied important positions in the public service. In 1925, Jews were appointed to the posts of Cabinet Minister and Senator. They also served as court officials and in other capacities.

Despite their comparatively high economic and—in part at least—civic position, Jews were discriminated against as regards nationality: very few foreign Jews were naturalized and the provisions of the Egyptian constitution never applied to Jews. These provided that persons born in Egypt automatically became Egyptian citizens, unless they acquired another nationality by birth; and that an Egyptian resident was regarded as an Egyptian national, except when he could prove that he possessed another citizenship.

An inkling of things to come was felt in 1941-42 when, due to Nazi propaganda and the advance of Hitler's armies in North Africa, the atmosphere became poisoned to such an extent that the Jews of Egypt grew fearful about their immediate future. Their fears receded, however, with the Allied victory at El Alamein.

The Situation Worsens

The situation changed in 1945 when, on November 2, an anti-Jewish pogrom took place in Cairo. A synagogue was burned down, twenty-seven Torah scrolls were desecrated, and a number of Jewish institutions (the Jewish hospital, a home for the aged, the premises of the Jewish Art Society and others) were destroyed.

The lull which ensued was broken in January, 1948, when police raids on Jewish homes and hotels in Cairo took place and many Jews were arrested. The domestic Egyptian difficulties which arose in April, 1948, led to the imposition of martial law in May. It was used to divert the growing dissatisfaction of the population by instituting a number of economic measures against Jews: the property of internees and of Jews residing in Palestine was placed in government custody. At the same time police surveillance was established over certain Jews, lists of Jews to be arrested were prepared, and indiscriminate arrests of Jews accused of Zionist or Communist activity were made in Cairo, Alexandria, and Port Said. Although no official data on the number of detainees in May and June were released, their number was reliably reported to have exceeded a thousand men and women. The men were put in internment camps and the women in detention camps under strong police guard. All suffered harsh treatment. Measures were also taken against the Jewish communities; police supervision and later prohibition of Jewish meetings were ordered, and the Jewish communities had to provide lists of all their members.

In June, 1948, bombs were thrown in the Jewish quarter of Cairo, resulting in the destruction of a dozen houses, the death of twenty, and the wounding of at least forty Jews. The quarter was thereafter attacked by Arabs, who forcibly removed Jews from streetcars, buses, and other vehicles, and beat and robbed them. The police not only did not interfere but even conducted searches in Jewish homes and synagogues. Further acts of violence occurred in July, the most extensive one on July 17, 19, and 20. Jews were attacked in the streets, their houses were plundered, bombs were thrown in a Jewish quarter, murders were committed. As a result, about 250 Jews were either killed or seriously wounded, hundreds more were arrested, and some 500 shops were damaged in addition to other property losses.

With the end of these outrages, a brief lull ensued during which some foreign Jews were released and some confiscated property was returned to the owners. However, on September 22, 1948, new bombings occurred in the Jewish quarter of Cairo. The death toll was nineteen, with sixty-two Jews injured. Large-scale looting took place. Although the police finally moved against the rioters, the Jews themselves were blamed for the disaster.

The last day of September witnessed fresh arrests of Jews. In October there was a new wave of excesses against the Jewish population, involving murders in Cairo and Alexandria, as well as the dynamiting of Jewish homes and stores.

The collected evidence shows that these excesses were the result not only of connivance by the authorities but also of systematic official propaganda against the Jews in the press, on the radio, and in the mosques. The government made extensive use of the state of siege decrees and sequestered millions of pounds worth of Jewish assets, including a considerable number of large Jewish businesses.

The Period of 1949-1954

The situation started to improve in the second half of 1949 when the Egyptian government began to grant exit visas to Jews and, especially since January, 1950, when the more moderate Wafd party came to power. The government rescinded a number of anti-Jewish orders, freed detainees, and restored sequestered assets to their owners. Exit visas were granted, but only on condition that the emigrants would never return to Egypt; in many instances the latter were glad to get out of Egypt and left their property behind. The number of emigrants between May, 1948, and January, 1950, was estimated at 20,000. Most of them found their way to Israel; others went to France, Italy, the Americas, South Africa, Australia, and elsewhere. Some of them were rather recent settlers but there were also some old residents—the richer strata. By 1950 the situation seemed to have quieted down somewhat and the remaining Jews appeared to have regained some faith in their position, although emigration continued, with about 10,000 leaving in the following years. To many Jewish leaders it was an accepted fact that time was working against them. On the other hand, there were some returnees from Europe, and the local Jewish communities resumed the operation of schools, hospitals, orphanages, etc., although the poorer Jewish youth had no schools to attend.

A further amelioration in the situation of the Jews of Egypt took place during the last months of 1950 and the first part of 1951. Reports from Cairo were to the effect that the tension between the Egyptians and the Jews in Egypt had eased considerably. Some of the wealthier families, though no longer popular in court circles, still wielded considerable influence in the social and economic life of the country. All Jews who had been interned during the Arab-Israeli war were released, with the exception of one Jew who was detained as a Communist. Sequestered property was returned to its rightful owners, although in many cases it had diminished in value due to the inefficiency and corruption of the officials who administered it. There remained, at that time, a fairly self-sufficient community and there seemed to be no move toward mass emigration. Although peace with Israel had not been achieved, tension in the Arab states had lessened and the Jews believed that the danger had passed and they were safe in remaining in Egypt.

A sign of this improvement was the announcement in June, 1951, that for the first time in four years Jews had again received Egyptian royal decorations. On the other hand, the fact that police still posted extra guards outside the synagogues during religious services on Friday and Saturday, and the re-legalization of the Moslem Brotherhood with its strongly anti-Jewish tendencies gave little comfort to the Jews of Egypt.

This temporary improvement in the lot of the Jews was probably due to economic reasons. There was a realization that in the banks of Cairo and the cotton market of Alexandria the Jews would be sorely missed if expelled. Owing to the Nationality Law and the difficulties experienced by many foreigners working in Egypt, replacements for the Jews could hardly be found. This was especially so because the Egyptians were known to be lamentably short of men trained for responsible work in the field of international finance and banking.

Jewish bankers and businessmen pursued their vocations once again; in the law courts Jewish lawyers were building up important practices; professional men were pursuing their careers in various fields of activity, including journalism. In the book-shops works by Jewish authors were displayed, and there still existed a Jewish weekly which even published news of Israel. The Maccabi basketball team was playing, and Jews were included in teams which represented Egypt in cricket and tennis matches. The rich still seemed to find life profitable in Egypt, which was by no means remarkable in a country where corruption in official quarters was the order of the day. The events of recent years, however, had hit the poorer people hard. In particular, the legislation against foreigners (especially the Company Act of 1947), had thrown many Jewish clerks and wage earners into unemployment and misery.

In the middle of July, 1951, an explosion rocked a synagogue at Ramleh, a suburb of Alexandria, but no casualties were reported.

In the years that followed, particularly in the first period after the accession to power of Naguib, the lull in anti-Jewish measures generally continued. Signs of friendliness toward the Jewish community were displayed by Naguib in 1953 even though some expulsions of foreign Jews took place from time to time, and in November, 1953, nine men and four women arrested for alleged Zionist and Communist activities, were tried and sentenced. Similarly, alien residents of Egypt who visited Israel were not re-admitted, or, if they had returned, were expelled. Emigration continued practically uninterrupted, reducing the Jewish population to about 30,000 in 1954.

In 1954, the situation worsened. Arrests for alleged Zionist and Communist activities took place, and three Jews were arrested on charges of allegedly setting fire to the U. S. library and a number of cinemas.

In July, 1954, 120 Jewish homes were raided by the police, and a number of Jews, accused of breaking the pledge not to learn Hebrew or engage in hachshara, were detained, but later released.

In September, 1954, new arrests of Jews started, including employees of Cairo banks. By October, the number of those detained rose to 150; further arrests took place in November and December. Jews were arrested on charges of trying to wreck the Anglo-Egyptian agreement on Suez, of espionage and subversion in favor of Israel, and of illegal imports from Israel.

The registration of all stateless Jews, allegedly as a preparatory step to their deportation, was ordered.

The Last Period (1955-1961)

The year 1955 was marked by extensive trials of Jews arrested in 1954. The sentences meted out were harsh, but neither the storm of indignation abroad nor the appeals for clemency by foreign governments moved Nasser; the sentences were executed as pronounced.

Although earlier in the year a percentage of those arrested in 1954 were released, new arrests of Jews took place in November, 1955. These followed an intense campaign by Egyptian newspapers against important Jewish businessmen, physicians, and officials who were branded as spies, saboteurs, and speculators.

Concentrated efforts to eliminate the Jews, step by step, from business and employment were launched. These efforts were accompanied by visits and searches of businesses and homes, the imposition of exorbitant taxes, and other coercive measures.

The last stage was reached with the Israel-Franco-British intervention in October, 1956. There followed large-scale expulsions and forced departures, wholesale sequestration and confiscation of property, arrests, and dismissals from positions. The nationality law was amended to denaturalize "Zionists." Everything was done by the authorities, the population was not allowed to interfere, so that there were only a few isolated instances of mob violence. The exodus went on during the whole year of 1957, (about 24,000 left up to the end of 1957) so that at the end of 1957 barely more than about 10,000 to 15,000 Jews remained in Egypt. Their number further declined somewhat in 1958.

In general, the worst treatment of Jews occurred in the last months of 1956. Since 1957, a certain relaxation in the export of goods for those departing became noticeable. In May, 1957, sequestration of property of Jews who remained in Egypt, except for British and French citizens was lifted, certain properties were restored to their Jewish owners, Jews were even permitted to rejoin clubs. Agreements between France and Great Britain on the one hand and Egypt on the other regarding sequestered property, were concluded recently, but their application to Jews meets with difficulties. However, those who had lost their employment were for the most part unable to find work; the whole communal structure was destroyed. There are at present practically no Jews outside Cairo and Alexandria. Nearly all synagogues have been closed down and some have been converted to mosques; the Jewish schools have been either shut down or, if still functioning, are reduced to shambles. The same applies to other Jewish institutions (hospitals, etc.) The Community Councils of Cairo and Alexandria lost their status as legal entities.

Two measures introduced in 1958 point in particular to the sad plight of Egyptian Jewry. The first was a law providing that any Jew leaving Egypt with the intention to settle abroad will be denied re-entry to Egypt. It does not apply to any other group. The second was a decree forbidding Jews to travel from Egypt to Syria and vice versa despite the union of the two countries which ended with Syria's revolt in 1961.

SYRIA

The number of Jews in Syria in the early 1930's was estimated at between 35,000 and 40,000. In 1943, the official census showed only 29,770 Jews; of these, 13,673 lived in Damascus, 15,066 in Aleppo, and 1,938, mostly engaged in agriculture, were in the Jezirah region. In all other towns and regions only 93 Jews were counted. Most of the Jews (in Damascus practically all of them), resided in the Jewish quarter. They were Orthodox and, in Aleppo, almost fanatically religious. They had no intellectual life of their own and numbered among the older generation no physicians, lawyers, or writers. The younger generation, thanks to the Alliance schools, spoke French. There was also much knowledge of Hebrew. B'nai B'rith lodges played an important role; in Damascus all social and philanthropic matters of the community were left to the lodge. Syria had a Jewish French-language newspaper and a Jewish library in Aleppo.

The economic position of Damascus' Jewry was always poor: the whole community was pauperized, hardly anyone could be ranked among the better-situated middle class. A considerable part of the Jews were artisans; some owned tiny factories turning out various Oriental wares, mostly of metal and textile. The situation was somewhat better in Aleppo, where a large portion of the trade with Turkey was in the hands of Jews.

The Jewish position had already begun to deteriorate under the French mandate, when Syria came under strong Nazi influence, in particular after the collapse of France; for that was the time the pro-Vichy forces were in control of the area.

With the end of the mandate the schools of the Alliance were shut down, although they were later re-established in part. The Jewish communal (religious) schools were at first not affected, except for changes in the curriculum.

Mob violence occurred in Damascus and Aleppo on many occasions.

A systematic anti-Jewish campaign started in 1945 which resulted, among other things, in the refusal of Syrian authorities to allow any Jew to enter Syria. On October 12, 1945, attacks upon Jews again took place in Damascus; in 1946, frequent arrests of Jews on charges of maintaining contacts with Zionists or Palestine occurred. Confiscation of Jewish-owned land took place somewhat later. On the other hand, Jews were still active in the political and economic life of the nation, and Syria for some time even facilitated the immigration of French Jews to assist in the building up of the country.

The planned anti-Jewish campaign assumed larger dimensions in 1947, with the Jewish community being forced to proclaim its opposition to Zionism, and with Jews being arrested and tortured by police without apparent reason. The death penalty was imposed for illegal emigration to Palestine. The outrages culminated in the Aleppo pogroms. These resulted in eight dead, several hundred wounded, twelve synagogues burnt down, 150 houses and a number of other buildings, including five schools, destroyed. All this took place after the U.N. decision on Palestine of November 29, 1947. The damage was estimated at $2.5 million. There were anti-Jewish demonstrations also in

Damascus, resulting in one Jewish fatality. These outrages were accompanied by governmental restrictions on the movement of Jews, denial of jobs in the government, withholding licenses, making virtually impossible admission to governmental schools, and the prohibition of land purchases, opening commercial establishments, and disposal of property. The pogroms caused an exodus to Lebanon but it was halted by the government. At the beginning of the Palestine war, 260 Jews were arrested in Damascus, but most of them had been released by the middle of May, 1949.

The poor economic conditions and the prevailing insecurity led to a considerable emigration of Jews from Syria to Palestine, Lebanon, and overseas. About 15,000 to 19,000 left Syria between 1943 and 1947. The intensified anti-Jewish acts also resulted in further emigration since 1948. By 1948, the number of Jews in Syria had decreased to about 9,000, and by 1950 to about 6,000. By that time almost the entire younger generation had left Syria.

Although the position of the Jews improved somewhat in March, 1949, with accession to power of Zaim, who abrogated the restrictions on the movements of Jews and on the sale of their property, the general atmosphere did not grow better. This was indicated among other things, by the bomb thrown on August 6, 1949, into the Damascus synagogue. New difficulties for the Jews arose in 1956 after the Sinai campaign.

Upon the restoration of freedom of movement, the constant stream of Jews to Lebanon was resumed and illegal emigration to Israel began. No exact number of emigrants is available, but Syrian newspapers spoke of hundreds of families going illegally to Israel. At present there are about 5,000 Jews left in Syria—about 2,000 each in Damascus and Aleppo and a few hundred in Kamishlia near the Turkish border. Restrictions in employment and acquisition of land continue to exist. Jewish bank accounts are frozen. Jews are not permitted to travel abroad, except against payment of high fees, and they are also restricted in their movements inside the country. They are not admitted to governmental schools; Jewish religious services are held under police supervision.

The Jews are impoverished. Most of them work as common laborers; only a few are engaged in clerical work. Already in 1950, over one-half of all the Jews in Aleppo and Damascus were dependent on local charity and foreign assistance. Damascus has an Alliance School and a Talmud Torah; Aleppo has two schools.

The Jews of Syria live in constant fear. The Syrian radio frequently broadcasts anti-Jewish tirades. With the borders closed and no prospects for an amelioration of the situation, the future is even darker than in other Middle East countries. It is, indeed, desperate.

LEBANON

The Jews of Lebanon on the eve of 1933 numbered about 3,500. They were mostly small traders, and only a small number were well-to-do. There were very few professionals. The community, however, was well organized. It had its own schools, a central synagogue, meeting halls, a library, and, in addition to the B'nai B'rith lodge, which dealt with social and philanthropic matters, a Bikur Cholim. The Jews, under the French mandate, acquired the French language and French culture.

The Jewish community over the years increased despite some emigration, mainly through the influx of Jews from Syria—under the French mandate there existed no restrictions on movements between Syria and Lebanon.

On December 31, 1944, there were 5,666 Jews in Lebanon: 5,022 in the district of Beirut and the rest in smaller towns, among them Tripoli, Tyre, and Sidon. In 1949, the number of Jews was estimated at 7,000, including 2,500 refugees from Aleppo and 1,000 from Damascus. By 1952, the number of Jews had risen to approximately 10,000: 5,920 Lebanese, 1,041 foreigners as "permanent" residents, and about 3,000 Syrian Jews living there as "tourists."

Until the outbreak of the Arab-Israel war, the position of the Lebanese Jews was considered good, despite sporadic anti-Jewish demonstrations and some official discriminatory acts. In 1945, two anti-Zionist demonstrations took place. On May 9,

1946, two persons were injured when Arab terrorists in Beirut threw bombs into the Jewish stores in the center of the city. On January 8, 1948, a Jewish merchant was stabbed to death by unidentified assailants one hour after the police had withdrawn special patrols which had been sent to the Jewish shop area following the "discovery" and seizure, a day earlier, of munitions in the garden of a Beirut synagogue. Shortly afterwards, a bomb exploded in the Alliance School in Beirut, smashing windows and ripping out part of a wall, but there were no casualties. It was alleged that the school was the headquarters of Zionists in Lebanon. The Jewish quarter in Beirut was attacked on three successive days, but there were no casualties.

In October, 1945, the Lebanese authorities withdrew the residence permits of eighteen Jews and assigned other Jews to special places of residence in accordance with the anti-Zionist attitude decided upon at a conference of Lebanese and Syrian statesmen. On the other hand, Lebanon early in 1946 consented to the admission of a small number of Jewish refugees who could not return to their homelands.

In January, 1948, the Lebanese government ordered all foreign Jews, including students at the American University, to leave Lebanon. On May 15, 1948, anti-Jewish demonstrations took place. The Jews, however, were aided by the Christian-Arab community, and armed troops prevented the rioters from entering the Jewish quarter. The police also forced Arabs in the Sidon region, who had seized Jewish-owned property for the benefit of Arab refugees, to restore it to the legal owners. However, some thirty to forty Jews were arrested and kept in a concentration camp; Jews were forbidden to travel abroad; and a number of Jewish officials were dismissed from their posts. In May, 1948, forty-one American and three Canadian Jews, together with twenty-three Palestinian Jews, were forcibly removed and transferred to a concentration camp, from the U. S. vessel "Marine Carp" which had anchored in Beirut, but were released on June 25.

During the same period anti-Jewish demonstrations took place in a village in southern Lebanon. However, the police fired on the demonstrators and killed four of them. Bombs were thrown into the homes of some Jews who had refused to make contributions to the Arab cause, although Jewish contributions to the Arab Palestine Fund amounted to some fifty million francs, allegedly as much as the total contributed by the rest of the population.

After the cessation of hostilities in Palestine, the government rescinded all measures against the Jews, freed the detainees, and reinstated the dismissed officials. Syrian and Iraqi Jews were permitted to leave for Israel. On the other hand, a serious attack on Jewish property occurred again in February, 1950, when a bomb exploded in the Alliance School causing three casualties.

The Jewish position worsened somewhat in 1952 as a result of the accession to power of the Camille Chamoun regime. The few Jews serving in the army were dismissed, a number of Jews were arrested on charges of "smuggling" and "spying" for or being in contact with Israel. In November of the same year, special permits for travel abroad were introduced and then were soon eliminated; the Maccabi and Jewish Boy Scouts were dissolved as allegedly providing military training, thereby endangering the security of the state. In the following years sporadic searches of Jewish homes occurred.

On the eve of the 1958 disturbances in Lebanon, the Jews were to a considerable extent well-to-do businessmen and professionals; the rest consisted of white collar workers and laborers. Jewish participation in the civil service had largely been eliminated—only fifteen Jews were so employed, all in minor positions. The Syrian Jews were less well-off and less represented in the professions. The Jews of Lebanon were able not only to provide for their own communities but also to assist the Jews of Syria. They possessed a well-organized community in Beirut, led by an elected Community Council; the elections were controlled by the government. The Council registered marriages, deaths, and births and represented the community before the government; the Grand Rabbi, who was actually the only rabbi in the country, was under the authority of the Council. The Council maintained a Talmud Torah (there were also Alliance Schools), and a variety of social and relief institutions.

The disturbances did not seriously affect the status of the community, although some Jewish families left the country early in the year for fear of persecution. In June, Moslem extremists threatened to blow up the Jewish quarter in Beirut on charges that arms and ammunition were stored in the synagogue. In September, 1958, seven Beirut Jews were kidnapped by Lebanese rebels, but returned safely after thirty-six hours.

In Lebanon the Christian-Arab population appears to be a stabilizing factor so that the Jewish situation has not deteriorated to the desperate extent it has in Iraq, Egypt, and Syria for the 6,000 Jews of Lebanon in 1960.

TURKEY

According to the census of 1927, about 82,000 Jews lived in Turkey. More than 46,000 of them resided in Istanbul, over 16,000 in Izmir, and 5,700 in Edirne. The rest lived in 14 other communities ranging from 100 to 2,000 Jews each. Ankara, the capital of Turkey, had about 650 Jews. In the middle of the 1930's the number of Jews was estimated at 78,000.

Economically the Jews suffered a certain number of disabilities. The ban on the acquisition of rural estates by foreigners was also applied to Turkish Jews; other non-Moslems also suffered this disability, but to a lesser extent. Since Turkish étatism excluded private initiative in heavy industries, Jews were engaged in a number of light industries (toys, perfumes, soap, etc.). This refers to owners only; the number of Jewish workers and employees even in Jewish enterprises was small, because of the requirement of Turkish citizenship, which, again, in practice meant Moslems. The law forbidding foreigners to engage in handicraft totally eliminated those Jews who did not possess Turkish nationality. There were some Jewish barbers, tailors, shoemakers, and, most of all, hatmakers. Even in handicraft there were small chances for the Jewish youth, because Turkish artisans did not accept Jewish apprentices and the formerly existing Jewish trade school was closed.

No restrictions on the exercise of commerce existed, but even so,

Jewish activities in this field of economic endeavor were limited:
Jews were not accepted in state-owned or state-subsidized commercial enterprises and could not serve as contractors for state
enterprises, except if associated with Moslems. Banks were mostly state-owned and they granted loans to Jews very sparingly;
the main source of credit was a Jewish loan association, founded
by the Joint Distribution Committee.

In the liberal professions, particularly medicine and law, Jews
still played a role, but their numbers were on the decline because admission to medical schools was becoming more and more
difficult for Jews. Although no such limitations existed in the
law schools, non-Moslems had few chances for advancement
in law. There were very few Jewish teachers in general high
schools; even in the Jewish schools, Jews were barred from
teaching the Turkish language. In the field of journalism, Jewish activity was restricted to the few still existing Jewish periodicals.

The situation described above was conducive to emigration.
Although no exact figures on the total number of emigrants are
available, by the middle of the 1930's about 2,000, and in the
years 1940-1945, 4,700 Jews had emigrated to Palestine. A number of Turkish Jews went to France, Rhodes, and South America.

The position of the Jews was aggravated considerably in
November, 1942, with the introduction of a capital levy on property and excess profits, known as the "Varlik." The payment of
this tax, which was imposed in secret meetings without con-
sultation with the taxpayer and had to be paid within fifteen
days, ruined a large portion of the Jews and other minorities.
Those who were unable to pay the tax (about one-third of Istanbul Jews), were deported to the mountains of Ashkale in Eastern Turkey for forced labor. Although theoretically the "Varlik"
applied to everyone, Moslems were either not taxed at all or at
a very low rate while Jews and other minorities were taxed
150 to 250 percent of their total resources. The "Varlik" was
abolished within a year, but the alienated and lost possessions
were not returned, nor was the tax itself ever refunded. It took
the Jews about ten years to recover from the economic ruin
which the tax wrought.

Since the abolition of the "Varlik," no official anti-Jewish measures have been introduced. The Zionist movement is banned and the Jews are not permitted to maintain formal contacts with foreign organizations. Nor are foreign Jewish organizations permitted to work in Turkey. However, the same restrictions apply to all Turkish citizens and to all foreign bodies.

Jews suffer from the general anti-minorities (in particular, anti-Greek) sentiments. There have also been some anti-Jewish articles in Turkish papers and there exists an anti-Semitic monthly, but the government is taking measures against such outbursts. Serious difficulties arose in 1955 in connection with the dispute between Turkey and Greece concerning Cyprus. The anti-Greek riots in September, 1955, in Istanbul and Izmir got out of hand, and considerable damage was also inflicted on Jewish property, although the riots were not directed against Jews. In the center of Istanbul 75 to 100 Jewish shops were destroyed; some stores in other parts of Istanbul were also damaged and windows were smashed in one synagogue. The damage to Jewish property was estimated at 140 million dollars. The Turkish government granted some financial assistance and banks provided some loans to rebuild the businesses. Minor incidents also occurred in the provinces. No further riots of this kind have occurred, but there were anti-Semitic attacks in local papers from time to time and arrests of Jews on charges of smuggling money abroad.

After the establishment of Israel, large-scale emigration took place. During the years 1948-1956, approximately 37,000 Jews emigrated to Israel, in addition to about 6,000 who emigrated to other countries. Some 3,000 to 3,500 returned from Israel. The mass exodus took place in 1949 and 1950. After 1955 the movement slowed down considerably.

The policy of the Turkish government toward emigration to Israel underwent several changes; at first, emigration to Israel was prohibited for all practical purposes. In October, 1948, the ban was lifted, but in November, 1948, it was restored. Emigration went on, but via French and Italian ports. The policy was liberalized in 1949.

The emigration reduced the number of Turkish Jews to

40,345 in 1955, according to the official census. Their present number is estimated at 48,000 to 55,000. About 40,000 to 45,000 live in Istanbul, some 5,000 in Izmir, the rest in smaller communities.

In general, the Jews suffer under minor discrimination only. The poorer elements emigrated in the years 1949-50. The economic position of those who stayed on is satisfactory; they are engaged mostly in commerce and the professions, but are poorly represented in the country's political, cultural, and administrative activities (there are very few Jewish officials, and these in minor positions only). In the last (1957) general elections, five Jewish candidates stood for election and two were elected. Previously there had been only a single Jewish member of Parliament.

The Jews of Istanbul are represented by two councils—the Secular Jewish Council with about 8,000 members including their families, and the Orthodox Jewish Council numbering 25,000 members including their families. A serious blow to Jewish organizational activities was the suppression in October, 1958, of all Jewish charitable, social, and cultural institutions linked to the Grand Rabbinate. While, under existing law religious organizations are purely restricted to religious matters, there existed in fact a coordinating body of Jewish welfare and educational organizations, which worked in the headquarters of the Grand Rabbi. Efforts have been made by the Jewish community to retain the old status, but the outcome is still unknown.

The overthrow of the Menderes regime and the assumption of the Premiership by General Cemal Gursel has not meant an improvement in the situation of the Jewish community. A governmental order in late 1960 broke up the communal organizations of the minority groups, including the Jews. Each Jewish institution or synagogue must have its own independent council. New rules in 1961 require every synagogue or institution to be conducted as a separate foundation with its own administration, with all meeting minutes in Turkish. There is also fear that the government may nationalize the Jewish hospital and orphanage.

IRAN (Persia)

At the beginning of the 1930's the Jews of Persia were still concentrated in their ancient ghettos, living in degradation and poverty. Two-thirds lived in the major cities of Teheran, Shiraz, Ispahan, and Hamadan, each of which had Jewish populations of 6,000 to 9,000, and in four smaller communities of about 1,000 to 2,000 each. The majority of the ghetto inhabitants were sickly and short-lived: eye and skin diseases were common; hunger and sickness took a heavy toll of lives.

In the ghetto of Teheran the Jews lived in indescribable squalor and filth. The ghetto streets and yards were heaped with refuse and the air filled with its stench. The houses were mean at best, and those of the poor were mere hovels built almost underground, their walls covered with smoke and grime. The same situation prevailed in most of the other ghettos, except for Kashan with 1,000 to 2,000 Jewish inhabitants, where the streets were clean and the houses were solid buildings.

At that time the Jews of Iran were mostly petty merchants apart from a few artisans. The Jews were engaged in moneylending and brokerage, or else sold charms and amulets. Few of the occupations provided anything like a normal subsistence; even the most skilful artisans barely earned a living. It is no wonder that the streets were full of beggars and cripples.

The Jews labored under no legal disabilities, but ancient customs and prejudices strongly influenced their lives. Jews were practically barred from the civil service, the legal profession, and some banking institutions. Governmental concessions were difficult to obtain and very few Jews were admitted to high schools and universities. Social ostracism was strong. Some of the Moslem law discriminations were still practiced; for instance, Moslems considered water touched by Jews as unclean.

By now a few Jews, most of them newcomers, have become substantial industrialists or merchants. There exist only comparatively small Jewish middle and working classes. About 80 percent of the total Jewish population belong among the poor. About seventy-five U. S. cents a day for a whole family is regarded as an ideal income. At the start of the last war there were Jews in the service of the government, but they were discharged under the influence of Nazi propaganda. No reinstatements took place after the war.

A change has taken place in the geographical distribution of the Jewish population. Of the total of some 75,000 to 85,000 Jews in Persia, approximately 50,000 now live in Teheran (as compared with about 10,000 to 11,000 in 1938); about 15,000 to 20,000 in Shiraz (11,000 to 12,000 in 1938); about 6,000 in Isfahan (8,000 to 9,000 in 1938); and about 5,000 in Hamadan (7,000 to 8,000 in 1938). The increase in the Jewish population of Teheran is due mainly to an increase in popular anti-Semitism in the smaller localities. The economic situation there is worse, and it is easier to emigrate to Israel from Teheran than from provincial towns.

Life in the ghettos has not become much more tolerable. Many buildings in the Teheran Jewish quarter are a thousand years old. On the average, six to ten persons live in a small room. The houses are dirty and unsanitary. Water comes from canals and is used for all purposes. Only a few inhabitants of the ghetto are in a position to buy potable water. The majority of the denizens are clad in rags, and beggars roam the streets. Most of the Jews are peddlers, a small portion are artisans or carpet weavers or shopkeepers, and many live on charity. The shops are small, dark shacks, whose whole stock can be purchased for a few dollars.

Communal life has progressed little. The majority of the Iranian Jews living in ghettos still lack the sense of self-respect which is required for normal social and communal life. Rather, they are marked by the inferior political, social, and economic status in which they have had to live for centuries. In 1957, the first Congress of Iranian Jewry took place. At long last it is creating organizations for Jewish affairs in the provinces under the supervision of the central organization "Iranian Jewish Congress." Until recently the main activities in the field of social, cultural, and health endeavors were carried on by foreign organizations (Alliance, Joint, ORT). Several local organizations (youth, hospital, etc.) have arisen in Teheran due to the activities of the wealthier Jews.

In 1956, widespread anti-Jewish violence occurred in the Kurdish regions; in consequence nearly all the Jews have left that area. The majority went to Israel. The period during which Mossadegh was in power was a time of considerable anxiety. His demand for a large loan from the poor Jewish community created an almost intolerable situation. Fortunately, he was forced to resign before he could realize his threats in case of non-payment.

The poor social and economic conditions have contributed to considerable emigration, particularly to Israel. Until 1948, only about 3,500 Iranian Jews arrived in Palestine and Israel. Since the establishment of the State of Israel to 1955, about 40,000 Jews have emigrated from Iran. Thereafter, emigration declined, partly because of the insufficient preparation of the Iranian Jews for proper integration in Israel. It now amounts to 5,000 to 6,000 annually.

AFGHANISTAN

Until the Hitler era, Afghanistan Jewry was a small community of several thousand persons whose general condition could be described as a live-and-let-live existence. In the early 1930's, however, the position of the Jews of Afghanistan deteriorated considerably as compared with what it had been in previous times, particularly in the economic field. This was due mainly to the requirement of governmental licenses for the import and export trade and the establishment of "indigenous" Afghanistan import and export associations. In 1936, all Jews were forcibly evacuated from a number of provincial towns, so that their economic positions could be taken over by governmentally established monopolies. The expulsion was accompanied by robbery and brutal treatment. Somewhat later, Jews were required to obtain permits to travel inside the country and they were barred from a number of trades.

The Afghan Jews have had to pay a special head tax, and have been subjected to insult added to injury, with the payment being accompanied by humiliating procedures. Previously, Jews were barred from active military services: they were not permitted to bear arms; instead, they had to do the meanest manual work. By 1952, they were forced to pay a special tax for being "exempt" from military service. They are also excluded from governmental services.

The Jews of Afghanistan, except for Kabul, have always lived in ghettos. Everywhere they keep together for fear of outrages. Women and children rarely leave their neighborhood.

Anti-Semitic propaganda and arrests of Jews after the establishment of Israel led to an appeal in 1950, by the Afghan Jews to Israel for assistance. In the appeal they complained of being systematically deprived of every possibility of earning a living and of soldiers and policemen oppressing them without interference. Interventions by the World Jewish Congress led to the release of at least part of those who had been imprisoned.

Emigration from Afghanistan went on all the time, mostly to England, Russia, and Germany. Emigration to Palestine began in 1923, but it was on a comparatively small scale. Approximately a thousand left in the 1940's for Palestine via India. Emigration to Israel was stepped up when the ban was lifted at the end of 1950: about 3,800 have arrived in Israel via Persia since the establishment of the Jewish State.

The present number of Jews in Afghanistan is estimated at a few hundred families only. They live in Kabul, Herat, and Balch.

MOROCCO

In 1933 (and until 1956) Morocco was divided into three parts: (a) the French Protectorate, (b) the Spanish Protectorate, and (c) the Free City of Tangier. The Jewish position in the three regions differed considerably.

The Jews were subjects of the Sultan (whose seat was in the French Zone but who theoretically also exercised his functions in the Spanish Zone) and as such depended on the whims of the Sherifian administration. They were not permitted to hold office in that administration, at least, in any position of authority, nor—under the Protectorate Treaty—could they acquire

French citizenship. They were obliged to settle all their disputes with Moslems before Moslem judges. However, the formerly existing prohibitions on residence outside the ghettos, attendance at general schools, and exercise of any profession they desired were abolished under the Protectorate.

There were about 140,000 Jews in the French zone of Morocco in 1933. The figure rose to over 161,000 in 1936. At that time, over 46 percent of all the Jews lived in the three cities of Casablanca, Marrakesch, and Fez, and another 13 percent inhabited three other cities. The rest were scattered all over the country in smaller groups. They were usually small storekeepers, peddlers, and artisans. Most Jews lived in ghettos, where conditions were appalling. Their quarters were overcrowded; six to seven persons per room was no rarity; in certain cases as many as ten squeezed together in a single room.

The status of the Jewish communities was as low as that of the Jews in general. The communities were under strict supervision of the authorities. They required governmental approval for the sale and acquisition of real estate and the filing of lawsuits; prior authorization for the use of the funds, income and expenses were needed. In 1945, certain Jews, who paid a special tax, were granted the right to elect the members of the community committees, but those elected needed the approval of the authorities to assume their posts. The liaison between the community and the protectorate administration was an Inspector of Jewish Institutions.

In general, Moroccan Jews enjoyed physical security until the pro-Vichy administration instituted anti-Jewish measures, including the mandatory yellow badge. In November, 1942, when the German army was about to march into Casablanca, a mass pogrom was planned by the Moroccan nationalists. Fortunately and fortuitously, the U. S. Army occupied Casablanca a few days in advance of the fixed date of November 15. Riots took place in Oujda in May, 1948, following the proclamation of of Israel as an independent Jewish state, with the result that sixty-five Jews were beaten up and a boycott was proclaimed. In June of that year, pogroms occurred in Oujda and Djerade, resulting in forty-three Jews killed and 155 wounded. These pogroms could have been averted if the appeals of the Jewish communities for protection and assistance had been heeded. Later the perpetrators were punished.

The struggle for Moroccan independence seriously affected the Jewish position. An indirect boycott of Jewish stores began in 1952. In August, 1953, riots again took place in Oujda, exacting a death toll of four Jews and the burning of a Jewish pharmacy. Attempts to storm the Jewish quarter of Rabat were frustrated by the French police. The year 1954 witnessed killings of Jews in Casablanca, stabbings in Rabat, and a pogrom in Petitjean, causing six fatalities and the sacking of the Jewish quarter. On the other hand, the Sultan promised to improve the Jewish status and four Jews were admitted to the Moroccan Higher Civil Service College.

With the establishment of Israel, the emigration of Moroccan Jews to the Jewish state began, despite the outlawing of Zionism and the ban on emigration proclaimed by the Sultan. The ban was lifted after Israel was recognized by France, by which time almost 20,000 had already left through Algeria and Marseilles. With the lifting of the ban, orderly emigration commenced. By 1952, the number of emigrants to Israel had increased to 35,000.

The Spanish zone of Morocco contained about 10,000 to 12,000 Jews during the 1930's. They resided in Tetuan and Melilla for the most part. The political and economic position of the Jews was better there than in the French zone.

Tangier had a native population estimated at about 8,000. Under the Statute of Tangier they enjoyed full equality with Moslems. The International Legislative Assembly comprised three native Jews, who were appointed from a list of nine submitted by the Jewish community. The Jews also elected three members of the municipality of Tangier.

In the last phase of Morocco's struggle for independence, Jewish organizations, and in particular the World Jewish Congress, exerted efforts to obtain guarantees for the Jewish population in a free Morocco. Assurances of equality and freedom of emigration were given by the Moroccan Office of Information and Documentation in New York, and in November, 1955, by the Sultan, when he returned to Rabat from his exile. A Jew was appointed to the cabinet and others were given positions of authority in the Moroccan administration. Today there is hardly a ministry without some Jewish personnel. Jews are valued as doctors, lawyers, teachers and other professionals, of whom there is a scarcity in Morocco. On the other hand, the general economic position in Morocco, which has worsened since independence, has especially affected the Jews. Many French and Jewish employees have since left Morocco and the departure of the French has undercut the Jewish clientele. Emigration has considerably depleted the smaller communities, creating there a sense of insecurity and an urge to move to larger cities, where employment and work are easier to obtain.

The communal position of the Moroccan Jews has not improved. The local autonomy which existed in the Spanish zone and the large cities of Rabat and Fez, has been replaced by stricter control on the part of the local governors. These arbitrary local officials sometimes refuse to recognize the elected presidents of communities, set aside referenda, etc.

Emigration was at first free and in 1955 a total of almost 25,000 Jews emigrated from Morocco to Israel. However, in May, 1956, official voices were heard denouncing emigration as anti-national. On May 13, 1956, the police, without warning, ordered the dissolution of the organization which was concerned with emigration—known as Kadima—and stopped emigration. There had accumulated in a camp near Casablanca over 7,000 would-be emigrants. Thanks to intervention by the WJC, an agreement was reached whereby they were permitted to leave for Israel in August-September, 1956. Despite formal promises that no restrictions would be placed on individual emigration, such restrictions are, in fact, extant. Although the pressure toward emigration has diminished somewhat, it is still very much in existence, especially in the smaller Jewish communities.

The hopes of Moroccan Jewry for political rights and social equality when Morocco became an independent state, were shattered by the pro-Arab league policy of the government in 1958. Jewish organizations came under stricter control, emigration to Israel was banned, and postal relations with Israel were severed in 1959. Since 1956 some 30,000 Jews are reported to have left Morocco despite the ban. The problem of Jewish emigration took a dramatic turn with the sinking of a small boat *Pisce* in January, 1961, carrying forty-three "illegal" Moroccan Jews to Gibraltar on their way to Israel. All were drowned.

The old King Mohammed V, kept a spark of Jewish hope alive with his expression of solicitude for Moroccan Jewry and his promise to end the bans of Jewish emigration. But his sudden death and the accession of his son, King Hassan II, to the throne in 1961 have sealed the exits. According to the census figures published by the Ministry of the Interior, the Jewish population has declined in recent years from 180,000 to 160,032. The largest Jewish community is in Casablanca and now numbers 71,175, the census reports. Some 14 percent of the total live in Sefron, 11 percent in Essaquira, and 5.2 percent in Marrakesch.

TUNISIA

On the eve of 1933, the 60,000 Jews of Tunisia consisted of two distinct groups: the indigenous Jews known as *twansa*, and the immigrants from Spain and Italy who were called *grana*. The two communities not only differed in their religious ritual, language, and culture, but were, in fact, two different communities with their separate temples, tribunals, cemeteries, butcher shops, etc. There was a Grand Rabbi of the *twansa* but none of the *grana*.

The Jewish community of Tunis, enjoying the status of a legal personality, was jointly elected by the two groups. In other places the council of the community was appointed by the local authorities. The right of election was, in time, somewhat expanded.

In Tunis the Community Council consisted of nine *twansa* and three *grana* and was divided into two sections: one concerned with cultural and the other with welfare affairs. The existing communities joined in 1948 in a Federation of Jewish Communities in Tunisia. The income of the community was derived from taxes on kosher meat and matzot, from donations, etc. There were rabbinical tribunals which had jurisdiction over religious and family affairs, the members being appointed by the Bey of Tunis as members of the Tunisian judiciary and paid by the Tunisian Treasury.

Politically the Jews, unless they were foreign nationals, were equal citizens of Tunisia, but they did not serve as judges nor did they hold any high office in the Tunisian administration. French citizens, however, were employed in the protectorate administration. Generally, the relations between Jews and Moslems were good, but the position of the small Jewish communities in the interior of the country was bad and growing worse. The Jews there were subjected to economic boycotts; they were frequently robbed, beaten, and sometimes were even killed by the Moslem population.

Almost a third of the gainfully employed Jews were engaged in commerce, and slightly over one-fourth were in industry and handicraft. One-fifth were manual workers and servants and the rest were professional men and officials, with only 0.3 percent engaged in agriculture. The trend, in general, was—as a result of the growth of a Moslem class—toward a larger proportion of manual workers and professionals, and a smaller proportion of those engaged in commerce. While there were well-to-do Jews outside the ghettos (haras), the residents of the Jewish quarters were very poor. Even in the city of Tunis one out of every three Jewish families lived in conditions of appalling poverty. The proportion in other cities was even higher. Most of the rooms in the haras were without windows and not infrequently as many as eight to twelve persons lived in one such room.

Until 1938, French naturalization was granted quite freely; thereafter it slowed down considerably so that from 1946 to 1951 only 382 Jews were naturalized. By 1949, about one out of every five Tunisian Jews was of French nationality.

During the war Tunisia came under the Vichy administration which instituted a number of anti-Jewish measures. In 1942-1943, Tunisia was under virtual German control. With Nuremberg efficiency they introduced compulsory labor and spoliation, took hostages, and imposed fines. Pillage, rape, and murder were frequent in the outlying regions.

Within twenty years the Jewish population increased to 100,000-110,000, of whom about 60,000 to 70,000 lived in the city of Tunis and about 20,000 in the interior of the country. The rest were scattered in smaller communities. However, the census of early 1956 showed only 57,000 Tunisian Jews, to which must be added about 25,000 foreign Jews. The total had thus declined to about 80,000. This was due—despite natural increase —to emigration, the departures for Israel alone between 1947 and 1956 amounting to 27,000. Economically the situation did not improve much—the largest portion still lived in dire poverty and the ghettos were as overcrowded as in earlier times. The trend of the Arabs taking over Jewish positions continued. Yet, on the other hand, a sizeable group of Tunisian Jewry rose into the merchant and professional classes.

The fight for Tunisian home rule and independence which started in 1952 had its repercussions on the Jewish scene. Boycott appeals by Tunisian nationalist leaders, the plunder of Jewish stores during the general riots, and the political rivalry in municipal elections, which were construed as a tug-of-war between the French and the Tunisians, were part of the difficulties. In January, 1953, a bomb exploded at the entrance to a Jewish house, and in May, 1953, disturbances occurred in the Jewish quarter of Tunis.

The Jewish position improved in 1954, with the stabilization of the general situation. The government gave assurances that Jews would be treated on a footing of equality with all the other inhabitants.

With the attainment of home rule, a Jew was appointed a cabinet minister, and orders were given for the appointment of Jews to the police force and administration. This was counterbalanced by the worsened economic position of the country, and the changeover from French Protectorate to a free Tunisia resulted in the squeezing out of Jews from their traditional positions as middlemen and professionals. The increased nationalistic tendencies resulted, among other thing, in certain opposition on the part of official Tunisian circles to Zionism. Emigration to Israel increased and resulted in the departure, in 1955, of 6,100 Jews for the Jewish State.

The attainment of full sovereignty for Tunisia did not result in spectacular changes on the Jewish scene, from the political point of view. It aggravated the organizational situation, however. In the program of laicization of Tunisia the rabbinical courts were abolished, although in practice they continued to function on a scale comparable with rabbinical courts in the West. The same policy led to the dissolution of the Federation of Jewish Communities. The Jews of Tunisia, in the view of the government, should distinguish themselves from other inhabitants only in religion. Therefore it was reasoned, the Jews need no organ which is engaged in other than religious affairs. The Federation was replaced by a temporary Central Jewish Consistory to deal with religious affairs only. In the same way all central Jewish welfare agencies were dissolved, and only local welfare bodies, under governmental control, are permitted.

Although the government proclaimed that the right of emigration to Israel was to be maintained, the exodus must not be organized. Jews were warned against Zionist tendencies, and those who either "dream of the Promised Land" or felt themselves French, it was intimated, had better leave the country.

The present Jewish population is estimated at about 67,000. The largest Jewish community is in Tunis and numbers approximately 50,000.

LIBYA

In the early 1930's Libya, then under Italian administration, and consisting of Tripolitania, Cyrenaica, and the Fezzan, comprised a Jewish population of approximately 25,000, of whom 22,000 lived in Tripolitania. The Jewish population rose to somewhat over 29,000 in 1937 and to 36,000 in 1948. Few of the Jews possessed Italian nationality; some were foreign citizens. The vast majority were Libyans and had the same status as the rest of the population. There were two legally constituted Jewish communities. There also existed rabbinical tribunals with jurisdiction over religious and family affairs insofar as Libyan Jews were concerned.

The economic position of Libyan Jewry was rather poor. Only one-third had adequate incomes and many lived on charity.

Living conditions were even worse: many lived in underground caves or dark shacks. Disease was widespread.

Politically, the situation was also unfavorable, because of the Italian policy of that period to curry favor with the Moslems. In 1938, the Italian racial laws were introduced in Libya. Italian citizenship granted to foreign Jews was revoked, the Jewish cultural institutions were closed, and Jews were prohibited from possessing businesses in the European parts of the principal cities. Somewhat later thousands of young Jews were put to forced labor and in the winter of 1942-1943, Jewish males from the ages of seventeen to forty-two were put into concentration camps, and females and children under a curfew. For a time Libyan Jews also suffered from German persecution and war acts when Rommel's divisions held the upper hand in the Desert campaign.

When the war ended, the country was under British occupation. Nevertheless, in November, 1945, large-scale savage pogroms occurred in Tripolitania. These resulted in 130 dead including babies and old men, some 190 wounded, and property losses estimated at £600,000 to £800,000. The British provided some financial relief but no adequate punishment of the guilty. An attack on the Jewish quarter in Tripoli occurred in June, 1948, instigated mainly by Tunisian volunteers on their way to Palestine. The cost was 14 dead, the desecration of synagogues, and considerable damage to property. In 1949, a bomb was thrown in the Jewish quarter of a provincial town.

Persecution and disorders caused the Jews from the provinces to seek refuge in Tripoli. Only a few hundred remained in the smaller places. The exodus from the provinces was accompanied by extensive emigration which by 1951—the year of the establishment of the State of Libya—had reduced the number of Jews in Libya to about 5,000-6,000. All told, approximately 32,500 Jews had left Libya for Israel. This emigration continued, so that by now only somewhat over 4,000 still live in Libya. There are about 4,000 in Tripoli, and some 300 to 400 in Benghazi. Their economic position is generally tolerable; some of those remaining are well-to-do people, but about one-half are poor. They live under restrictions with respect to travel and communication with people abroad. Their social and sport clubs are closed. There are two Jewish communities in Tripoli and Benghazi, but they do not enjoy the previous legal status authorizing them to collect taxes. Late in 1958 the Tripoli Community was placed under governmental supervision.

YEMEN

Of all the Moslem countries, Yemen enforced the Moslem anti-Jewish laws most strictly. Thus all Jews of Yemen over thirteen years of age had to pay a special higher tax. They were debarred from the army and not accepted in government services even in the lowest ranks. In law courts their evidence against Moslems was not accepted. The Jews had to wear long side curls, a special turban, a long black shirt, and no shoes. They were not permitted to touch a Moslem; they were not allowed to raise their voices in the presence of Moslems or when praying, and had to stand up in the company of Moslems. They were always at the call of any Moslem, even when in synagogue. One of the most humiliating requirements was to clean the public latrines. Jews were prohibited from bestriding an animal or from riding on it; from building houses higher than those of Moslems; from having lights on in the night or from stirring from their quarters at night. A Jew was not to be beaten to death, but every Moslem could pull a Jew by his curls or spit in his face with impunity.

Economically, their position was almost as bad. Jews even began to be self-eliminated from their traditional trades as soap-makers and weavers, as they had to train Moslems in these fields. Their main occupations were as blacksmiths, potters, gold and silversmiths, basket weavers, etc.

The tragic position of the Yemenite Jews forced them to emigrate in masses, mostly to Palestine, despite the existing prohibition and the confiscation of property for "illegal" emigration. Large-scale migration to Palestine, the Holy Land of Yemenite Jews, through Aden, started in 1933, amounting to 4,000 between 1933 and 1935, and 1,100 in the next three years. In the first few years of the last war, emigration, except for a trickle, stopped; but between 1942 and 1944 another 2,000 escaped from Yemen. All in all, about 17,000 left Yemen between 1923 and 1946, but there were almost no emigrants in the years 1946-1948. The only way open was Aden, where by 1944 about 3,000 were crowded. The figure rose to 4,000 in 1947 and 8,000 in October 1948.

By the end of 1948, six Yemenite Jews were arrested on charges of having killed two Arab girls for ritual purposes. Outbreaks of violence and plunder followed. In the meantime, the evacuation of the Yemen Jews from Aden by airlift—an operation which became known as "Operation Magic Carpet"— began and the flow of Yemenite Jews to Aden increased. The first phase, until July 1, 1949, embraced about 4,500 and the second, the largest, over 29,000 between July 1 and November 14, 1949. About 15,000 left Yemen for Israel in the next few years. Since then only small groups emigrated.

All in all, between May 15, 1948, and the end of 1956, over 45,700 Yemenite Jews arrived in Israel.

After the exodus a certain number remained, mostly to prepare for emigration, but stayed on. The Iman then decreed that all Jews must leave Yemen. Although the district governors began to press the Jews to emigrate, the decree was not enforced everywhere. In some places the Jews had to embrace Mohammedanism in order to be able to stay on.

The present number of Jews in Yemen is not known exactly; probably no more than several hundred are left by now. They are mostly craftsmen and earn an adequate living. But for all practical purposes there has been an end to Galut Yemen.

Similar hopes for an exodus of Moroccon Jews were ended on December 19, 1961, after political parties in Rabat attacked the government for having tolerated "Zionist-inspired" emigration. Some 2,000 Jews left Morocco in the short span of three weeks when all travel restrictions were lifted. But 20,000 Jews who had received passports were affected by the stoppage.

CHAPTER FOUR

THE JEWS IN THE SOVIET UNION
I.   1917-1939

by JACOB ROBINSON

Before the outbreak of the Russian revolution more than one-third of the world's Jews dwelt within the borders of the sprawling Russian empire. From the Baltic Sea to the Black Sea, in a wide belt across Eastern Europe, were the most thickly settled Jewish communities in the world. For many generations the Jews of Russia and Poland had formed the backbone of Judaism. They had built great seats of religious learning; they had developed a major literature in Hebrew and Yiddish; they had provided the Haskalah movement, Zionism, and Jewish Socialism with some of their most brilliant leaders. And from their teeming towns and cities there flowed a constant stream of immigrants who brought new energies and vitality to Jewish religious and communal life in all the countries to which they came.

After the collapse of the Russian empire, several of her westernmost provinces with large Jewish populations became independent countries. A large segment of pre-war Russian Jewry, however, remained within the borders of the new Russian state. Until the Nazis swept without warning across the borders of Russia in June, 1941, the fate of Russian Jewry lay hidden behind the barriers which the U.S.S.R. had placed between herself and a world she considered unsympathetic or hostile. For twenty years Russia's 3,000,000 Jews—almost one-third of Europe's pre-war total of 9,500,000 Jews—were cut off from Jewish communities in other countries.

91

Before the war, 2,100,000 Jews lived in those parts of Russia later invaded and occupied by the Nazis. After the last remnants of the German armies had been rolled back from the desolated plains of occupied Russia, only 600,000 Jews (including those who had been evacuated) remained alive.

In all of Russia there were, at the end of World War II, 1,800,000 Jews. Approximately 600,000 more lived in countries bordering on Russia and were subject to strong Russian influence. Thus, over two-thirds of Europe's surviving Jews were within the orbit of the Soviet system.

The reopening of some of the lines of communications with Russia—slender though these were after the war, enabled us to estimate more clearly than before some of the effects which Soviet society has had on Russian Jewry. In 1939, a census was taken in the Soviet Union and, while only fragmentary returns have so far been published, these, together with facts already known, make possible a more or less detailed account of the fortunes of the Russian Jews from the downfall of the empire to the Nazi invasion.

Within the Pale

The Jews of Czarist Russia were, in the mass, a poverty-stricken people, subject to special taxes; confined by law to certain parts of the country known as the Pale of Settlement; prohibited from owning or renting farms; forced to choose among a limited number of occupations because they were barred from others. Yiddish was the language of their daily life and they adhered to orthodox Judaism with intense piety. Their birth rate was high and from 1881, when government-inspired pogroms erupted throughout the country, tens of thousands emigrated annually.

World War I brought disaster to the Jewish population, as the battles of the eastern zone were waged mostly in the Pale of Settlement and in the thickly settled Jewish regions of Poland. Many refugees fled into the interior of old Russia and the restriction of Jews to the Pale of Settlement was practically broken as a result. In addition, thousands of Polish Jews were deported to areas outside the battle zones. Forcibly uprooted from their established life, hundreds of thousands of Jews lived precariously in cities of the dying Russian empire.

The March Revolution

The revolution of March, 1917, took over from the Czarist regime a backward country with undeveloped industry, a largely illiterate population with little experience in self-government, but, at the same time, a people bursting with creative energies which had been stifled by centuries of oppression. The Jews of Russia were similarly endowed. When on April 3, 1917, the Provisional Democratic Government issued a decree abolishing at one stroke all the legal disabilities of the Jews, the latent forces of their group-consciousness found immediate expression.

New Jewish social and educational institutions and other expressions of their distinctive communal life sprang into existence. It was not long before the leading Jewish political parties—the Zionists, the Socialist-Zionists, the Bundists and others—were demanding a regime of cultural autonomy. Their program called for equality of rights and organic integration in the economic and political organization of the state. They also demanded the establishment of self-governing communal institutions, to be legally recognized and supported by government funds.

Communist Revolution

The new freedom was short-lived. Hardly eight months after the Provisional Democratic Government had assumed power Russia was plunged into bloody civil strife by the Communist revolution. The Jews suffered more than any other group of the population. Most of them lived where the fighting was heaviest. More than 80 percent of Russia's Jews, only 14 percent of the non-Jews, lived in the cities—always the chief war sufferers. From 1918 to 1922, pogroms, instigated by the anti-Bolshevist forces, took place in some 900 cities and villages of the Ukraine and White Russia. At least 75,000 Jews, mostly men of middle age, were slain in these outbreaks. Between 500,000 and 600,000 fled from their homes to the comparative safety of Russia proper despite widespread famine.

Throughout these tragic years the Jewish Communists, with greater partisan zeal than the Communists of other Russian nationalities, conducted a relentless drive against the Jewish religion, Jewish communal life, and other distinctively Jewish activities. At their instigation, cultural institutions like "Tarbut" (the Hebrew school system) and the Jewish Educational Association (OPE) were liquidated and even such relief agencies as YEKOPO, ORT, and OZE were bolshevized and later forced to discontinue their work. Rabbis and other religious functionaries were persecuted. Zionism, considered a tool of British imperialism, was outlawed and its leaders were arrested and deported to remote parts of Siberia. Instruction in Hebrew was suspect, and Hebrew books were confiscated.

There was no place in the Soviet system for individual craftsmen and businessmen who constituted 70 percent of the Jewish population. These became automatically "declassed." In contrast, the overwhelming majority of the non-Jewish population were peasants and industrial workers and the ratio of "declassed" elements among them was relatively small. After the Soviet regime was securely established, the Jewish problem became predominantly a problem of "declassed" people.

The manner in which the mass of Russia's "declassed" Jews was absorbed in the new economic order was determined partly by factors which affected the Russian people as a whole and partly by deliberate government action to solve the problems of the Jewish population in particular.

THE ECONOMIC STRUCTURE

During the two decades following the Communist Revolution, hundreds of thousands of "declassed" Jews died in the struggle to keep alive in the midst of civil war, pogroms, and prolonged starvation. The deaths of many of the older people were undoubtedly hastened by continuous lack of appropriate housing, food and medical care, and by their inability to face the tremendous difficulties involved in adjustment to the new social order.

Breakdown of the Pale

During the years of militant communism, civil war, and the Five-Year Plans, the whole country experienced widespread population movements to meet changing economic objectives. The Jews also took part in these population shifts. At the beginning of 1939, no fewer than 1,200,000 out of a total of 3,100,000 Soviet Jews were to be found in regions which before the Revolution would have been practically inaccessible to them. Most of them lived in Leningrad, with an estimated Jewish population of 275,000 and Moscow with about 400,000, and other large industrial cities of the Russian Soviet Federated Republic.

However, even in 1939 the majority of the Jewish population still lived in the traditional Jewish regions of the Ukraine and White Russia. There were 1,532,000 in the Ukraine (of whom 180,000 were in Odessa, 175,000 in Kiev, 150,000 in Kharkov and 100,000 in Dnepropetrovsk), and 375,000 in White Russia.

Large-scale migrations of Jews to the metropolitan centers served before 1929, when the Soviet government began its massive program of industrialization, to alleviate the lot of the Jews who remained in the regions and enabled those who migrated to enter occupations which had previously been closed to them.

Jewish Five-Year Plan

Social planning accounted for the greatest changes in the economic structure of Russian Jewry. After a few years of "planning" on a minor scale, involving special legislation favoring Jewish settlement on the soil, the Soviet government in 1930 lauched a major program for Jewish reconstruction. The program was part of the nationwide plan for general economic reconstruction. The Jewish Five-Year Plan had four specific objectives: It sought to liquidate the Jewish small towns; to place as many Jews as possible on the land and to collectivize individual farmers; to enroll craftsmen into cooperatives; to draw large numbers of Jews into industry.

According to official information, the program resulted in the disappearance of "unproductive" elements among the Jewish population and a marked increase in the percentage of industrial laborers and "intellectuals"—lawyers, engineers, doctors, scientists, teachers, etc. The extent of the changes involved may be measured by the fact that some 50 percent of the Jewish occupations in the pre-Revolutionary period had been classed as "unproductive."

Jewish Town Vanishes

Under the Czars, the Jews of Russia had for centuries lived chiefly in small towns which were predominantly Jewish in population and in character. These towns functioned as trading and supply centers for the peasants and the big land-owners in the surrounding farms. In Soviet Russia the small Jewish town has practically disappeared as an administrative unit, and if it still exists as a geographical entity, its character has completely changed. Instead of functioning as a source of supplies for the surrounding farm population, it has become an industrial center. The greater part of its population has either been moved in the course of attempts to settle the Jewish townsman on the land, or has migrated to other regions and found its place in the expanding Civil Service and in industry.

Not only has the Jewish small town disappeared, but cities which for centuries had been predominantly Jewish gradually lost their Jewish character. The total number of inhabitants increased, but the Jewish population remained practically stationary, with the result that the percentage of Jews in these towns dropped precipitously.

In 1926, for example, Minsk had 53,000 Jews in its total population of 131,000; in 1939 its total population had risen to 238,000 while the number of Jews had remained almost stationary. During the same period the population of Kiev rose from 512,000 to 850,000, but its 1926 population of 175,000 Jews remained practically unchanged. The same is true of other large cities.

While the cities and the small towns, which once had large concentrations of Jews, were losing their Jewish character, the great masses of Jews were pouring into the metropolitan centers of Russia proper. It was estimated that 42 percent of the pre-war Jewish population in the Soviet Union lived in six great cities.

The Working Class

The number of Jewish industrial workers from 1897 to 1939 increased from 50,000 to 400,000.

The increase in the number of Jewish industrial workers was one of the by-products of the tremendous efforts to industrialize Russia during the three Five-Year Plans. How many of the 400,000 Jewish industrial workers are manual workers or technicians cannot be ascertained, since the term "industry" in the 1939 census covers all factory employees, whatever their function. The process of industrializing the Jews was accompanied by opposition on the part of non-Jewish workers to having Jews placed in their workshops. In some instances this opposition led to open clashes.

Jewish craftsmen tended to become members of craft cooperatives if they did not transfer to industry. In 1939 the number of craftsmen in cooperatives was four times as great as those outside the cooperatives. But the percentage of craftsmen in the Jewish population in 1939 was smaller than in 1897.

Farming

The authorities made strenuous efforts to attract Jews to the land. Jewish farming had a long tradition in Russia. In 1897, 2.4 percent of the Jews were in agriculture, with some 15,000 Jewish farmer families—94,402 persons altogether. During the early years of militant communism and of the "New Economic Policy" agrarianization was primarily a spontaneous movement of declassed people seeking a livelihood. It became a predominately planned process only after 1924. The first major project was that of Jewish mass colonization in the Crimea. The Crimean project was soon dropped, however, and the existing farms were collectivized. After 1930 all efforts were directed toward resettlement in Biro-Bidjan, which was scheduled, eventually, to become a kind of Jewish "national home."

Agricultural resettlement, directed by the organization first known as "KOMERD," and later as "GESERD," was the only field in which foreign financial assistance was solicited. Funds were collected through Agrojoint, a special agency sponsored by the Joint Distribution Committee. For several years, American Jewish organizations cooperated with the Soviet government in agricultural settlement but withdrew their cooperation in the late thirties without official explanation. That withdrawal may have been due to the doubtful success of the plan, the collectivization of Jewish farms in the Crimea and to the difficulties the agricultural experts experienced in their dealings with the government.

In addition to these major land settlement schemes, special measures were taken in the late twenties to encourage agriculture as a subsidiary occupation in the small towns. In 1934, there were only 25,000 Jewish farm families—some 100,000 persons altogether—or not more than 3 percent of the total Jewish population. While the official census of 1939 listed 6 percent of the Jewish population in agriculture, this figure probably included Jews living on collective farms but doing some other work.

Jews on the Land

The path of collectivization was not a smooth one. The official historian of USSR Jewry, L. Singer, summarized the conflicts it involved as follows:

> Naturally, the development of the Jewish migrants' collective farming, like the whole agricultural collectivization in the country, encountered violent resistance from the class enemy. Jewish *kulaks* (prosperous farmers) who managed to slip into the ranks of the emigrants, fought at first openly and then clandestinely against the social reconstruction of agriculture. The class enemy would not only infiltrate into the collective farms, but also entered their administrations, inspection commissions, and so on, and carried on their work of undermining. However, the enemy was crushed, and the emigrants' collective farms, too, are solid and forever committed to the Bolshevist road to a high level of

prosperity and culture. The one-time Luftmenschen and unskilled workers, formerly apathetic and backward, have now become active and conscious builders of socialism and communism.

The Professions

One of the most striking results of the breakup of the old Jewish economic structure was the influx of Jews into many intellectual and professional fields from which they had been previously barred. Here, perhaps, the element of spontaneous choice played a greater role than planning. The great majority of the 350,000 Jewish salaried employees are listed as "intellectuals," since there are practically no private liberal professions in the Soviet regime. A comparison of the figures for 1897 with those of 1939, though obscured by the difference in terminology, shows the tremendous progress made by Jews in these fields. In 1897 there were 42,000 Jews in the professions; there are now 230,000. In addition, the types of professional activity in which Jews once engaged have changed radically. The census of 1897 registered 1,034 writers, scientists, and artists, 9,766 medical personnel, 35,263 teachers (most of them *melamdim,* i.e., elementary Hebrew teachers), and some 75,000 business employees. In 1939, the official census listed 25,000 Jewish engineers, architects and constructors, 60,000 auxiliary technical personnel, 1,000 other agricultural technicians, 7,000 scientists, 46,000 teachers in elementary and grammar schools, 30,000 engaged in cultural activities (journalists, librarians, club managers), 17,000 in art, 21,000 doctors, and 31,000 auxiliary medical personnel. The growth in various professional groups between 1926 and 1939 has been between 200 and 500 percent.

Certainly figures alone do not tell the whole story. An adequate picture of the Jewish contributions to Russian culture would have to embrace all fields of science, literature, and the arts. There are, for example, such world-famous names as Abraham Joffe, the physicist, and Alexander Gurevitch, the discoverer of mythogenetic rays.

A new phenomenon is the achievements of Jews in the literature and culture of the "minor" Soviet nationalities. The national poet of White Russia, Z. Biadule (pseudonym of Samuel Plavnik) is a Jew who began his career in the field of Hebrew and Yiddish letters.

THE JEW IN SOVIET SOCIETY

In pre-revolutionary Russia, Jews were primarily identified by their religion and only baptism opened avenues to advancement. The Soviet state, at least until World War II, adopted a negative attitude toward religion. Since religion is neither a matter of public record nor an element of public organization, the Jew had to find another niche in Russian society. Here a difficult problem faced Soviet theorists, the final solution for which has not yet been found. The Jews were classed as a nationality. But according to Soviet theory, nationality implies that a group possesses its own territory, language, and economic organization. The last criterion is irrelevant since the economy of the whole Union is centrally planned and directed. Yet even the classification of Jews as a nationality under the criteria of territory and language presents certain difficulties.

The criterion of language was not consistently applied in the case of Jews. Every Soviet citizen who so desired could declare himself a Jew and be recorded as such under the rubric of nationality on his passport, even if his mother tongue was not Yiddish. In fact, many Russian-speaking Jews, some of them in high positions, did so. Yet, if there is any specific Jewish culture in Russia, it is almost exclusively in Yiddish. Thus, the Soviet Union is the only country in the world where there is not a single Jewish periodical in the dominant language of the country, though hundreds of thousands of Jews speak Russian exclusively and probably all understand it. The last issue of "Tribuna," a Russian-language magazine devoted to the Jewish agrarian problem, was published in 1933. Since then, no other Russian-language magazines for Jews have appeared. The tendency has been for those linguistically assimilated to lose interest in specifically Jewish affairs. It is significant that whatever studies of the Jewish situation and of Jewish problems were published in the Soviet Union have been almost exclusively in Yiddish. Linguistic assimilation, it would therefore appear, has far greater significance with respect to Jews in Russia than anywhere else.

"Territorial" Nationality

While the territorial criterion of nationality is largely inapplicable in the case of the Soviet Jews, a substitute for it has been found. The government gave expression to the "territorial" aspect of Jewish nationality by setting up, in line with general Soviet legislation on national minorities, special Jewish administrative and court districts in those parts of the Ukraine and White Russia with predominantly Jewish populations and where Yiddish is one of the official languages.

Before the war, there were five Jewish national districts; three in the Ukraine (Kalinindorf, New Zlotopol and Stalindorf) and two in the Crimea (Friedorf and Larindorf). The population of these areas was about 90,000, of whom 60,000 were Jews. The number of Jewish local (village) Soviets was 224 with a population of about 300,000.

Schools with Yiddish as the language of instruction were not confined to these districts but were set up by the government wherever the population desired them. According to official estimates, there were some 425,000 Jewish pupils in the elementary, junior high and high schools in the third year of the Second Five-Year Plan. Little more than 20 percent of this number were in Yiddish schools.

Fight Against the Past

On the basis of scattered information in the Soviet press, it seems that attendance at Yiddish schools was steadily declining in 1946. Owing to the militant anti-traditional character of these schools, many parents obviously preferred to send their children to non-Jewish schools where they would not be so indoctrinated against Jewish tradition.

In their attempt to create a new "Soviet Jewry" the Jewish section of the Communist Party (*Yevsektsia*) sought to separate Russian Jewry both from its historical past and from Jewish communities in other countries. The lengths to which they were prepared to go in achieving these aims is illustrated by their adoption of a phonetic Yiddish spelling intended to obscure the connection of Yiddish with Hebrew.

Before the war, the government spent large sums on Jewish cultural activities, especially in the field of research. Two special Jewish research institutes existed, one in Minsk and the other in Kiev. A survey of their publications reveals an imposing array of studies on the Yiddish language, Yiddish literature, and Yiddish folklore. It is not easy to ascertain whether there was any popular interest in these studies or whether they were "official" works. The official historian of Soviet Jewry sees the greatest achievements of Yiddish culture in the Soviet Union in the fields of literature and dramatic art—there were ten Yiddish state theatres and two dramatic schools. The growth of book production may be an indication of that success. While only forty-three books were published in the Ukraine in 1913, the number published in 1939 was 339. Much Marxist-Leninist literature has been published in Yiddish editions. Within a period of two years, 45,200 copies of the "Abridged Course in the History of the Communist Party" were printed in Yiddish. Well over 3,000,000 copies of the works of the great Jewish humorist, Sholem Aleichem, were published in ten languages in the period from 1917 to 1939. The works of modern Yiddish writers seem to have a large circulation but it is impossible to ascertain how much of this has been in the Yiddish language and how much in translation.

Assimilation

Despite the encouragement of Yiddish, assimilation has gone forward at a tremendous rate. The process of assimilation is not only a linguistic, but a political and social development as well. The life of the Soviet citizen—Jew and non-Jew alike—is almost completely absorbed by the state and subject to strong, uniform cultural influences. In the case of the Jew, this has resulted in a rate of assimilation not paralleled elsewhere. There is no official data about intermarriage. As early as 1926, however, when this tendency was only in its initial stages, 25 percent of the

Jews in Russia proper who married, married non-Jewish women; in the Ukraine 4.6 percent married non-Jews, and 2 percent married outside their faith in White Russia. According to all impartial observers this percentage increased in subsequent years.

Biro-Bidjan

The so-called Jewish Soviets are not purely Jewish. They embrace all the population of a certain district, Jews and non-Jews alike. They are classified as Jewish because of the predominance of Jews in the particular district. While the other nationalities have found a medium of self-expression either in federated national states, national autonomous republics, autonomous regions or national districts, and in national sections of the all-Union Communist Party, the Jewish situation has been different. Until 1930 the Communist Party had a special Jewish section, the so-called *Yevsektsia,* but for reasons never made public, it was dissolved in 1930. Most of its leaders were subsequently liquidated. Since then, there has been no special Jewish political group. Jews continued to be active in the regional Communist parties in the various districts in which they lived.

"Autonomous District"

It is difficult to ascertain which of two factors, the economic —the settlement of Jews on the land, or the political—the creation of some form of state for the Jewish population, influenced the Soviet decision to create a Jewish region in Biro-Bidjan. The project was started in 1928 with the decree of the Central Executive Committee of the U.S.S.R. to "strengthen the district of Biro-Bidjan for the needs of immigration." In 1934 this "unit" was transformed into a Jewish "autonomous region," which is the normal Soviet constitutional form for a territorial minority living within a heterogeneous national state. The results of colonization in Biro-Bidjan were disappointing. Its total population—Jewish and non-Jewish—is 109,000, according to the 1939 census. No more than 23,000 of the more than 60,000 Jews who went there have remained and scarcely 3,000 Jewish families are quoted by Singer as able to make a living from the soil, while the others are working in business and factories. The rest maintain themselves as artisans or casual laborers. Only a small proportion of Jewish children attend Jewish schools. While the general population has grown, the Jewish population has not. Russian is the dominant language in the offices, collective farms and workers' clubs.

The Soviet government was fully aware of the fact that the authorities directly responsible for the settlement of the toiling Jews on the land were in large degree to blame for the failure of the Biro-Bidjan experiment. Thus, the Decree of September 27, 1933, read:

> The Praesidium of the Central Executive Committee of the U.S.S.R. notes that the KOMZET (The Committee for the Establishment of the toiling Jews on the Land) did not shift to a sufficient extent its work to the fundamental district of Biro-Bidjan and did not strive to eliminate the great defects in the process of establishing toiling Jews in it. . . .

The nature of these "great defects" was clearly revealed by the whole history of the Biro-Bidjan settlement; incompetent and inexperienced management, paralyzing red tape and lack of understanding of the vital needs of the settlers are the most important among them. A special decree of the Council of People's Commissars on October 1, 1934, was required in order to urge the completion, by November 1, 1935, of a hospital with seventy-five beds in the city of Biro-Bidjan. The same decree demanded the construction in Biro-Bidjan during 1935 and during the first half of 1936, of:

a) Five elementary schools
b) Two incomplete middle schools, each with accommodations for 210 students
c) Two middle schools
d) Two kindergartens, each with accommodations for seventy children

The Council's recognition of the need for these institutions came fully six years after the region had been settled.

Anti-Semitism

At the end of World War II, Jews still believed that the Soviet government, as a government embodying the socialist tradition of tolerance in national matters, had from the very beginning taken a strong stand against anti-Semitism. The proclamation of the Council of People's Commissars under the leadership of Lenin (dated July 27, 1918) had condemned anti-Semitism in strongest terms, it was pointed out. As in other fights with enemies of the Soviet regime and with long-standing prejudices, Lenin employed two methods of combatting anti-Semitism: persuasion and coercion, it was argued. Jews cited a tremendous literature created in order to teach the working class that anti-Semitism, like other forms of racial and national hatred, was primarily a means of sowing discord among the workers and diverting their hatred from class enemies to their fellows of other races or nationalities. Moreover, the criminal code of the RSFR (Art. 59, Par. 7) provided severe penalties for any attempt to incite national or religious hatred. This law was later incorporated into the Criminal Code of the Union; its basic principle was embodied in Art. 123 of the Stalin Constitution. It has been consistently, even rigorously, enforced by the Soviet courts.

Few sociological surveys would have been more fascinating or fruitful than large-scale studies of the effects of Soviet legislation and economic policies on anti-Semitism in the Soviet Union—the former land of the Czars. Unfortunately, no such data was made available by Soviet authorities. But there was no doubt that the Soviet regime was officially committed to eradicate anti-Semitism wherever it might show itself.

It thus took two decades, from 1939-1959, before the true story of the Jews in the Soviet Union was known.

THE JEWS IN THE SOVIET UNION
II.   Since 1939

by SAMUEL LEVITAS and the Editors of the "New Leader"

THE SOVIET PATTERN IN PERSPECTIVE

Throughout modern history, the treatment of national, racial and religious minorities has been a barometer of social sanity and moral decency. During the past quarter-century in particular, the world has become keenly sensitive, especially as a result of the Nazi experience, to the symbolic role of minorities. It is thus with increasingly troubled spirits that men of conscience have come to feel and express growing concern in recent years for the plight of the Jews in the Soviet Union.

That plight, it must be stressed, is not to be compared with their tragic destiny under the Nazis: Covert discrimination, even the most serious deprivation of guaranteed minority rights, is still a far cry from extermination. The Nazis, in their anti-Semitism as in all their crimes, appealed to the basest instincts of their followers, and Hitler's barbarities were entirely consistent with the ideology of his movement. His regime was not really embarrassed by revelations concerning its policy toward the Jews; at most, it attempted to conceal the proportions and the more grisly aspects of the policy, but not its existence.

It is quite different with Soviet policy toward the Jews, for that policy clearly conflicts with both Soviet constitutional doctrine and the basic internationalist, egalitarian tenets of Marxist-Leninist ideology. The Soviet government, as the documents in this report reveal, singles out the Jews for special, differential treatment. It formally considers the Jews a nationality, as is clear from the internal passport which every Soviet citizen must carry and which lists vital statistical information about the individual. On this passport, which serves as an identity card, there is a space—"Paragraph 5"—for the specification of the citizen's nationality. Every Soviet Jew is required to specify as his nationality: *"Yevrei"*—*"Jew."*

Yet despite this formal recognition, the Soviet government deprives its Jewish citizens of the bulk of even the minimal cultural and spiritual privileges enjoyed by all other Soviet nationalities and religious groups. It provides the Jews with neither the means for maintaining a full cultural life nor the opportunity to assimilate completely. In short, the effect of its policy has been to constitute Soviet Jewry a peculiarly marginal category of citizens and to isolate them from normal existence.

This policy has a history, and it is related to the development of the Soviet nationalities policy as a whole. The more than 200 distinct nationalities and ethnic groups in the USSR have for centuries inhabited the geographical regions in which they reside and have retained their national consciousness, languages, literatures, folklore and customs. In Czarist days, government policy was, with some variations and fluctuations, to Russify the other nationalities forcibly. This policy failed utterly, and the bolsheviks inherited all the problems of rule in a multi-national state. The need of the Soviet state to rule effectively did not differ essentially from the needs of the Czars. The utopian philosophy of cosmopolitan socialism foundered, as had Czarist policy, on the rock of reality. This reality was that the various national groups refused to be extirpated. They clung to their traditions and cultures and remained obdurately irreducible. Effective statecraft on the part of the Communists required that they accommodate their theories to this reality.

It took the Communist party and state a decade and more to hammer out this accommodation. By the late 1920's, a full-fledged, quite new philosophy emerged, signified by Stalin's famous slogan—"national in form, Socialist in content." The consequences of this policy were felt primarily in the political and linguistic spheres. In theory, this policy should have enabled the various national cultures to flourish. In practice, the opposite has been true. "National in form" remained an empty formality; "Socialist in content" was the decisive formulation.

It meant that the newspapers, schools, books, party and state organs in the national republics became carbon copies of their Russian counterparts, exactly aping in their own languages the formulae of Moscow.

Nevertheless, the forms and formalities did exist. The various nationalities did have their own territorial republics, their own schools, newspapers and cultural activities in their own languages—and even, where they lived as a large enough minority in another republic, specially established schools or, at the very last, additional school lessons in their own languages. (A case in point is that of the Tadjiks—a people of some 1.8 million who, though they have their own republic of Tadjikistan, also live in part as a dispersed minority in neighboring Uzbekistan. They have their own schools in Uzbekistan, and where there are too few of them for that purpose, their children are given special lessons in the Tadjik language and history in the Uzbek schools.)

The policy even went so far that linguistic experts were assigned to create whole alphabets and even vocabularies for a number of small, dispersed ethnic groups just emerging from backward, semi-nomadic existence. No doubt such an extension of the policy had both an economic reason (literacy is indispensable to modern industrialization) and a political reason (literacy facilitates the penetration of the Party line to the masses). But the case of the 3,000-odd Udege, in Eastern Siberia, is still striking, for they not only had an alphabet and a culture created for them, but had one of their tribesmen, Dransy Komonko, educated at government expense to become the "national" poet.

The three million Jews of the Soviet Union have now reached such a pass that they are deprived of the national prerogatives which even the 3,000 primitive Udege have. But it was not always so, even during the first two-and-one-half decades of the Soviet regime. At the outbreak of World War I, there were some five million Jews in the Russian Empire. Czarist policy had for a century and one-half been openly, unmitigatedly and violently anti-Semitic. Wholly deprived of the exceedingly few political rights available anywhere in autocratic Russia, the Jews were required to live in a restricted "Pale of Settlement," which consisted chiefly of parts of White Russia, the Ukraine, Bessarabia, Lithuania, Poland and a few other narrow strips of Russian-held territory. There they existed in teeming destitution and thorough-going pauperism.

Despite these extraordinary desperate economic and political circumstances, Jewish cultural, spiritual and intellectual life was at its zenith. Communal organizations of every description flourished. Countless academies of traditional Jewish learning existed side-by-side with modern, advanced Hebrew and Yiddish schools. The forty-year period from 1880 to the Revolution witnessed a virtual renascence of Hebrew and Yiddish literature, led by poets, novelists and essayists of genuine distinction. Large printing establishments existed in all the centers of Jewish population for the publication of daily newspapers, weekly and monthly journals and hundreds of books, in Yiddish and Hebrew. Exciting new ideas, philosophies and movements captured the imagination and inspired the younger generation.

Most of this came to an abrupt end with the Bolshevik Revolution. The Jewish life that was permitted to remain was an attenuated version of its predecessor. To the "Jewish problem," as to the larger nationalities problem, the bolsheviks brought a rigid ideological orientation: They categorically denied the existence of a Jewish nationality. The Jews were a mere "caste," a vestigial anachronism. Grant them political equality and the opportunity to engage in modern, productive economic pursuits, eliminate their religious benightedness—and they would quickly disappear as a group. Such opportunities were indeed created for the Jews as individuals after the Revolution. But as in the case of the other nationalities, the Jews failed to disappear as a group, and the regime found itself forced into working out an accommodation with irreducible realities, and to recognize the existence of the Jewish national entity, no matter how severely restricted the forms it was allowed to take.

Religious practice and instruction were drastically curtailed and virtually driven underground. The Hebrew language was banned, and publication of the Bible in Hebrew was prohibited. The Zionist movement was outlawed, and contacts between

Soviet Jewry and other Jewish communities throughout the world were largely eliminated. Autonomous communal and cultural organizations were increasingly disbanded. And yet, a Jewish cultural life of sorts was nonetheless permitted—in the Yiddish language. A network of Yiddish schools, under party and state supervision, was established. Yiddish newspapers, journals and books were published. Above all, a first-rate Yiddish theater flourished.

But even this came to a sudden and violent end thirteen years ago. With one sweeping administrative decree late in 1948, Stalin and his cultural commissar, Andrei Zhdanov, eliminated every facet of secular Jewish cultural life and physically exterminated more than 450 Jewish writers, artists and intellectuals —the cream of the Soviet Jewish intelligentsia. This shattering blow was, however, only the culmination of a policy that had its beginning more than a decade earlier, in 1936. And the five years after 1948—which came to be known among Soviet Jews as "the Black Years"—were characterized by a marked heightening of the anti-Semitic content and tone of official policy. It was a period when Jewish intellectuals were attacked as "rootless cosmopolitans," when Rudolf Slansky and his comrades in Czechoslovakia were tried not only for opposing Moscow but for being agents of an international Jewish conspiracy in the service of Western intelligence, when a group of Soviet Jewish doctors were falsely accused of killing two leading Soviet officials and plotting to kill others, when Jewish leaders were arrested, tried and executed on trumped-up charges of disloyalty and treason, when it was widely believed by Jews and non-Jews alike that Stalin planned to deport the whole of Soviet Jewry to Eastern Siberia—and all of this to the tune of an anti-Semitic propaganda campaign reminiscent of the Protocols of the Elders of Zion.

The shift of Soviet policy toward the Jews beginning in the late thirties is explainable largely in terms of the Soviet leadership's estimate of the relative loyalty of the Jews under changing world circumstances. In the first decade and a half, however unmalleable the Jewish group might have been, it could be counted on to be loyal to the regime in preference to Czarist,

White Guardist and reactionary forces. But with the purges against the Old Bolsheviks, many of whom were Jews, and especially with the growing possibility of a rapprochement with Nazi Germany in 1938-39, the loyalty of the Jews and their preference for the Soviet regime over the West were called into question.

Beginning in 1938, therefore, a number of Jewish cultural institutions—schools, newspapers, etc.—were forcibly closed down, and part of Jewish communal leadership (which had loyally carried through its assigned task of implementing previous Soviet policy to the Jewish community) was liquidated. This policy, temporarily halted and reversed during the war, when once again full Jewish loyalty was relied upon in the war against the Nazis, was reinstated and expanded with the war's end. More forcefully than ever, then, the Soviet leadership came to suspect Jewish loyalty at a time of heightened tension with the West and of growing Soviet antipathy to the new State of Israel.

The period, 1948-52, was also marked by the heightening of Stalin's paranoid megalomania, as Premier Nikita Khrushchev amply revealed in his famous "secret speech" at the 20th Congress of the Soviet Communist party. We need only recall some of the highlights of that period: the Communist coup in Czechoslovakia; the fight against "revisionists" in the world Communist movement and the expulsion of Marshal Tito from the Cominform; the drive toward rigid conformity in Soviet arts and sciences; the Soviet-directed campaign in Italy and France against the Marshall Plan and the North Atlantic Treaty Organization; the Berlin Blockade; the Korean War. As Stalin sharpened the cold war against the West, he simultaneously sharpened the war against that group of Soviet citizens whom he believed had the closest contacts with and sentiments for the West—the Jews.

Though the situation has eased considerably since Stalin's death in 1953, the basic pattern of the policy remains essentially unchanged. Its tragic lineaments are ironically illustrated by the fact that the Jews today are deprived even of the prerogatives presently enjoyed by the Volga Germans, who were deported and dispersed by Stalin during the days of the Nazi invasion of the USSR. For the Volga Germans now have German schools, radio broadcasts in their own language, and even two newspapers. *Neues Leben* and *Arbeit*, in their places of dispersion.

The Soviet government cannot, of course, admit its discriminatory policy toward the Jews. To do so would reveal a sharp clash between Soviet constitutional doctrine and the real situation, and, more significantly, a profound contradiction of basic ideology. And this would be no small thing in a country where Marxist-Leninist ideology, however distorted and diluted, still holds sway—an ideology that makes a fetish of "the unity of theory and practice," the correspondence of doctrine to facts and vice versa.

And yet, as the documents in this report demonstrate, the contradiction exists, and it is manifestly a source of deep embarrassment to the Kremlin. For one thing, the Soviet leadership is far from indifferent to the serious process of disintegration that has been under way for several years in the West European, British, Latin American and North American Communist movements—the result, in no small measure, of the traumatic impact of the revelations about Soviet Jewry. The situation is all the more damaging to the self-assumed Soviet role of champion of democracy of the disadvantaged minorities everywhere in the non-Communist world and of the newly-independent Asian and African nations which still retain memories of discrimination at the hands of their former colonial masters. It is above all embarrassing to the Soviet government at the very time it is engaged in a major campaign for the good will of the Western world.

Soviet sensitivity on this question has increased as the factual revelations have accumulated in recent years and as the expressions of concern in the non-Communist world have grown more serious and more persistent. The irony in this situation is that Moscow risks major obloquy for a policy which has proved to be impracticable and untenable. For underlying Soviet policy of the past twenty years and more has been the unwarranted, irrational suspicion that Soviet Jewry is a potentially or actually disloyal group which can be rendered harmless only when it has been fragmented. Based on this suspicion, the tacit assumption of the policy has been that discrimination is both inevitable and essential. But a major, though unanticipated, consequence has been a defensive reaction in the form of greater Jewish group consciousness, and alienation from the regime. It is the old story of fear of a bogey leading to repression, which in turn makes the bogey real and provides an apparent basis for the fear. And so the vicious circle is closed.

Journalists, political figures and other informed parties in the non-Communist world have repeatedly questioned Soviet leaders about the status of Soviet Jewry. Their replies, especially those of Premier Khrushchev and Deputy Premier Anastas I. Mikoyan, are given later in this report. It is precisely because the Soviet leadership has been so embarrassed by these approaches that it has believed it necessary to deny on every occasion the existence of "a Jewish problem" in the Soviet Union, and of a pattern of anti-Jewish policies.

The pattern is irrefutably revealed in the accompanying documents: a pattern of differential treatment in cultural and religious affairs, of discrimination in education and government employment, of denigration of the Jew's social image, of scarcely concealed anti-Semitic prejudices. The documents are grouped around four main themes: "The Absence of Cultural Freedom" —as already discussed—"Judaism," "Discrimination in Government and Education," and "Prospects and Alternatives." The unique virtue and value of these documents is that they are based almost entirely on Soviet or non-Soviet Communist sources.

Status of Religious Practice

Jews are singled out for differential treatment where religion is concerned. But documentation is more difficult to obtain for religion than for culture. Communists who are troubled about the Jewish question, like Messrs. Sloves, Waterman, Salsberg, Suller, and the British Party delegation, are secularists themselves and are not particularly interested in religious developments. As a result, Communist sources on religion are virtually non-existent.

Nevertheless, from the information provided by interested

parties, such as Western religious figures and journalists who
have visited the Soviet Union in recent months and years, it is
possible to piece together a coherent picture of the status of
Jewish religious life there.

The Russian Orthodox Church is permitted to maintain a cen-
tralized, nation-wide organization of religious congregations, with
the Patriarch as its head. Similar systems exist on a nation-wide
basis for the other two major denominations, Moslem and Baptist. Only the Jews are kept in an organizationally atomized
condition. There is no federation of Jewish communities and
no Chief Rabbi. Contact between local congregations is made
difficult, if not impossible.

There are only some sixty rabbis, many of them improperly
ordained, for the Jewish population of three million. Many communities have no synagogues at all and must hold services, when
permission is granted, in other locations. Considerable government aid has gone into the reconstruction of damaged Orthodox
churches; many sequestered churches have been returned to the
religious authorities. Similarly, a number of sequestered Moslem
mosques have been returned. But not one synagogue has been
rebuilt or returned to the Jewish communities since the end
of the war.

There are ten Orthodox seminaries for the training of priests,
with a total of some one thousand students. There are also
several Moslem seminaries and one Baptist seminary. But it
was not until 1957 that the Jews were permitted to open a
seminary, for the first time since the Revolution, and the number of students is restricted to twenty. The average age of the
sixty rabbis serving the Jewish community is well over seventy.
This means that at the present rate of training, the Jewish seminary will be unable to provide replacements as rapidly as the
older rabbis die or retire, further depriving the Jewish communities of necessary religious leaders.

The same discriminatory pattern prevails for religious publishing facilities. The Russian Orthodox and Baptist churches
were permitted to print Bibles last year, and the Moslems
brought out a new edition of the Koran. But no Hebrew Bible
has been allowed since 1917. Similarly, the Baptists recently

put out an edition of 25,000 hymnals, which is the equivalent
of one for every twenty-one of the faithful. Last year the Jewish community was given permission, for the first time in many
years, to print an edition of 3,000 prayer books—the only Hebrew book permitted in the Soviet Union—which is the equivalent of one for every 500 practicing Jews. And this does not
take into account the sizeable number of these prayer books
that were shipped abroad for propaganda purposes. The Baptists, Moslems and Russian Orthodox are free to print and distribute their religious calendars and almanacs. The Jews have
been given permission only to produce a photocopy edition of
a handwritten calendar.

Because of the thirty-year-old ban on the teaching of the
Hebrew language, young Jews and Jewish children are at a
further disadvantage, compared to their Russian Orthodox and
Baptist counterparts, in participation in religious services. Though
religious education for children under eighteen is prohibited for
all faiths, the Russian Orthodox and Baptist children can at
least take part in their church services in the language they
are taught in the public schools. But the Jewish children are
unable to follow the Hebrew prayers of the synagogue service.

Against this background of discrimination, which itself is in
large part based on the suspicion and distrust revealed in the
articles cited earlier, the recent campaign against many aspects
of Jewish religious practice becomes understandable. The campaign reached its height between September 1958 and July
1959. Three major news stories, in the New York *Times* on May
21 and June 19, and the New York *Herald Tribune* of July 26,
carried most of the details. Citation of these non-Communist
sources, however reputable they are, is a departure from the
procedure followed in this special study up to this point. But
the accuracy of these newspaper accounts is doubly enhanced
by the fact that they evoked repeated denials from Soviet
sources—denials which by their very nature served to confirm
the accounts.

The reported facts can be summarized as follows:

The synagogues of Chernovtsky, Bobruisk, Korosten, Baranovich, Rakhov, Novoselitsa, Orenburg, Chernigov, Stalino, Ba-

bushkin and other cities were closed down by the security authorities.

The rabbi of Chernovtsky traveled to Moscow to intervene with the authorities, but in vain. The synagogue was closed down, and its Holy Scrolls transferred to two small huts on the edge of town where services were thereafter to be conducted. The synagogue officials were forced to promise they would tell outsiders the synagogue was closed down because it had been used for "non-religious and illegal purposes."

The synagogue at Voronezh, which escaped destruction during the war when the city was under heavy attack, has been taken over by the authorities for use as a grain warehouse. The Jewish community has been unable to raise the money required to redeem it. The windows have been bricked up and the Star of David removed from the building.

Prayer meetings in private apartments, in places that have no synagogues or where the synagogues lack sufficient space, were forcibly dispersed in Kharkov, Olevsk, Tula, Bobruisk, Vitebsk and other places.

In Kharkov, twenty such groups were dispersed in September 1958 during the Jewish New Year services. All the Holy Scrolls were confiscated, and a policeman told one of the Jews, "You eat Russian bread, but you pray for Israel."

In Korosten, the community had saved enough money to build a synagogue. Unable to obtain an official permit to build, the Jews proceeded to build it anyway. The building was confiscated.

In Yevpatoriya, in the Crimea, the authorities confiscated 25,000 rubles raised by the Jewish community to rent a building for a synagogue.

In Baranovich, in White Russia, the Great Synagogue has been taken over by the State Security Committee. Since then, the rabbi has not been permitted to function, and ritual slaughter of cattle and all other Jewish rites have been forbidden.

Last Passover, a number of Jews in Chernavtsy, in the Ukraine, including synagogue officials, were arrested on charges of having participated in "Zionist propaganda." This was based on the fact that at the conclusion of the Passover Feast, Jews traditionally repeat the centuries-old statement, "Next year in Jerusalem."

(The ban on private prayer meetings has come as a real blow to Russian Jews. With the increasing closing of synagogues, Jews have taken to gathering in each other's homes for prayers. In the Jewish faith, a service, as well as the hallowed repetition of the memorial for the dead, requires a quorum of ten men. Thus, a ban on private prayer meetings is tantamount to a ban on prayer.)

In Vitebsk, White Russia, all twelve private prayer meetings were closed on May 16, 1959 and the Jews were threatened with ten years in prison if they resumed the meetings. They were told, "Your religion is hostile to the Soviet government."

In Baranovich, a memorial erected to 4,000 Jewish victims of the Nazis has been destroyed. A public lavatory has been built in its place.

In Minsk, White Russia, Jewish inscriptions have been effaced from a memorial in the former ghetto, which, with its inhabitants was destroyed by the Nazis.

In Kiev, Kharkov, Kuibyshev, Rostov, Kishinev, Odessa and Lvov, a ban was imposed on the baking of *matzoh*, the unleavened bread eaten during Passover.

In Bendery, Baranovich, Minsk, Kishinev, Voronezh and Kiev, Jewish cemeteries were desecrated and memorials defaced.

Soviet Deputy Premier Frol Kozlov was touring the U.S. at the very time that some of these reports were reaching this country. When queried about them, Kozlov replied with what was a clear evasion, and his lead was followed by other Soviet sources. On July 3, in San Francisco, Kozlov said, "These charges are slander. There are synagogues in Moscow, Leningrad and Kiev." Of course, the claim had never been made that there were no synagogues in those three cities. Kozlov very carefully avoided meeting the actual charges.

Ten days later, at his final press conference, Kozlov again adverted to this question: "Just recently," he said, "I visited Kiev, and I saw the Jews there leading a happy life in their usual pursuits and bathing in the Dnieper. And they looked no worse than you." This observation obviously had no bearing on the closing of synagogues or the dispersal of private prayer meetings anywhere; the happy reference to Kiev was clearly calculated to obscure the issue. Two weeks later, a statement signed by Kiev Jews appeared in *Izvestia*, vouching for the fact that their synagogue was still open.

Kozlov made another inadvertently revealing statement on July 3. Commenting on the reported ban on the baking of *matzoh*, he said: "I personally know a rabbi in Leningrad. When I worked there, he approached me and asked that the necessary ingredients for *matzoh* be put on sale there. We did sell these ingredients, and the Jews were free to celebrate the holiday in the traditional way." But, Leningrad was not one of the towns where a ban on *matzoh* had been reported. Moreover, the Kozlov statement indirectly confirmed the report that bans were in effect. Otherwise, why should a rabbi in a city of almost 200,000 Jews have to make the appeal which Kozlov himself described in 1959?

Similar confirmation of a *Times* report came from an article in the July 23 issue of *Sovietskaya Moldavia*, published in Kishinev. The *Times* had reported on July 19 that a number of Kishinev Jews had been arrested for violating a government decree by baking *matzoh* in preparation for the Passover holiday. *Sovietskaya Moldavia* wrote:

> Religious rituals contribute significantly to the propagation of religious ideology. They are cultivated not only by ministers of religion but by swindlers and crooks, who exploit the ignorance and credulity of the faithful. It is known, for instance, that the celebration of Passover requires the use of *matzoh*. A number of Jews, hoping to fill their purses, baked *matzoh* for sale in their homes, under unsanitary conditions and without prior registration and medical checkup. They thus openly violated Paragraphs 127 and 129 of the MSSR Penal Code.

> Such speculators were, for example, the following inhabitants of Beltsy: Rakhnes (33 Melnichaya Street), Peisakh Belenko (35 Pervomaiskaya Street), Isser Taliuk (6 Steppnaya Street), Peisakh Shneider (26 Krasnaya Street), and others. The driver, Boris Spector (34 Chapayeva Street)

served this clique. The *matzoh* was transported from Beltsy to various towns and sold to believers. But the Beltsy speculators were not alone. Bokhlin, the former chairman of the Bessarabskaya community, and his subordinate did not limit themselves to the unregistered mass production of *matzoh;* they contrived to sell it through the stores of the district and the railway supply union. . . .

The peculiar characteristic of most Jewish holidays is their clear expression of nationalism. Such festivals as Passover, for example . . . give rise to nationalist feelings and poison the minds of Jews by diverting their thoughts to Israel, "the land of their fathers". . . . Judaism kills love for the Soviet motherland.

Quite apart from the invidious remarks about Judaism and the insinuation of disloyalty on the part of believing Jews, this article begs the obvious question: Why would the "speculators" have endangered themselves by baking *matzoh* secretly, were there not in fact an official ban on the baking of *matzoh?*

The Kozlov pattern of evasion also was followed in two Moscow radio broadcasts dealing with these questions on July 25 and September 3. The latter broadcast, in the English language, denied religious discrimination against Jews and added that there are synagogues in such cities as Odessa, Kiev and Lvov. Once again, there have been no reports of synagogues being closed in those cities. The July 25 broadcast was more interesting and detailed; it was reprinted in the August 2 issue of the *Morgen Freiheit,* over the signature of one S. Rabinovich, described in the broadcast as "a Soviet journalist of Jewish origin."

Rabinovich, referring specifically to the *Times* reports, says that the Ukraine, which was described as one of the centers of attacks on the Jewish religion, actually has many synagogues— in Kiev, Vinnitsa, Lvov, Odessa, Kherson, Nikolayev, Berditchev, Dniepropetrovsk, Kirovograd. Comparison with the list of cities in the original report shows that Rabinovich failed to mention any one of them in his "refutation," and that none of the cities he cites had appeared in the *Times* and *Herald Tribune* reports.

Rabinovich also claimed that synagogues are active in "the regions" of Zhitomir, Poltava, Khmelnik, Transcarpathia, Chernigov and Moldavia, but he carefully avoids mentioning the names of the towns in those regions. Actually, the central cities of two of the seven regions he named have had their synagogues closed down; again, Rabinovich was careful not to mention those cities, but only their regions. The Moscow radio broadcast then continued:

> There is, however, another reason why in this or that township there may not be a synagogue. . . . Each religious community in the Soviet Union may freely organize its activities. But in order to do so, it must fulfill certain conditions. One of these conditions is the registration of every religious community or organization with the local authorities. The State does not interfere with the internal affairs of the communities. If, however, the community does not bother to register itself or if it breaks the Soviet law in question, then—whether it be of the Jewish or other faith—it loses its right to open a house of worship.

The fact is, however, that in the cases cited in the newspaper reports the local authorities had repeatedly been requested to grant the Jews the right to open a synagogue (in some instances, it was even a question of returning a sequestered synagogue). But they not only refused all the requests, they then proceeded to break up the private prayer meetings under various pretexts, including the charge that such gatherings were not part of an officially registered religious community. What is more, before a group can register there must be a synagogue in existence, and this the local officials had themselves refused to authorize.

It is clear from the evasions, indirect admissions and transparent refutations that a discriminatory policy, including a physical campaign against houses of prayer, cemeteries and religious rites, is being conducted in the Soviet Union against the Jewish religion, based on the assumption that it is hostile to the State. No other religion has been subjected to a like campaign; on the contrary, there has even been a certain relaxation as far as the Russian Orthodox and the Baptists are concerned.

The Feeling for Israel

It is not surprising that the Jewish community, isolated as it is, has developed special feelings of warmth for and interest in the State of Israel during the past decade. A striking instance was provided by the spontaneously demonstrative reaction of Soviet Jews to the appearance at the Moscow synagogue of Israeli Ambassador Golda Meir in 1948. They reacted similarly to Israel's Zionist delegation (as distinguished from its Communist delegation) at the 1957 Moscow Youth Festival. These reactions are, at least in part, the result of persistent Soviet anti-Israel propaganda, which Soviet Jews inevitably feel also reflects on themselves. Yet the Soviet need to present Israel in the worst possible light is itself based on the official assumption of the alien, hostile and suspect character of the Jews and on the concomitant conviction that the new State of Israel would serve as a magnet of attraction for this group. And so the vicious circle closes.

Analysis of the unprecedented Soviet propaganda campaign against Israel since 1948—conducted primarily in the Russian, White Russian and Ukrainian languages in provincial organs most widely read by local populations—reveals that it has far less to do with the Middle East situation than with the attitudes and position of Soviet Jewry. The violent attacks on Israel and Zionism that characterized "the Black Years" from 1948 to 1953 are of a piece with the above mentioned 1957 article, "Behind the Screen of Zionism," by A. Leonidov.

It must have become apparent to Soviet authorities, however, that the violent and persistent descriptions of Israel as an enemy of the Communist world and a link in the "imperialist" chain only served to attract the alienated Soviet Jewish community further to Israel. For early in 1958, the nature of this campaign changed, and Soviet Jews began to be overwhelmed with a barrage of articles, news items, radio broadcasts and letters to the editor, seeking to persuade them that East European Jews who had migrated to Israel were suffering horrible conditions. Two of the vast number of such articles that might be mentioned were "Hell in the Israeli 'Paradise'" by P. Yulski, published in the March 25, 1958 issue of *Sovietskaya Kultura,* and

"The Price of Recovered Sight" by N. Nedialkov, in the July 26, 1958 issue of *Pravda Ukrainy*. The import of the whole campaign addressed to Soviet Jewry at this time had the effect of warning—"However badly off you may consider yourselves here, you would be worse off there."

A further shift in the nature of the propaganda effort, evidently reflecting the imperviousness of Soviet Jews to this "persuasion," was inadvertently revealed in the second half of 1958: the establishment of a special propaganda bureau to deal with Jewish affairs. The existence of such an agency came to light in *Unzer Freint*, a Yiddish Communist newspaper in Montevideo which published an article called "A Jewish Parcel from the Soviet Union" in its issue of August 2, 1958. The article revealed, by an evident slip-up, that the Soviet Embassy in Uruguay had been supplying the press with "informational" material about Soviet Jewish cultural life, and it added: "A Press Bureau dealing with this matter in Moscow is sending information and photographs concerning Jewish cultural activities in the Soviet Union to the various Soviet embassies abroad, and they in turn distribute it to the press of the various countries." It seems likely that it was this office that embarked on the next stage of the effort to influence Soviet Jewish attitudes on Israel.

In the summer of 1958, a group of more than a dozen "tourists" applied for visas to visit Israel. Significantly, all these tourists were Jews. Upon their return home a spate of "eyewitness" anti-Israel articles appeared in the press. (It is also known, from cautiously formulated private letters written by Soviet Jews that meetings of Soviet Jews were drummed together in various cities to hear lectures by these tourists.) All the tourists' articles engaged in systematic vilification of Israel and conditions of life there. Among these articles were the following:

"Myth and Reality About 'Flourishing' Israel" by G. Plotkin, in the popular Moscow evening paper, *Vechernaya Moskva*, August 8, 1958.

"A Journey to Israel," a two-part article by G. Plotkin in *Literaturnaya Gazeta*, August 26, 30, 1958.

"The Truth About the Israeli 'Paradise'" by P. Zhurba, in the *Minskaya Pravda* (Minsk, White Russia), November 18, 1958.

"Ten Days in Israel," two articles by S. Fry in *Trud,* November 27-28, 1958.

The campaign was capped by a document that appeared in *Trud* on May 26, 1959. Entitled "The Victims of Zionist Propaganda," it purported to be the text of a letter from 107 individuals in Israel to Marshal Klimenti Voroshilov, Chairman of the Supreme Soviet. In the letter, the signers state that they are of Russian origin; they bitterly complain of conditions in Israel and express a desire to return to the Soviet Union. But this latest twist in the anti-Israel campaign shows no more signs of success than its earlier versions.

DISCRIMINATION IN GOVERNMENT
AND EDUCATION

The Background

There are, of course, no independent agencies inside Russia to probe and challenge official denials of discrimination against Jews in higher education and government employment. But sufficient evidence has accumulated over the years, from students of the subject, from knowledgeable visitors and from defectors, to prove that such a policy exists and is thoroughly implemented.

Significant light on the background of the discriminatory policy against Jews in government was provided by Bernard Turner, a journalist who survived a ten-year sentence at a forced labor camp in Bratsk, Siberia. At the camp, he encountered David Bergelson and Itzik Feffer, two distinguished Soviet Jewish writers victimized by the 1948 purge. Bergelson and Feffer had also been leading Jewish communal figures and prominent members of the Jewish Anti-Fascist Committee. The following excerpt is from an article by Turner in Number 25 (1956) of

Di Goldene Kayt, a well-known Yiddish magazine published in Tel Aviv:

> Feffer and Bergelson told me that their arrest was a culmination of developments that went back to 1944. It was then that they learned for the first time of the anti-Semitic policy pursued by Party and State in the Soviet Union. In 1944, the Soviet Foreign Ministry suffered from a dearth of diplomats. . . . A foreign service training institute was opened in Moscow, headed by Deputy Foreign Minister Vladimir G. Dekanozov (who later shared the fate of his comrade, Beria). [Dekanozov had been Soviet Ambassador in Berlin during the Nazi-Soviet Pact.] The institute had a rigid quota for Jewish students. Feffer and Bergelson raised this question at a closed meeting. . . . [Deputy Foreign Minister] A. L. Lozovsky vainly brought the matter to the attention of Dekanozov. He later conferred with Foreign Minister Andrei Vishinsky, who denied the very existence of any discrimination against Jews. Lazar Kaganovich [the only Jew on the Politburo] refused even to talk about the matter.
>
> Subsequently, Bergelson went on to say, it became crystal-clear that the anti-Semitic policy in the internal affairs of the Soviet Union had been fully sanctioned by Stalin and the Politburo. Jewish Communist circles learned of a top-secret decree issued by the Central Committee of the Party that Jews, Communist or not, were to be excluded from the Polish and Czechoslovakian "national armies" which had been formed by Colonel Berling and General Svoboda on Soviet soil.
>
> The decree expressly stated that every Jew of typical Jewish appearance (a "Jewish nose," curly hair, Yiddish accent) was to be excluded from the Polish Army of Liberation, the Red Army and the NKVD units attached to the Polish Army. Jews of "good" appearance could remain in the Polish Army, but would have to change their names to pure Polish and eradicate any trace of their Jewish identity.

Statements made by top Soviet leaders, including Khrushchev himself, leave no doubt that the Jews are considered alien in

Soviet society and that a policy of discrimination in "sensitive" positions is conducted against them. One such inadvertent admission was made by Khrushchev, accompanied by Mikhail Pervukhin, a member of the Party Presidium, in the interview with the French Socialist delegation in May 1956. This was part of the text of the interview published in *Réalités* in May 1957:

> KHRUSHCHEV: Anti-Semitic sentiments still exist here. This is a complicated problem because of the position of the Jews and their relations with the other peoples. At the outset of the Revolution, we had many Jews in the leadership of the Party and of the State. They were more educated, maybe more revolutionary than the average Russian. In due course, we have created new cadres. . . .

> PERVUKHIN: . . . our own intelligentsia.

> KHRUSHCHEV: Should the Jews want to occupy the foremost positions in our republic now, it would naturally be taken amiss by the indigenous inhabitants. The latter would not accept these pretensions at all well, especially since they do not consider themselves less intelligent or less capable than the Jews. Or, for instance, when a Jew in the Ukraine is appointed to an important post and he surrounds himself with Jewish collaborators, it is understandable that this should create jealousy and hostility toward the Jews.

In an interview published in the pro-Soviet New York weekly, *National Guardian,* on June 25, 1956, Madame Ekaterina Furtseva, a member of the Party Presidium, replied to a question concerning the implications of the Khrushchev statement to the French Socialists:

> She said that some years back, talk of anti-Semitism here [in Russia] was stirred as a result of misinterpretations of certain government actions. The government had found in some of its departments a heavy concentration of Jewish people, upwards of 50 percent of the staff. Steps were taken to transfer them to other enterprises, giving them equally good positions and without jeopardizing their rights.

The furor created by the Furtseva statement, clearly if indirectly admitting that government policies of discrimination in employment were directed at Jews as such, led to a clarification by the then press chief of the Soviet Foreign Ministry, Leonid Ilychev. This was reported by *National Guardian* the following September:

> Mr. Ilychev secured from Mme. Furtseva this explanation: In her interview she meant that if at some time there had taken place changes in office personnel, these changes were dictated by the economic needs of the country and under no circumstances were aimed at any discrimination of persons of any nationality. If a chief of an office or department found that in his office there existed over-saturation of a certain group of specialists, then proceeding from the economic needs of the country and with no reference to nationality, some of the specialists were given other posts in industry, agriculture and other branches. Never at any time during the Soviet power were there any quotas for Jews or persons of some other nationality, and there are not now.

> Ilychev used the same occasion to set the *National Guardian* straight on Khrushchev's views. What Khrushchev said, he explained, was that after the Revolution some of the USSR's national republics did not have their own national trained core of key people, that these cadres at the time were largely Russian. But now the Revolution was almost forty years old, new cadres had been created and the people of these republics were demanding a place for them. It is quite understandable that any people should want to create their own cadres and prefer their leading ones to be of their own nationality. But this does not mean that able Jewish people are not and will not be promoted.

The manifestly exclusionary implications of the repeated references, by Khrushchev, Pervukhin, Furtseva and Ilychev, to "their own" and "indigenous" cadres was deeply resented by the Canadian Communist, J. B. Salsberg, as he reported it in his articles. He states that he inquired about the Furtseva interview at one of the official sessions he had with top Soviet leaders, among them Khrushchev and Suslov:

To my great regret and shame, I must record the fact that, though one of the main leaders who answered neither confirmed nor denied Mme. Furtseva's words, his own explanation more than corroborated the essence of her statement.

He tried terribly hard to prove to me with examples that the transfer or dismissal of Jewish employes in once-backward republics that now have "their own" intelligentsia and professional people capable of occupying the posts previously held by Jews or Russians has nothing to do with anti-Semitism. But what is the meaning of "their own" in a Socialist country? Why yield to the demands of undemocratic elements?

Worse still was the argument that a state which has many nationalities must always consider the sensitivities of these nationalities and peoples. He described the problem that came up when six gifted music students were sent by the government to an international music competition. It happened that all the six chosen were Jews. But for the sake of good relations among peoples, the authorities intervened and only two Jews were sent, the other four being chosen from among other nationalities. . . .

The explanation is full of enormous contradictions. How does it jibe with the "integration" theory and with the assertion that the Jews "are expressing themselves in the culture of the people among whom they live"?. . . Who examined, and why, the student chosen from Minsk, Moscow and Kiev, to determine whether he was a 100 percent White Russian, Great Russian or Ukrainian, or only a Jewish White Russian, a Jewish Great Russian or a Jewish Ukrainian? Are there two classes of citizens in the Soviet Union?

Soviet Statistics on Jews

It has become a persistent Soviet policy to conceal the part played by Jews in various spheres of Russian life—as if Jews did not exist there, or as if the Communist party and government had adopted a dual policy of denigration, on the one hand, and silence about Jewish achievements, on the other.

A striking example is provided in a widely-distributed book

issued by the State Publishing House for Statistics—*The Achievements of the Soviet Regime in 40 Years in Figures*—published in 1957 as part of the 40th anniversary celebration of the Bolshevik Revolution. The 358 pages of this book include statistics and tables on virtually every aspect of Soviet life. But nowhere do the words, "Jew" or "Jewish," appear.

Two other glaring examples of concealment are reflected in this book:

On page 294, a table entitled "Publication of Books in the Different Languages of the Soviet Peoples" provides comparative figures for 1913 and 1956, in terms of the number of published items and their aggregate circulation. A footnote adds: "During the years of the Soviet regime, there have been published in the USSR books in 124 languages of the peoples of the Soviet Union, as well as of foreign countries."

Yiddish is not listed in this table. It was not found to be even as deserving as "Tat," the language of a small Daghestan tribe, which boasted of the publication of a single item in 1956, with a circulation of 1,000 copies. It is, of course, well known that no Yiddish work was published in 1956. But in 1913, literally hundreds of Jewish publications appeared in Yiddish (as well as Hebrew), for it was the springtide of the Jewish cultural renascence in Russia.

On page 285, there is a table (for the year 1955) entitled "Division of Scientific Workers in Institutes of Higher Learning, Scientific and Other Institutions. According to Nationality." It quotes the very same figures cited by another official periodical, *Voprosy Filosofii* (*Problems of Philosophy*)—which had, however, a much more limited circulation than the popularly produced statistical book. *Voprosy Filosofii* lists 24,620 Jews among a total of 223,893 scientific and academic workers. In this list, Jews occupy second place among the nationalities, and constitute almost 10 percent of the total number. But the other publication—*Achievements of the Soviet Regime*—much more widely distributed and read, entirely omits even the mention of Jews. Either these 24,620 Jews have disappeared from their fields (which may, in part, be true, as a result of exclusionary processes) or honorable mention of them has disappeared—or a combination of the two developments has occurred.

Another example of official silence on Jewish achievements is provided by an official Soviet booklet called *The National Traditions of the Peoples of the Soviet Union,* issued by the State Publishing House in Moscow in April 1957. Here, it is stated that 10,940 soldiers and officers received the order, "Hero of the Soviet Union," for their courage and heroism during World War II. There follows a statistical breakdown of these honors, by nationalities. The total comes to 10,543; thus, 397 persons are unaccounted for. No Jews are listed, which helps to explain the discrepancy.

In April 1944, at the Third Conference of the Jewish Anti-Fascist Committee, it was announced that as of April 1, 1944, there were 3,517 recipients of the distinction, "Hero of the Soviet Union," among whom were more than 100 Jews. In subsequent years, Jews were again similarly mentioned in various Soviet publications, so that it is quite reasonable to suppose that Jews represent the major portion of the 397 "Heroes of the Soviet Union" whose nationality is unspecified in the above table.

Political Exclusion

A graphic index of the exclusion of Jews from Soviet political life is provided by the figures for Jewish representation in both Houses of the Supreme Soviet during the past 22 years. These figures are available for December 1937, January 1946, March 1950 and April 1958.

In December 1937, 32 of the 569 members (5.6 percent) of the Soviet of the Union, and 15 of the 574 members (2.6 percent) of the Soviet of Nationalities, were Jews—thus constituting 4.1 percent of the Supreme Soviet's total membership.

In January 1946, five of the 801 members (.8 percent) of the Soviet of the Union were Jews. An official tabulation for the Soviet of Nationalities for that year was never made, on the ground that the ravages of the war, especially in the western regions of the country, precluded it. But the rapporteur of the

Soviet of Nationalities indicated that Jewish numerical representation in that House had dropped from 11th to 26th place—this, despite the known fact that the Jews occupy somewhere between seventh and tenth place among the population of the many Soviet nationalities. At that time, then, Jews constituted no more than .8 percent of the Supreme Soviet's total membership.

In March 1950, two of the 678 members (.3 percent) of the Soviet of the Union, and three of the 638 members (.5 percent) of the Soviet of Nationalities, were Jews—thus constituting .4 percent of the Supreme Soviet's total membership. In April 1958, only three members of both Houses could be identified as Jews, out of a total of 1,364. Thus the Jews constituted no more than .25 percent of the Supreme Soviet's total membership.

The Soviet Union's three million Jews represent about 1.5 percent of the country's total population. The above figures show that in the postwar period, Jewish representation in the Supreme Soviet has been reduced from .8 percent in 1946 (one-half of the pro rata proportion) to .4 percent in 1950 (one-third of the pro rata proportion) to .25 percent in 1958 (one-sixth of the pro rata proportion).

Of the 255 members of the Communist party's powerful Central Committee, only one is known and has been publicly identified as a Jew—Mark Mitin. Premier Khrushchev himself has on several occasions pointed to Mitin as an example of a Soviet Jew in a prominent public position, evidently seeking by this means to refute aspersions of discrimination. Mitin has distinguished himself throughout his career as an astutely inflexible sounding-board of Soviet policies. His worthiness to be singled out as a leading representative Jew is brought into question, however, by the following characteristic statement he made on the Doctors' Plot in an early 1953 issue of the Cominform journal, *For A Lasting Peace, For A People's Democracy:*

> The names of the doctor-killers who, on orders from the U.S. and British secret services, killed Comrades A. A. Zhdanov and A. S. Shcherbakov, outstanding leaders of the Soviet Communist party, will be cursed forever. Pro-

gressive mankind will never forget these black crimes of the Zionist lackeys of the imperialist secret services. The evil crimes of the group of doctor-killers, like the activities of the Zionists—participants in the anti-State conspiratorial center in Czechoslovakia and in the act of terror against the Soviet Legation in Tel Aviv—are all links in the same chain.

Higher Education

The existence of a *numerus clausus*, a quota for Jewish students, in the universities and in the specialized, advanced technical and academic institutes, has been widely reported since 1955. With the intensification of competition for admission to institutions of higher learning in recent years, there is ample ground to believe that the tacit exclusion of Jewish applicants, readily recognizable by their identity cards, has proceeded apace. An illuminating indication of these exclusionary practices was provided by the late Leon Crystal, a prominent Jewish journalist who specialized in East European and Soviet Jewish affairs for the New York *Jewish Daily Forward*.

Crystal visited Minsk, the capital of White Russia, in the spring of 1958 and noted down statistics that appeared on the bulletin board of the University of Minsk, the Republic's leading school. These figures concern the number and nationalities of the students who were graduated that year from the University's history and chemistry faculties.

As a basis for comparison, it is interesting to note the population figures for the four leading cities of White Russia. Minsk itself, with a population of 412,000, has 40,000 Jews. Bobruisk—total population, 150,000; Jewish population, about 60,000. Gomel—total population, 144,000; Jewish population, 15,000. Mogilev—total population, 106,000; Jewish population, approximately 12,000. The Jewish population of these four major White Russian cities constitutes 10-12 percent of the total population of those cities. It might be expected, therefore, that this proportion would be generally reflected at the University, especially in a region such as White Russia, where Jews were traditionally bearers of a high educational and cultural standard.

This expectation is not borne out by the figures. The history faculty at the University of Minsk graduated 213 White Russians, 70 Russians, 40 Ukrainians and seven Jews. The chemistry faculty graduated 224 White Russians, 76 Russians, 41 Ukrainians and eight Jews.

Several points emerge from these statistics. First, the proportions represented by the students of the three other nationalities, besides the Jewish, reflect quite closely the general distribution of nationality populations in White Russia. Secondly, the figures for the students in both faculties are extremely close, which suggests a tacit official policy of fixed nationality ratios at the University. Finally, within this context, the proportion of Jewish student representation has been fixed at a remarkably lower ratio (about 2 percent) than is warranted by Jewish population statistics—so low, in fact, as to be virtually exclusionary.

Additional light on this situation has been shed by David Burg, a brilliant young intellectual who was graduated from a Soviet university in 1956 and who is now pursuing advanced scholarly work in international affairs at St. Anthony's College in Oxford. In the December 1957 issue of *Sotsialisticheski Vestnik,* Burg wrote:

> At the same time that the limitation of the right to work was being practiced, measures to restrict the right to education were, and still are, being put into effect. Although Jews are admitted into secondary schools without restriction, their admission into institutes of higher learning is governed by a *numerus clausus.* The instructions are obviously such that Jews are, as a rule, not to be admitted into universities and the more important institutes, while only a limited number of their most capable applicants may be admitted into second-rate institutes. Even those who are graduated from secondary schools with honors and who, therefore, have the right of admission without entrance examinations into any institution of higher learning in the country, are able to enter universities only thanks to their good connections or an unusually lucky chain of circumstances.
>
> Suffice it to say that at Moscow University's philology faculty, where before the war the proportion of Jewish

students was as high as 40 percent, only three of the 250 applicants admitted to the first-year course in 1951 were Jews, and only five or seven in 1955. It is easier to gain admission to institutes for the study of mechanics or pedagogics than to universities. But even there, all other things being equal, it is easier for a non-Jew to gain admission than a Jew.

If it is still possible, though difficult, to enter a university, the road to a scientific career is practically barred to Jewish youth. This road in the Soviet Union usually leads through a fellowship position (*aspirantura*), from which Jews are barred. Even in cases recommended by the Scientists' Council, admission is refused on the ground of a "lack of vacancy." Notwithstanding all these hardships, people still managed to live somehow.

Analysis of pre-war Soviet statistics suggests that in the late 1930's at least 9 percent of all students in institutions of higher learning were Jewish. This is not a surprising figure, considering that at that time, and to a certain extent even today, university student bodies were largely recruited from the urban population, particularly from the children of the intelligentsia—the very strata in which Soviet Jewry was most heavily represented. Though no figures concerning Jews in institutions of higher learning today have been published, the available evidence indicates that their proportion is between 2 and 3 percent. The irony of the situation is made all the more graphic if it is recalled that even in Czarist days, when an official *numerus clausus* obtained, Jews constituted an average of 5 percent of all university students throughout Russia, and twice as much in the Jewish Pale. The sharp contrast with the 1930's and even with the Czarist period is inescapable.

The resultant bitterness of Soviet Jewish youth has been described by Sally Belfrage in her 1958 book, *A Room in Moscow,* written after she had spent many months in the Soviet Union. The daughter of Cedric Belfrage, a long-time editor of the pro-Soviet New York weekly, *National Guardian,* Miss Belfrage's testimony is of peculiar interest:

I had seen how bad it could be. . . . Actual discrimination went only [sic] so far as sometimes barring them from certain key professions—diplomacy and the nuclear sciences—but the general individual attitude of prejudice was often terribly discouraging. Their biggest resentment, however, was that since 3,000,000 of them had to be classified a separate nationality and were compelled continually to identify themselves as something apart, they should not be allowed the privileges of a nationality. . . . As bad as anti-Semitic attitudes can be elsewhere, they seemed to me to be worse in Russia. It was a traditional thing, I realized—Russia was the country of the pogrom—but in the context of the present it was hypocritical coming from the same mouths that constantly intoned the major criticism of America, discrimination toward Negroes. I could almost never hear a Jew described except with the apologetic preface, "He's a Jew, but . . . (he's very nice, he's very intelligent)." And frequent anti-Semitic jokes, Rabinovich this, Rabinovich that (always Rabinovich). Some Russians spent a great deal of their verbal energy on attacking anything and everything Jewish.

The resurgence of popular anti-Semitism can hardly be explained away, as Soviet leaders have frequently attempted to do, as a residue of pre-Communist attitudes alone. It is a hardly surprising phenomenon in view of the consistent pattern of Soviet policy in the past decade and a half. This policy must act as a kind of muted but unmistakable incitement of a population with an ancient tradition of anti-Semitism and with decades of accumulated experience in inferring official attitudes from the authorities' acts of omission and commission. Additionally, current policies and attitudes stand in sharp contrast to the policies of the 1920's and early 1930's. In earlier periods, the authorities repeatedly recalled the condemnation of anti-Semitism by Lenin and other bolshevik founding fathers; and at that time, the Soviet population could hardly have overlooked the prominent part played by Jews in Government and Party. The import of official isolation, exclusion, denigration and deprivation of rights is not likely to be lost on the population at large today.

THE 1960'S, PROSPECTS AND ALTERNATIVES

The anti-Jewish policy continues today. But it is a trap which the Soviet authorities have got themselves into. Distrustful of the alien, they have produced alienation. Fearful of the hostile, they have created hostility. The limbo of isolation into which Soviet assumptions, attitudes and policies have forced the Jews is increasingly awkward for the Kremlin and increasingly bitter for the Jews. For the Kremlin it is awkward simply because to perpetuate this policy of discrimination through indirection and concealment is cumbersome and inefficient, and embarrassing vis-à-vis the world Communist movement, the Afro-Asian world, and the West. It is awkward, above all, because it has failed as a solution to the problem which it has itself created. Moscow's special, differential approach to the Jews has only served to induce a reaction within the Soviet Jewish community reminiscent of the crypto-Jewish marrano community produced by the Spanish and Portuguese Inquisition.

What, then, are the prospects for Soviet Jewry? What alternative courses of action are realistically open to the Soviet rulers to escape the vicious circle of their own making? There would appear to be only four alternatives, each with its own limitations: (1) complete implementation of Jewish nationality rights; (2) unimpaired opportunities for full assimilation and elimination of discrimination; (3) emigration; (4) a combination of these three.

The implementation of Jewish nationality rights would constitute no divergence from Soviet ideological considerations or from the prevailing practice in regard to all other nationalities. It would give the Jews the full benefit in all cultural and religious matters of their present, officially recognized national status: schools, press, publishing houses, theaters, institutions of higher learning, religious freedom no less than that accorded to other religious groups, and communal associations and organizations.

The limitation inherent in this course is that it is precisely what the Soviet authorities fear most. They are prepared to regard Jews as harmless only if they live as a fragmented group; any kind of larger Jewish organization, cultural or religious, would be viewed suspiciously as a security risk. Thus, the only form of easement that has been allowed the Jews in the past year or so is such that it represents no permanent institutionalization: disparate Jewish concerts, a limited edition of one volume of Sholom Aleichem's works—but no theater, no publishing house, no press, no nationwide communal organization. For the time being, therefore, this does not appear to be the direction in which Soviet policy is likely to move.

The opposite alternative—the opportunity for full assimilation —would mean free choice of nationality for all individual Jews. This, and the concomitant elimination of discrimination, could most efficiently and quickly be effected by the abolition of Paragraph 5 of the identity card, as it pertains to Jews. But such a policy would run head on against the basic assumption underlying present Soviet attitudes to the Jews. The very *raison d'être* of this policy has been to remove Jews from all security-sensitive positions in public life. The right of assimilation would not result in the disappearance of Jews as such for at least several generations, but it would mean that they could readily filter back into the very positions from which they are steadily being ejected. This process, furthermore, would conflict with the current Soviet policy of decentralization, which grants at least superficial concessions to the very elements, especially the Ukrainians and White Russians, who would object most strenuously to merging with the Jews. Such a policy would mean that a million new, formerly Jewish "Ukrainians" would presumably be free to resume the leading part they once played in the Ukraine's public life. There is little doubt that such a policy would meet strenuous objection in the Ukraine. This course, then, seems no more likely a prospect than the restoration of full nationality rights.

The third alternative—emigration—is usually considered the

least feasible from the point of view of the Soviet regime. The unquestionably powerful arguments brought against the likelihood of such a course are that it is unprecedented in Soviet history, that its adoption would represent an admission of ideological and political failure in domestic policy, that it would have a deleterious impact on the other national groups in the USSR, that it would have an adverse effect on Soviet relations with the Arab countries, since a large proportion of Soviet Jews who would emigrate would presumably settle in Israel.

There is something to be said, however, against each of these objections. Emigration is not wholly unprecedented in Soviet and East European Communist experience, as witness the "repatriation" of the Hellenic minority to Greece from the Ukraine's Black Sea coast at the end of World War II, the "repatriation" in the reverse direction of large numbers of Armenians from the Middle East to the Soviet Armenian Republic during the war (in both cases, these minorities had had no direct relation with their ancient motherlands for many centuries), or Rumania's "repatriation" of the *Volksdeutsche* from Transylvania to West Germany, although their ancestors originally came from the Austria of Hapsburg days.

Such a move, then, would not constitute an admission of ideological failure precisely because it is not unprecedented. Nor would the consideration of its possible impact on the other Soviet nationalities be decisive, since it was not so in the other case; moreover, unlike the Jews, the majority of all the other Soviet nationalities live inside the USSR. Finally, the adverse effect on Soviet-Arab relations could be exaggerated: The Arab countries, as it happens, are already a major source of Jewish immigration into Israel; nor are the Arabs likely to endanger their major source of arms because of even as sharp a difference as this might arouse with the Soviet Union; finally, the Kremlin has rarely allowed such purely external considerations to determine or prevent a policy decision considered necessary for internal reasons.

All of the foregoing, of course, is obviously too speculative to permit a guess to be hazarded as to which side of the argument on emigration is the more powerful in the Kremlin's calculations. There remains a fourth alternative course which could combine elements of the other three. Permission for a substantial number of Soviet Jews to emigrate could result in an easing of the profound Soviet suspicion toward the Jews who remain. With a larger number of Soviet Jews outside rather than in the USSR, the remainder could conceivably be relieved of their security risk status. And this in turn could lead both to the reconstitution of minority rights for those who choose to exercise them and the opportunity of full integration for those who choose to assimilate.

The prospect must naturally be faced that the Soviet government will persist in its present policy, however embarrassing, irrational and self-defeating it may be.* If so, the prospects for Soviet Jewry are ominous indeed. Although the possibilities of reversing this trend through external influence are obviously small, the Soviet leadership has shown itself sensitive to just such influence. Surely the civilized world has the moral obligation to undertake initiatives that hold even the smallest promise of success. Men of decency and good conscience have ever persisted, regardless of the odds.

* Hopes were raised in 1961 by the establishment of a Yiddish-language magazine, the distribution of limited editions of Sholom Aleichem's writings, and the publication of a poem "Babi Yar," denouncing Russian anti-Semitism, by the non-Jewish Soviet poet, Yevgeny Yevtushenko. These hopes were dashed by the subsequent arrest of Jewish leaders in Moscow and Leningrad.

CHAPTER FIVE

JEWS IN LATIN AMERICA

by JACOB FREID

Jews have been living in Central and South America for over 400 years. Today some 735,000 Jews—one out of every seventeen in the world—live in the lands of Latin America. They have settled in every part of this geographical area, from the Rio Grande to the Straits of Magellan and in all the Caribbean islands.

During the years 1926-1947 more than 190,000 Jewish immigrants from Europe found sanctuary in the countries within this Western Hemisphere territory, and Jews throughout the United States and Canada became increasingly conscious of their fellow Jewish-Americans to the South. In the context of recent world events and Jewish history, the Jews south of the Rio Grande have become a major and important segment of the Jewish people.

Fifteen years ago the Jews of Latin America comprised no more than some 3 percent of the Jewish people; today they are more than 5½ percent of all Jews. But their importance is not merely numerical. Because the Latin American countries constitute one of the largest blocs in the United Nations, the attitude of these countries toward their Jewish citizens finds important reflection in world politics. In addition, one result of the European Jewish tragedy has been to shift the centers of aid to the Western Hemisphere, and, like the Jews to the North, Latin American Jewry has also become a most important reservoir of economic help, both in the relief, rehabilitation and resettlement of Jewish refugees and in the building up of Israel. Finally, so many disquieting developments have occurred with the recent contagion of military coups in Latin America and the resultant

fall of governments and rise of new regimes, that the status of
Central and South American Jewry has become of serious concern to Jews everywhere.

Who are these Jewish neighbors of ours: what is their history
and immigration; their occupational and population structure;
their political, economic and social problems; their cultural and
spiritual needs; their contributions to Latin-American culture
and civilization?

In the Beginning

The history of the Jews in Latin America begins where the
Jewish history of Spain ends. Jews not only helped in the discovery and exploration of the New World, but were among its
pioneering colonists. Jewish communities existed as early as
1504 in the West Indies, 1524 in Peru and 1540 in Chile. In the
sixteenth and seventeenth centuries Jews were already playing
an essential role in the commercial life of Latin America. The
discovery of America meant a haven to the marrano Jews fleeing
the Inquisition in Spain and Portugal. They emigrated to Central and South America in considerable numbers and were in-
strumental in developing the great plantations which formed
the basis for the entire colonization of that part of the world.
A marrano exile from Spain, Juan Sanchez, established the first
trading posts in the lands of Santo Domingo, Haiti and Mexico.

However, the Church of Spain abhorred this marrano exodus.
Its long inquisitorial arm reached out to destroy these early
American roots of Judaism by a persistent persecution that
ended the rapid progress and the promise of a secure and creative life for the first Jews who came to the New World.

The adherents of the forbidden faith, together with their
hopes of fresh opportunity for initiative and enterprise, were
consumed in the fires of two hundred years of periodic auto-da-
fés. There was one escape—mass conversion. Many took the
way out. By 1800 the fading Jewish communities in Latin
America had almost disappeared.

The result is that the history of the Jews in Latin America is
a palimpsest—a document erased and then written on again—
this time by new authors and after many years.

Modern Immigration

Toward the end of the nineteenth century the story of Latin American Jewry began anew when large groups of Jewish immigrants came once again to a South America which had swallowed the traces of the descendants of the Sephardic refugees from Spain.

This modern Jewish immigration to Latin America began in the 1880's when the new Sephardim came from the Mediterranean—from Turkey, from Morocco and other regions of North Africa and the Middle East—to settle almost exclusively in Argentina. In the 1890's they were joined by several thousand East European Jews under the aegis of the Jewish Colonization Association, and the widening stream reached the shores of Brazil and Uruguay as well.

Jews had four principal reasons for coming: first, the economic, political and social dislocation of Jews in Europe, especially in Poland, the Balkans and Turkey. Most of them came from Poland, Lithuania, Latvia, Rumania and what is now Soviet Russia. They abandoned the Old World because of discrimination, starvation or pogroms. Second, the Jewish Colonization Association, founded by Baron de Hirsch, subsidized immigration to Argentina, and in smaller measure to Brazil. Third, whereas the United States imposed quota restrictions after 1924, Latin America had liberal immigration policies in the pre-Hitler years. Fourth, Latin America was a new land hardly touched by the industrial revolution, inviting both immigrant ingenuity and development.

So the Jews emigrated. The first stream was followed by two others, for like the pattern of Jewish immigration to the United States, the Jews also came to Latin America in three main waves of immigration.

The principal influx began years later. Only after World War I, and particularly after the adoption of the American quota law in 1924, did Jewish immigration to the South, and in part also to the Central American countries become very large. It then increased so rapidly that during the early 1930's this second stream of immigrants spilled over into all of the republics, more than a score in number, wherever there was

Jewish Immigration to Latin America

	Number of Immigrants	Percentage of Total World Jewish Immigration	Yearly Average
1847 to 1900	30,000	3.0	500
1901 to 1925	168,000	8.0	6,700
1926 to 1930	73,000	43.5	14,600
1931 to 1939	92,000	18.2	11,500
1940 to 1947	27,000	9.0	3,750
Total 1847 to 1947	390,000	9.7	3,645

the slightest chance of admission. The third influx was of Central European Jews who fled the continent during the years of the Nazi plague. Thus altogether, some 400,000 came to Central and South America in the past century. Since 1947 there has been little significant immigration except to Brazil. Here in the early fifties 6,000 to 8,000 Jews from Israel, mostly via Germany entered, and in 1957 some 3,000 Egyptian and Hungarian Jews came in.

Population

The comparative growth of Latin American Jewry since the year 1900 and especially as a result of the extermination of Jews in Europe has given its people increasing importance in the total Jewish world population.

This steady increase has paralleled the general population growth. Today about 160,000,000 people live in the twenty-five countries of Latin America.

Eighteen of these countries have Jewish communities of at least 1,000 Jews, but there are barely 2,000 Jews altogether in

Estimated Jewish Population of Latin America

	Year	Jewish Population of Latin America	Percentage of Jewish World Population
1)	1900	50,000	0.46
2)	1925	250,000	1.70
3)	1939	550,000	3.29
4)	1947	620,000	5.54
5)	1960	735,000	5.82

all the seven other Latin American countries. Argentina is the only nation in which Jews comprise more than 2 percent of the total population, and only in one other country, Uruguay, are they more than 1 percent.

In every other land their percentage of the total population is infinitesimal. Thus apart from two exceptions, the Jewish communities are veritable tiny islands. The following table reveals them as small clusters of population, statistically scarcely noticeable in the teeming human haystacks in which they are embedded. This is their demographic status today.

So will it probably remain, for the sealed doors of Latin America give little promise of any substantial increase by immigration. With the close of the DP camps, most of the concentration camp survivors went to the new state of Israel after 1947.

Jewish Centers in Latin America

		Estimated Jewish Population	
		(1947)	(1960)
1.	Argentina	380,000	450,000
2.	Brazil	110,000	130,000
3.	Uruguay	35,000	50,000
4.	Chile	30,000	30,000
5.	Mexico	20,000	26,000
6.	Cuba	10,000	11,000*
7.	Colombia	8,000	9,000
8.	Bolivia	5,000	4,000
9.	Ecuador	4,000	2,000
10.	Venezuela	4,000	8,000
11.	Peru	3,000	4,000
12.	Paraguay	3,000	2,000
13.	Jamaica	2,000	2,200
14.	British Guiana	1,000	130
15.	Dominican Republic	1,000	600
16.	Guatemala	1,000	1,000
17.	Panama	1,000	2,500
18.	Surinam	1,000	1,000
19.	Others**	2,000	2,000
	Total	621,000	735,430

* Less than 9,000 in 1962 in Castro's Cuba.

** Curacao, Puerto Rico, Trinidad, Nicaragua, Salvador, Haiti, Honduras. In the 1949-1959 decade, about half the Jews of Ecuador emigrated, mainly to the United States. Today's Jewish population in the Dominican Republic is only about half of what it was in 1939, estimates varying between 400 to 600.

The hope that the immigration restrictions enacted during the world crisis of the 1930's would be repealed appears to have been unjustified. Immigration in the Central and South American countries remains selective. Although the vast expanse of Latin America offers ample opportunities for immigration, and governments eagerly welcome European immigrants, Jewish immigration is tacitly discouraged.

On the eve of the end of World War II and the liberation of the concentration camp inmates, the Inter-American Conference on War and Peace, February 21—March 8, 1945, stated that "it is inadvisable that compact and homogeneous nuclei settle on territories of the Americas who might represent an extension of their countries, parties or sects, and might claim . . . the status of minorities."

The Latin American countries regard Jews as unassimilable. Jews are kept out by their selective immigration geared to admit those who fulfill prerequisites in which Jewish DP's are deficient, i.e., experienced farmers and technicians who at the same time possess such a linguistic and cultural background as will make them swiftly assimilable. Few Jews need apply.

Finally, Latin American Jewry is concentrated in large urban communities. Here, too, as evident in the following table, the Jews are again seen to be a people of the cities.

Thus, with the exception of Brazil and Argentina, more than three-quarters of the entire Jewish population in these countries live in the capital city. Even in Brazil the Jews remain a metro-

Urban Concentration of Latin American Jews

City	Country	Estimated Jewish Population
Buenos Aires	Argentina	280,000
Rio de Janeiro	Brazil	41,000
Sao Paulo	Brazil	50,000
Montevideo	Uruguay	46,000
Santiago	Chile	25,000
Mexico	Mexico	24,000
Havana	Cuba	10,000
Bogota	Colombia	5,000
La Paz	Bolivia	3,000

politan people par excellence concentrated in the two largest
centers of Brazilian commerce, industry and culture.

Economic Situation: The Colonists

The first wave of East European Jewish immigration to the
Central and South American countries, particularly to the latter, which laid the foundation for the larger Jewish settlements
in this part of America, began with impressive colonization
projects. The initiative came from humble Ukrainian Jews.

One of the colonists, Yitzhak Kaplan, described the hegira of
these pioneers and founders of modern Argentine Jewry who
took the Old World with them and transplanted it across the
seas in the New:

> Well-established people of means, as well as artisans and
> petty traders, with their wives and children, left their
> homes, taking with them their rabbis, cantors, shochtim,
> scrolls of the law and sacred Hebrew books, and went to
> a far-away wilderness to found a new home. A small com-
> pany of the army of Israel, carrying with it the ancient
> Jewish impediments, started for a place hitherto untrodden
> by any Jewish foot—the wild steppes of Argentina. There
> they starved and suffered from diseases, there their children
> met an untimely death. They lived in the most primitive
> circumstances, and yet they remained loyal to the new, un-
> known and till then uncultivated soil. They didn't desert.

The first ten years of the pioneering trials of colonization in
the Argentine up to 1900 saw a considerable turnover, because
the European colonists from the ghettos were unprepared for
the wild pampas, which took its toll.

Today the colonists are prosperous, but their population is
shrinking. There is a steady exodus of the younger generations
who leave the comparative dullness of rural life for the attrac-
tions of the large city. The colonies have their own cultural institutions, libraries, synagogues and theatres, but these exert
an insufficient counter-attraction to the appeal of big town life.

In addition, many of the more prosperous colonists took their
profits from the products of the soil to become city merchants
and manufacturers of the products of the machine.

True, in spite of severe hardships, the founders made great sacrifices and proved that much could be achieved through stubbornness, sweat and will power. But the far-reaching plans of Baron de Hirsch, who aimed to colonize millions of Jews, were not realized. The future of Jewish colonization is questionable.

In 1940, only twenty-five colonies existed, nineteen founded by the Jewish Colonization Association (JCA) and seven by independent colonists. All the colonies combined owned 1,533,502 acres of land. Over 5,000 families were placed and settled on the land by JCA. In 1960, some 2,000 families remained. These and other Jews living in and around the settlements totaled some 15,000. But their farm production has not declined. These were the bulk of those who were in the JCA colonies. Others who were earning a living in the Jewish colonies were artisans, tradesmen and professionals.

This is the sum total of half a century of Jewish colonization: During the past seventeen years several hundred more new Jewish farmer families may have been added, but the population today is only half of what it was at the height of JCA's activities. The JCA still owns more than 499,000 acres, but it would seem to have very few applications for settlement on its land. At a time when Jews all over Europe were seeking havens of refuge, from 1933 to 1940, barely 398 families, less than 50 families a year, were settled on its land.

What are the main reasons for the bankruptcy of an undertaking which had at its disposal large sums of money, large stretches of good land and also fairly good political conditions, since the Argentine government was very sympathetic toward Jewish colonization? Perhaps the most important reason was the lack of faith in the possibility of establishing a Jewish future in the colonies. It is characteristic of the JCA colonization that the colonists were thinly spread over the country. The JCA colonies were scattered over the provinces of Entre Rios, Santa Fe, Buenos Aires, Pampa and Santiago del Estro. This was no accident. "The JCA did it deliberately," said a colonist, "because it thought that it would be politically wiser for us not to occupy one large stretch of undivided Argentine land."

In a Spanish pamphlet it recently issued, the JCA admits that "in order to ease the process of assimilation of the colonizing element it was necessary to establish contact with the native population, and for this reason the founder of the project desired that the colonies be scattered all over the country."

The future outlook is not promising. In 1948 an Argentine Jewish physician, Eliyahu Singer, born and reared in the colonies commented:

> The first generation of pioneers gradually died out. In the neglected cemeteries near the colonies almost all of them lie under bent, sometimes grass-covered tombstones with inscriptions that are no longer legible. Their numerous children who grew up in the fields together with the saplings the colonists had planted, are now scattered throughout the cities and towns of the country. They are merchants, doctors, lawyers, bankers, artists, writers (Spanish, naturally), deputies in parliament, etc. The present generation of colonists leads a monotonous existence without joy or sorrow, lonely, torn away from Jewish life.

Economic and Social Structure

Although there are no official figures on the economic, professional or social divisions among the Jews of Central and South America, there is sufficient material to permit an estimate of the economic and social structure of Latin American Jewry.

The Jewish communities of Central and South America can generally be divided into three groups. These are the larger Jewish communities, those of Argentina and Brazil; the medium-sized Jewries of Uruguay, Mexico, Chile and Cuba, and the smaller communities of less than 5,000 Jews each as indicated in the table on Jewish centers.

Outside of Argentina, where Jewish agriculturists constituted about 2,000 families in 1960, there are no Jewish farmers in those countries except for a scattered handful.* It is thus clear that the socio-economic structure of Latin American Jews is radically different from their non-Jewish neighbors. Its unique-

---

* In the early years of this century there was a fairly prosperous agricultural Jewish colony in Brazil, but it has since steadily declined.

ness marks the Jewish group conspicuously in the eyes of its countrymen. Even in the large communities it is overwhelmingly made up of a trading element, nearly three times larger than the Jewish laboring and industrial classes.†

The present security and the future status of these Jewish communities largely depend upon their function in the Latin American economy. The important questions to be answered are: What is the role played by the Jew, and whom does he encounter and compete with in his struggle for a livelihood in these countries where he is only a recent arrival?

In the very small Jewish communities containing 1000 Jews or less, employees are almost all white-collar clerks. In the larger communities the employee group is divided into two-thirds commercial and factory employees and one-third manual workers, while in the middle and smaller communities it consists almost entirely of industrial and commercial employees.

Economic Adjustment

The Jewish immigrant has certainly played a significant role in the economic development of Latin America. The Jews in Central and South America have, in fact, not only made remarkable progress in integrating themselves within, but also in positively contributing to the economies of their new homelands—to the mutual reward of these countries and themselves. To Latin American lands, tardily experiencing the industrial revolution, the Jews brought economic ingenuity, new enterprises, and new skills in trade, merchandising, light industry, as

† In the larger Jewish communities the percentage of Jews who are engaged in trade is between 45 and 55; in the medium-sized communities it is between 60 and 70, and in the small communities, between 80 and 90. In industry and manufactures 15 to 20 percent of the Jewish population in the large communities are gainfully employed, in contrast to 10 to 20 percent in the medium communities, and 5 to 10 percent in the smallest communities. Jewish participation in the liberal professions fluctuates from 5 to 10 percent in all communities.

As to the social-economic division, the following estimates are made. In the large communities the working elements, laborers and clerks, are 25 to 30 percent of all gainfully employed Jews; in the middle group they are only 10 to 15 percent of the Jewish population; in the small Jewish communities they are less than 10 percent.

well as in the arts, sciences and professions. With the Jews the
nascent process of modern consumer goods and commercial
expansion was accelerated. Their reward was the second chance
—the opportunity to reconstruct their Jewish lives on new soil.

The Jews were innovators. They introduced new local industries and businesses. They initiated the manufacture of furniture, textiles, clothing and leather goods; they increased the
flow of imports and exports; they developed new business
methods and techniques of credit, marketing and merchandising
which multiplied trade, made possible distribution to every part
of these countries, increased consumption and raised the living
standards of entire Latin American populations.

By means of a wonderfully organized credit and distribution
system they brought the poorest classes of the population into
the buyers' market. Indeed the Jewish immigrants helped to
revolutionize Latin American economic life. Through their system of home delivery they were able to penetrate into off-the-
beaten track communities with modern furniture, clothing, shoes,
and jewelry to people who had never imagined such things existed. Through installment plan methods this merchandise was
brought within the reach of these new markets.

Moreover, these energetic Jewish entrepreneurs did not limit
themselves to the organization of a market for imported goods,
but very soon began to produce these goods themselves. They
set up factories to manufacture home products which created
new work opportunities in the cities for large numbers of native
villagers and of immigrants. As the market for these goods broad-
ened, they became cheaper and even more accessible to the
broad masses of Latin Americans. Even in the medium-sized
and smaller Jewish communities, such as Santiago, Chile, the
Jewish immigrants were supporting themselves and many native
Chileans with some eight hundred enterprises producing mat-
tresses, glassware, electrical appliances, ladies' garments—which
for the first time in the country's history bore the stamp "Made
in Chile." In Bolivia they are not only hard-working pioneer
farmers, but also the first microscope to be made in the country
was manufactured by a recent Jewish arrival. In Colombia, new
plants mainly manned by native hands, produce cosmetics, dyes,

lamp shades, clothing, cutlery, combs, belts, gloves, boxes, and knitted goods previously imported in great part.

World War II brought on particularly favorable circumstances in this respect by ridding local industry of foreign competition. Because of this, all branches of industry, especially those founded by Jewish initiative, telescoped into five years a process of development which normally might have taken four times as long.

Competition

Jews, however, were not the only people in the field. True, they took the initiative in most cases. But they soon had rivals—people who competed with them not so much in either the quality or the price of goods but upon the basis of pedigree, of native against foreigner. These competitors were recruited from the classes of traders and artisans infected with the bubbling energy of the Jews. A second process also led to the growth of claimants to Jewish economic positions—the rise of other segments of the population, of the children of more prosperous peasants, higher paid workers, and officials. The stakes involved were not only large-scale commerce and large-scale industry, where considerable capital and experience are necessary. There also was competition for the small merchant and manufacturing positions open to the masses.

This question, which is at the core of the Jewish problem in these countries, has not been adequately studied. There are, however, data on the typical Jewish communities in Mexico City and Buenos Aires.

Mexican Example

For a long time, Mexico was outside the stream of Jewish immigration. It was not until 1920 that large numbers of European Jews from Poland, Lithuania, Rumania and Russia arrived. Few settled on the land. For the most part they followed the general pattern of adjustment of their U. S. kinsmen. They concentrated in the poor sections of the large cities just as they had in New York City's East Side, and made use of their old world trades and skills in earning a livelihood. Those who

lacked special skills or experience took up peddling, retail trade
and small-scale manufactures.

As itinerant pack peddlers from village to village, many
Jews were a combination of talmudic scholar, Daniel Boone
and Trader Horn. Like the Jewish peddler of our own frontier
a century ago, they were intermediaries of exchange between
city and country and in this case also between the descendants
of the Spanish conquerors and the native Indians.

Those Jewish peddlers and small merchants first appeared
in Mexico in 1921-22 and soon began to import diverse articles,
such as clothing, hosiery, underwear, etc. They offered strong
competition to the old-established foreign firms in many branches of commerce. Thanks to the Jewish merchant, shirts, hosiery,
handkerchiefs, toothbrushes, formerly regarded as unobtainable
luxuries by most people, became articles of daily use.

From selling, Jews gradually turned to producing these consumer goods and introduced new industries such as knitted
goods, shoes and hats. This was natural because the Jewish immigrants in the era between the two wars came mainly from
Poland where Jews were so prominent in small industry. Jewish
participation in Mexican industry made vital contributions to
ready-made clothing, textiles, shirts and hosiery manufacturing.

Today there is considerable participation of non-Jews in the
production of articles first introduced by Jews. These industries
also give employment to many non-Jewish Mexicans.

There are very few Jewish manual workers in Mexico, even
in Jewish factories. The occupational structure of the Jews of
Mexico City includes a majority of merchants followed by
white-collar workers and manufacturers in sizeable numbers.
Independent artisans and the liberal professions are also fairly
well represented.

The social structure is completely middle-class.

Argentinian Example

Peddling has been more extensive in Argentina than in any
other country. It is an important segment of the nation's economic life and its successful competition with the regular stores
has become as normal a phenomenon as the chain-store's com-

petition with the ordinary retailer in other lands. There is also a large number of Jewish middle-class and rich manufacturers. The occupational and social structure of the Jewish population of Buenos Aires are important because it is here in the principal city that the majority of Argentine Jewry is concentrated.

Business occupies approximately one-half the economically active Jews in the Argentine capital city of Buenos Aires. Small business and peddling accounts for about one-fifth of the entire Jewish occupational population, as does the group of business employees and clerks. Medium and wholesale business engages about 10 percent of Buenos Aires' employed Jews. In the category of industry and labor, medium and large manufacturers and laborers include some 16 percent each; artisans are a significant group of more than 10 percent; small industrialists and clerks are small segments. The remainder of the working population is made up of the Jews in the liberal professions, in the field of communications and rentiers. In the cities of the provinces, the percentage of those engaged in business is even higher. Of the total occupational structure, Jewish wage earning groups in Buenos Aires constitute more than 40 percent of all gainfully occupied Jews.

Textiles

In most European countries Jews pioneered in the establishment of textile mills and in the marketing of textile goods. In the New World, Jewish history repeated itself. Here again, Jews became very active in this field, performing the same miracles of initiative and achievement as in Europe. In these new countries of Jewish immigration the process of development has been much swifter than in the Old World, Argentina being the best example. Behind the development of the textile industry in Argentina lies a fascinating story of Jewish creative energy.

The Jewish weavers of Bialystock, Poland, who began to participate actively in the textile industry about twenty-three to twenty-six years ago, arrived in Argentina penniless, worked extremely hard at the beginning, but with the purpose of saving enough money to become economically independent. As soon as they had attained that independence, their rise in the industry was swift.

By 1942 the Bialystock Jews developed Vija Linch, which had been nothing but a muddy swamp area near Buenos Aires only some eight years before, into an important textile center destined to become the Manchester of Argentina. Here, in less than a decade, over a hundred textile mills, open day and night, produced more than 20,000,000 meters of woolen and silk goods annually. The day is too short for Vija Linch.

The pioneers were the Ruthenbergs, the Poniman brothers, Kulish, Epstein, Kantor—it has now become difficult to enumerate them all. The entire surrounding territory has come to life, like an early western boomtown. Restaurants, cafes, barber shops have opened to service the hundreds of working men and women who found employment in the mills.

Mutual Credit

Where did these poor immigrants get the capital to develop these industries? The answer lies in the capacity of Jews to adjust to new circumstances and to organize for mutual aid. The Old World spiritual heritage played an important part. The Jewish immigrant who came to the United States during the 1880's did not bring with him the leaven of the Jewish national revival or the experience either of the cooperative loan-funds that were later developed in Eastern Europe, or of the struggles for political and national freedom. Unlike him, however, the Argentine immigrant, who came after World War I, generally participated personally, in active or passive form, in all these movements which so strongly altered the cultural and even economic institutions of the Jew.

Besides Buenos Aires, almost every fair-sized Jewish community has one or two people's banks. These were the first institutions set up by the newcomers for purposes of mutual aid. The Jewish immigrant to Buenos Aires, Montevideo, Santiago, or Mexico City felt completely helpless, since he had neither capital nor the slightest possibility of obtaining a loan in any of the existing credit institutions. Mutual aid was the only solution. The result was a score or more of Jewish people's cooperative banks which played a vital role in helping the immigrants establish themselves in their new countries. Later, as in Buenos Aires, they became important economic institutions as large-scale Jewish industry developed, and were transformed into small shareholder's banks.

These institutions began to do business with extremely low sums. The "Banco Industrial," one of the oldest Jewish people's banks, was established in 1917, with 120 pesos. At its twentieth anniversary in 1937 it had a capital of 351,000 pesos, and its credits reached four million pesos.

The development of the Jewish people's banks is the best example of the rapid rise of Jewish credit in all the countries of Central and South America. This development reached its greatest height in Argentina.

Cooperatives

In Buenos Aires, Jewish peddlers created two great trading cooperatives which have now been in business for more than a quarter-century. Their sales are very large and are steadily growing. They have saved a considerable reserve fund to be used in times of depression, and have a reputation for strict honesty.

Anti-Semitism

Latin American populations include Indians, Negroes, Creoles, Portuguese, Spaniards, Dutch, Italians, and English, and are considerably tolerant of differences in nationality and race. Indeed, before 1933, the year of Hitler's ascent, anti-Semitism was rarely encountered in that part of the globe. Though present, it was quite dormant until spread by Nazi and fascist agents well supplied with funds, who built up Latin American fifth columns of co-nationals and sympathetic cultural groups, and recruited native ultra-nationalist societies, using anti-Semitism as an Axis political weapon. They infiltrated government bureaus, won over important officials and suborned venal editors. Also, adapting political tactics to local conditions, the Nazi agents in Roman-Catholic Latin America eschewed the anti-

Catholic chant and won over an impressive number of Catholic priests and laity, although the top echelons of the hierarchy condemned anti-Jewish activities. A significant and unique fact is that anti-Jewish attacks in a Catholic Latin America, couple Jews and Protestants as "a Jewish-Protestant alliance threatening domination of the world."

The Nazi influence in Latin American became particularly powerful in the most advanced republics where the great majority of Jews lived: in Argentina, Brazil, Chile, Bolivia, Peru, and Colombia. In Bolivia alone, the Axis controlled 80 percent of all business and industrial enterprises, using this power to accelerate anti-Semitic pressure. Today, more than sixteen years after the Axis defeat, the effects of its efforts still remain as a Nazi legacy to worry the Jews, although despite intermittent local outbursts in some countries, Jewish legal rights, property, and lives are not seriously threatened.

In recent years, and especially since the war for Israel's independence, the Arab elements, mostly Christians of Syrian and Lebanese origin, have begun to stir up anti-Jewish propaganda. These Arabs had also been pro-Axis. Their anti-Jewishness is not without its economic causes. They, too, are merchants and compete with the Jews. For this very reason, however, the Arabs themselves are not popular with the native merchant class, and ultra-nationalist groups have attacked them as well as the Jews. Therefore, although persons of Arab origin are seated in the Senate and in local governments in Argentina, and they also hold important positions in Bolivia, Chile and Brazil, their influence must not be overestimated.

In Mexico there is rivalry between the non-Jewish-owned large department stores and the Jewish stores and street bazaars. In Chile, Bolivia, and Venezuela, anti-Semitism was to some extent due to the fact that Jews who came as farmers established themselves as peddlers selling articles in the streets in the center of towns and giving the impression of suddenly invading the country in great numbers so that native merchants raised an outcry against them. Anti-Semitic propaganda stresses this factor of Jewish economic competition. Its seeds take root under unfavorable economic conditions, when anti-Semitic elements in Latin America, as elsewhere, attempt to make the Jews the scapegoat for the people's economic misfortunes.

Of special import in assessing anti-Semitism today, are the ABC countries—Argentina, Brazil, and Chile—because they are the most important countries of South America and contain the largest Jewish communities with Uruguay.

Argentina

In 1960, the Jewish population of Argentina was estimated to be about 450,000. The majority is Ashkenazim; the Sephardic community numbers some 40,000 whose tongue is Arabic and an additional 15,000 who speak Spanish. Buenos Aires is by far the largest Jewish community, with some 280,000. Rosaria has about 15,000 Jews, Cordoba over 8,000 and Santa Fe over 4,000. Immigration has been restricted since the last war.

DAIA—the Delegacion de Asociaciones Israelitas Argentina— is the central representative organization. It was established in 1935 and is made up of delegates from all existing Jewish organizations, except those following the Communist line. Buenos Aires has an elected Kehillah which deals with communal social and cultural matters. But its 45,000 members are all Ashkenazic Jews. All Jewish communities, including Buenos Aires, are affiliated with the Vaad Hakehilloth which was established several years ago, and now includes about one hundred such community affiliates.

Zionist organizations are well established, functioning, prolific and as varied in their convictions as their Israeli counterparts. The non-Zionist organizations are also represented, but their role is a minor one.

During World War II, and immediately in its wake, anti-Semitism pervaded the press; anti-Jewish demonstrations and attacks were frequent; arrests and fines occurred. In the government's effort to eliminate "foreign influences" from public life, the use of other languages in print and at public meetings has often been impeded. During the war there was a ban on the public use of Yiddish as a result, and in 1943 Yiddish papers were prohibited for a time. However, while the ban is still in effect, special permission for the use of Yiddish is liberally granted.

Argentina's Religious Education Bill of 1947 made the teaching of Roman Catholicism obligatory in all public schools. Until it was discontinued recently, ministers of other denominations were not authorized to teach.

President Juan Peron came to power in 1946 as the candidate of the "Labor Party," which was a coalition of bolters from Argentina's old democratic Radical Party and from the National Liberty Alliance's extremist wing. Jews were worried when he assumed power. Discrimination against Jewish students and instructors at the universities, against Jewish doctors in the city hospitals of Buenos Aires, and outbursts against Jewish persons and property fed this anxiety. Although the attackers went unpunished, Peron publicly expressed his regret over the incidents, and afterwards he spoke out for racial tolerance on several occasions. However, Peron's strongest statement against anti-Semitism on August 21, 1948 was made to a pro-Peronist stooge organization, the Organizacion Israelita Argentina. Its leaders boasted that Peron had promised to give special consideration to immigration applications of relatives of Argentina Jews submitted through OIA. The situation did change for the better that year when the status of illegal immigrants was legalized and naturalization was expedited. Anti-Semitic propaganda was still carried on by Peron's supporters, but Dr. Ricardo Dubrovsky who was then president of DAIA, in his report of December, 1948 stated that anti-Semitic activities had decreased that year.

With Peron's overthrow in September, 1955, the situation improved and Jews who had been dismissed from positions in universities and other schools because of their opposition to Peronism were reinstated. Difficulties in immigration still remain, and the universities continue to be the seed-bed of Argentina's severest expression of anti-Semitism. This is especially so in the medical schools, which have a high percentage of Jewish students. Jewish doctors must interne at Jewish hospitals since they can not gain admittance elsewhere.[*]

---

[*] Chaim Finkelstein (principal of the Shalom Aleichem School in Buenos Aires), "The Jewry of South America," Forum IV, World Zionist Organization, (Jerusalem, Spring 1959) p. 326.

The community has a problem in coordinating the activities of its constituency which is divided into three parts—the Sephardic Jews from the Mediterranean area, the Yiddish-speaking Ashkenazim from Eastern Europe, and the German-speaking Jews from Central Europe. The Vaad Hakehilloth (Council of Communities) came into being in 1952 in response to the need for a central Jewish body in Argentina to establish contact with some fifty-six community councils. Its emissaries have gone from Buenos Aires into every province to knit together Argentina's Jews. National congresses have also been held under its aegis.

The Jewish community in Buenos Aires pays subventions to a network of 59 Jewish primary schools with an enrollment of about 10,000. These are administered together with the schools in the provinces by the Vaad Hachinuch (Central Educational Board).* About 35 to 40 percent of all Jewish children of school age attend Jewish schools in Buenos Aires. There are some 14 schools in its suburbs and 67 in the provinces. Some 1,500 attend the suburban schools, and about 4,000 go to provincial schools. Advanced courses for adults are given in certain primary schools. The Sephardic communities maintain primary schools for about 1,500 children. There is one secondary school, a teachers' seminary, and a school to train nursery and kindergarten teachers. Their total enrollment is about 1,200. A Hebrew Midrasha and a Machon are also maintained as institutions of higher Jewish learning.

While each Jewish community has at least one synagogue, the provinces are a barren desert as far as religious education and rabbis are concerned. In 1956, a beginning was made to develop religious institutions. Jewish provincial communities, some with thousands of families, were without a single rabbi, and the smaller communities often were without *mohelim* and *shochtim.*

The immigrants who peopled Baron Hirsch's rural settlement projects struggled to wrest a life and a living from the soil. Their children and grandchildren abandoned the farms for the

---

* Only 139 pupils out of 7,340 in all classes remained to finish their studies in the top grades of elementary schools in 1960.

lure of the cities and its opportunities for a liberal education, training in the professions, and social betterment. The number of farmers is decreasing. Some leave, some become cattlemen, some lease their land to non-Jews. The settlements are no longer the center of Jewish life in Argentina. Bereft of religious leaders and education, they are becoming assimilated to the surrounding non-Jewish life.

Economic deproletarization was even more accelerated than in the United States. The Jews supplied vitally necessary economic functions to Argentine trade and industry and the door to the middle class was wide open for them. Today the Jewish trade unions, such as carpenters and tailors, no longer exist. The middle-class entrepreneur and businessmen have taken their place. There are now organizations of Jewish manufacturers of furniture and garments; retail, jeweler and fur cooperatives; bankers and retailers.

While the important Jewish contribution to Argentina's economic growth continues, the Jews are an economic enclave whose enterprises are insulated from the general environment. To Chaim Finkelstein "It is not a matter of language. It has deep cultural roots, familiar to us in the long history of the Galut."*

The Yiddish language which has played so central a role in Diaspora life and Jewish culture, is today at its virile best and most prolific in Argentina. The extensive Jewish press includes two dailies and twelve other periodicals in Yiddish; ten periodicals in Spanish; five periodicals in Yiddish and Spanish, and one each in German, Hebrew and Hungarian. The press is expressive of a vital national consciousness and the desire to create a Jewish life.

Will it succeed? The future will tell. Today in 1962 the Jews of Argentina share the culture of the country. Up to almost two-thirds of the Jewish youth take advantage of the free educational system of Argentina. Even the third to two-fifths of Jewish youth who attend Jewish schools are subjected to the pressures of assimilation by osmosis exerted by the majority

* "The Jewry of South America," *Forum IV*, World Zionist Organization, (Jerusalem, Spring, 1959), pp. 325-26.

culture. And particularly in the provincial towns there is Jewish rootlessness and ignorance of Jewish history, customs, tradition, literature or religion. Yet the Vaad Hakehilloth is alive
to the problem. It is only four years since the first all-Argentine
Jewish educational congress took place on March 16-17, 1957.

Argentine Jewry marked its Centenary in 1960. The Congress
of the Vaad Hakehilloth convened a special session attended by
246 delegates during the last week in August. The delegates
requested the Argentine government to take stern measures to
eradicate recent attacks on Jewish students fomented by the
Nazi-fascist movement in Argentina. Cognizant of the threat
of assimilation and the increasing number of mixed marriages
in the Argentine Jewish community, the delegates supported
measures for the strengthening of religious life and broadening
the Jewish educational network on an integrated full-time basis.
In a significant action the Congress adopted a program designed
to increase contact between the Ashkenazic and Sephardic communities, and to coordinate these two groups.

As for the difficulties caused by the abduction of Adolf
Eichmann to the smooth course of relations between the Arturo
Frondizi government and Israel, they have since returned to
normal. As a warm gesture of esteem, friendship and its wish
to smooth the ruffled feathers of Argentines, Israel staged an
impressive cultural and archaeological exhibit in Buenos Aires,
after the heat generated by the incident had simmered down
somewhat.

Brazil

There are about 130,000 Jews in Brazil, the great majority of
whom (86 to 88 percent) are Ashkenazim. Sao Paulo is the
largest Jewish community, with a population of 47,000 to 50,000.
Rio de Janeiro numbers 39,000 to 41,000 Jews, Porto Alegre
has 12,000 and Recife has 1,600 to 2,000. Brazilian Jewry is
organized nationally and has as its official spokesman the Con-
federation of Jewish Representative Institutions to which more
than 100 affiliated institutions and all the local federations
belong.

The advent of Hitler stimulated considerable Jewish immigration to Brazil after 1933 and a smaller wave after the end of World War II. In the early nineteen fifties some 6,000 to 8,000 Jews from Israel (mostly via Germany) entered. This immigration is continuing, though now slowed to a trickle. In 1957 more than 2,800 Jews entered Brazil from Egypt and Hungary, and in 1960 over 2,000 arrived.

In the 1955 presidential elections, the Fascist Integralist Party polled 700,000 votes—9 percent of the total—and the party, which had virtually disintegrated, was reorganized. Neither anti-Semitic publications nor special movements exist, although sporadic attacks occur in lesser periodicals and in some pamphlets. In August, 1955, the Archbishop of São Paulo uttered anti-Jewish remarks in his pastoral letter to the effect that Jews had clandestinely infiltrated the universities and were preaching "imperialist proselytism" there. Subsequently, he partially retracted this statement and explained it as not biased or directed against Jews.

Jews have held important positions in government such as the post of Minister of Finance, and they have been elected to parliament and to municipal office.

Brazilian Zionism is strong. There is a United Zionist Organization, the Unificada. The Zionist Organization's National Council for Education and Culture finances and directs Jewish education in Rio de Janeiro. In São Paulo it is supervised by the Vaad Hachinuch of the Federation of Jewish Societies. Virtually the entire educational system and the core of Jewish communal and cultural effort is bound up with Zionism and the State of Israel. In 1952 a corps of teachers came to Brazil from the young Jewish state. These Israeli teachers rejuvenated the Jewish educational system of Brazil, expanded the program into new schools and shored up the old schools threatened with a shortage of Yiddish and Hebrew teachers. Within five years about 5,000 children were studying in these full-time schools throughout Brazil. Both Rio de Janeiro and São Paulo also had institutes for Hebrew culture with a wide offering of adult courses of study.

Obviously these teachers brought to Brazil from Israel by the Jewish Agency permeated their teaching with Zionism and the story of their homeland.

The non-Zionists had their own schools in Rio and São Paulo, but the Zionist influence was most important. General subjects followed the official Brazilian school curriculum as in the American day schools and bi-cultural institutions. These were taught in Portuguese. Yiddish and Hebrew studies received two to three hours daily in addition. Besides the two largest cities, there are also Jewish schools in Porto Alegre, Recife, Curitiba, Salvador, Bela Horizonte and several smaller localities. All are day schools. Rio has ten primary, four secondary, one professional school and three kindergartens with a total enrollment of about 2,200; São Paulo has eleven primary and three secondary schools with an enrollment of 2,800.

The strong ties with Israel are revealed in the emigration of groups of Brazilian Jews to the new state and in an Israel-Brazilian cultural institute. There are ten important congregations and a number of smaller ones in Brazil. The community is active in both Brazilian and Jewish social, political, economic, intellectual and cultural life. The Jewish press includes five weeklies—two Yiddish, two Portuguese, one Portuguese-German; two Yiddish semi-weeklies; one Portuguese and one Portuguese-Yiddish fortnightly and two monthlies in Portuguese.

Chile

There are about 30,000 Jews in Chile, 90 percent of whom are Ashkenazim. About half of this number arrived between 1934 and 1946–3,000 after the start of World War II. Since then only 200 to 300 arrived annually until 1952. From then on there has been virtually no immigration except for a small group of Hungarian refugees in 1957. The largest Jewish communities are in Santiago where some 20,000 to 25,000 Jews live, and Valparaiso which numbers 1,200 to 1,500.

Chilean Jewry is represented by the Representative Committee of the Jewish Collective, with about forty affiliated organizations. While some of the first families of Chile are descended from Jews—Caho, Matte, Vicuna, Rodrigruez, Hurtado

—Jews as a group do not play any role in the political life of the country apart from individual outstanding politicians. The Zionist Federation represents all groups from Herut to Mapam and embraces virtually the entire Jewish community. This is the only Jewish political movement.

Apart from some anti-Semitic outbursts more than a quarter century ago, sparked by Nazi propaganda, aggravated by local economic conditions, and continuing sporadically until its renewed manifestation during the Arab-Israeli war, there has been little overt anti-Semitism.

The Vaad Hachinuch conducts five Hebrew schools, three of them in Santiago. The all-day school has an enrollment of some 1,000 pupils, including some 210 in advanced classes. The German Jewish Sunday School has about 400 and the Sephardic religious school some 50 pupils. Spanish is the language of instruction. There is one school in Valparaiso and another in Concepcion.

Chile suffers from a dearth of rabbis and cantors. Four rabbis and three cantors, all in Santiago, are all there are for twelve synagogues, (six in Santiago and six in the provinces). In Santiago three are separate East European, German and Sephardic congregations.

The Jewish press consists of one Yiddish-Spanish weekly, one Spanish weekly and several Spanish monthlies.

Liberal Uruguay is friendly to Jews. There is considerable anti-Jewish agitation in Argentina, Peru, Colombia, and Bolivia, but present sporadic incidents, demonstrations and attempts at discrimination are not an accurate indicator of future danger.

Mexico, the Dominican Republic, Dutch Guiana, and San Salvador at present offer no cause for alarm. But Guatemala and Costa Rica have witnessed anti-Jewish agitation, and in Cuba their economic situation is difficult since Castro.

The fact is, that anti-Jewish activities in Latin America are today passing through a phase in which future trends have not yet coalesced sufficiently to permit finite conclusions. Certainly the twelve years of feverish anti-Jewish activities until 1945 have left a deep imprint on the public life of Latin America. Contra-

dictory appraisals characterize these Latin-American manifestations of anti-Jewish acts, discrimination and propaganda either
as forerunners of unbridled anti-Semitism, or conversely, as
merely sporadic, minor incidents. Although the situation is
worsening, the truth still appears to lie in between these ex-
tremes.

Counter-Action

The policy of Latin-American Jewry in itself is one of preventive vigilance and counter-action. The central organizations
of the Jewish communities maintain close relations with the
government authorities. They have intervened effectively, when
it was necessary, with their governments in Argentina, Mexico,
Colombia, Bolivia and Peru.

Prompt, active intervention is of extreme importance. As a
case in point, instant and effective action by the World Jewish
Congress resulted in the abrogation of the first anti-Semitic
decree enacted in the Western Hemisphere. The anti-Jewish
decree had been ordained in Bolivia; it authorized a special investigation of the financial assets of recent "Semitic" arrivals in
Bolivia, and was followed by serious restrictions on Jewish economic activity.

In summation, Latin American governments as a rule maintain a correct or even friendly attitude toward their Jewish
inhabitants. The presidents and high ranking officials of Chile
and Uruguay, have in fact, publicly expressed good will toward
Jews. In Argentina too, important government spokesmen and
public opinion molders have opposed the introduction of anti-
Semitism. In addition, Latin American statesmen, journalists
and religious and cultural leaders are faithful proponents of
liberal and humanitarian traditions and democratic policies.

On the other hand, the situation in some countries parallels
that of European nations whose governments maintain a correct
or even friendly attitude as regards Jews, but which are either
not able or else for political reasons are very hesitant to curb
anti-Jewish activities. It is this political basis of anti-Semitism
bequeathed to Latin America by the Third Reich which is re-

sponsible for making this area one of the political danger zones on the contemporary Jewish map of the world. Therefore, despite favorable aspects, the situation of Jews in Latin America as regards anti-Semitism today may be presently regarded as deteriorating and requiring vigilance together with preventive and counter-action on their part.

Institutions

In the past decade, Jewish consciousness and communal activity has achieved a new impetus in Latin America. This is reflected in all spheres.

In Buenos Aires which is typical of the Latin American Jewish communities, many new communal buildings were constructed within the past twenty years at a cost of millions of pesos.

The Chevra Kadisha of Buenos Aires, as its Hebrew name implies, started as a burial society in 1894 with 185 members and an annual budget of 1,155 pesos. Today it numbers its members in tens of thousands and its annual budget has reached several million pesos. Exceeding its original aims, the society's activities encompass virtually every branch of Jewish communal endeavor. It maintains numerous institutions, including a teachers seminary.

The Circulo Israelita, which is the Jewish community organization of Santiago, Chile, conducts a loan "Kasse," a library, a Hebrew Institute for education and culture, and is engaged in Jewish political work—all in addition to maintaining a cemetery, synagogues and conducting charitable activities.

In contrast to the Buenos Aires community of a quarter-million Jews which recently celebrated its sixtieth anniversary, the Jewish community of Mexico City is still young. Its Jewish population comprises some 24,000, yet its communal possessions include splendid synagogues, buildings, cemeteries, a cultural center and social welfare and health institutions.

Jewish political-communal activity in Latin America is concerned with both local Jewish interests and world-wide Jewish movements. No matter how small a community, it contains Jew-

ish parties and factions of all shades of political opinion. But
the basis of Jewish life, and the nerve center of Jewish spiritual
activity, especially among Jewish youth, is Zionism.

Press and Education

The press is a barometer of active Jewishness. In this part of
the world, with only 620,000 Jewish souls, Yiddish daily newspapers, more than a dozen Yiddish weeklies and three monthlies, are published—besides twenty Jewish weeklies in Spanish
and Portuguese, some ten monthlies in Spanish and three in
Hebrew. Four of the dailies are published in Buenos Aires, including the two most important, *Di Yidische Zaitung* and *Die
Presse,* and two in Montevideo. The overwhelming majority are
Zionist.

The Daily Yiddish press of Latin America maintains high
standards, both with respect to general and Jewish information
and to serious comment upon general and Jewish questions.

The Jewish school is another community standard. Teachers
must still be imported from Europe. Here, chance took a hand.
A small community such as Mexico was more fortunate in obtaining good pedagogues than much larger communities, and
holds first place in the percentage of Jewish children of school
age who receive a Jewish education. 3,800 of its Jewish children
receive their full education in Jewish day schools. These are the
first generation native-born children of Sephardic and Arabian-
Jewish parents. Their annual budget for organized Jewish education amounts to hundred of thousands of pesos, a tremendous
sum for such a small community.

The Mexican provinces follow the capital city pattern. The
100 Jewish families of Monterey maintain a day school with 60
pupils. In the provincial cities of Argentina with much larger
Jewish communities there are no day schools and the percentage of Jewish children receiving some sort of a Jewish education
is no higher than in the capital. In Buenos Aires, which still
has old-time "chedarim" with their "melamdim" besides its
more modern schools, the number of pupils has risen during
the past two years and today totals some 10,000. There were
no modern Jewish day schools in this center of modern Jewish

culture until 1949 when the first one was opened by the Sephardic community. About 35 to 40 percent of Jewish children attended Jewish schools in Buenos Aires in 1960.

These are examples of the degree of Jewish school attendance in Latin America. The entire Jewish school population of Rio de Janeiro is approximately 2,200 with several hundred more receiving private Jewish instruction. Rio has day schools and a Hebrew high school. The latter, in existence for some thirty years, is considered one of the model Jewish schools of South America. Rio de Janeiro also has Yiddish schools, and one other school whose language of instruction is Hebrew. Thus, about one-third of Rio's Jewish children of school age receive the benefit of some sort of Jewish education.

Montevideo has ten Jewish schools: several are all-Hebrew; others use Yiddish as the language of instruction, but also teach Hebrew; and one uses Hebrew as the language of instruction and also teaches Yiddish. There are about 1,550 students. There is also a Yeshivah with some 110 students.

Santiago has five Jewish day schools with about 1,000 pupils, totaling some 30 percent of all Jewish children of school age. Hebrew is the principal language in which Jewish subjects are taught. In all Jewish day schools in Latin America, general subjects are taught in Spanish. In Brazil of course they are taught in Portuguese.

The condition of Jewish education in some of the small communities is pathetic, although there is an attempt now to raise it from its low estate. Even in such a fair-sized community as Colombia, with its 9,000 Jews, there are only two day and two afternoon schools. In Venezuela, El Salvador, Ecuador and several other communities, schools were only recently founded. However, Latin America has proportionately more Jewish day schools than the United States, where Jewish schools are overwhelmingly only supplementary to the public school.

Culture

Jewish cultural activity in Latin America is not limited to schools. All the larger communities have Jewish libraries. Intensive cultural activity is carried on by the youth organizations,

particularly by the young Zionists. The "Yivo"* section of Buenos Aires has issued five volumes that make an important contribution to knowledge of the history of Argentine Jewry. It has
also established a large and important library and archives for
the gathering of material on the history of Jewish communities
in all Latin American countries.

Indeed, Latin America today seethes with Jewish creative
talent. In Argentina alone there are several hundred Yiddish
poets, novelists, short story writers and journalists. Jews have
attained eminence in Spanish literature and journalism, and in
the arts, sciences and professions. Among them, Alberto Ger-
shunoff is considered one of the foremost contemporary political
writers in the Spanish language. His novel "The Jewish Gau-
chos" is a Latin American classic which opened new literary
perspectives.

Leon Duchobny is an outstanding authority on Spinoza. Fried-
rick Oppler, writer and historian has brought home to Latin
American Jewry an understanding and appreciation of the heritage and contemporary role of the Jew in his book Os Judeus
eo Munda de Hoje (The Jews and the World of Today). In
politics, Dr. Enrico Dickman is an important Argentine Socialist
leader. Natalie Berman, Socialist, and Anchel Fibuvitch, Radical, were members of the Chilean Parliament. There are many
Jewish professors of medicine, chemistry, technology and law.
Dr. Richard Dubrovsky, president of DAIA, official representative body of Argentine Jewry, and an affiliate of the World
Jewish Congress was chosen from a large list of candidates
for a Buenos Aires State Clinic professorship. Dr. Mine Chase-
levitch is professor of clinical medicine at Buenos Aires University.

The works of Yiddish classicists—I. L. Peretz, Sholem Asch,
Peretz Hirschbein, among others, have been translated into Spanish. Jews are also found as prominent Latin American sculptors,
painters, musicians, engineers, and lawyers.**

---

* Yiddish Scientific Institute to disseminate Yiddish culture and scholarship.
** The host of important names is too long for recital. Among those
deserving mention are: Bernardo Verbitsky, editor Davar, a monthly re-

Conclusion

The typical Latin-American Jewish community is made up of three separate bodies whose members have gravitated toward one another as "landsleit" (kinsmen): the Sephardim, the Central Europeans and the East Europeans. This reflects the historic fact that its founders arrived as distinct groups, and the sociological fact that national origin and its pattern of religious observance have strongly influenced Jewish communal organization.

The three groups have remained divided by differences in language and customs, despite increased need for mutual cooperation. As a result there is a great deal of separatism and duplication in communal activities, and there has been no central planning for total Jewish community needs.

Still there are trends toward unity. Zionism has been a common denominator uniting the leaders, if not the members as yet of the diverse groups. Anti-Semitism has served to unify the communities into Central Committees affiliated with the World Jewish Congress, which like DAIA in Argentina, is the officially representative body of the community. The membership of Jewish youth organizations in sports and culture also cuts across the country-of-origin lines of their elders.

The Spanish-speaking Sephardim found their language facility, and their social customs a bridge to easy assimilation. A visitor to their community finds little apart from their synagogue and religious life to distinguish them from their non-Jewish neighbors, and their synagogue, the spiritual and communal center of their activities, is a diminishing influence. Their youth has received little or no Jewish education and many have been lost to the Jewish faith.

The Central and East European community groups, while learning the language and history of their new countries, at the same time feel the need for identification with the Jewish

view in Spanish; Benno Weiser, editor *Dos Mundos;* Solomon Resznick, editor of *Judaica,* a scholarly Jewish monthly; Dr. Joseph Mirelman, Jewish book publisher; Carlos M. Grumberg, noted poet; Lazaro Schellman, writer; and Lazar Segal in Brazil and Dr. Robert Singer who fled Germany in 1938, in Uruguay, leading Latin American modern painters.

cultural heritage. The psychological shock of Hitlerism has built up in these Jews a stronger resistance to assimilation, and has helped to knit the community together.

Assimilation through intermarriage is a disturbing factor in the smaller communities, such as Venezuela, Nicaragua and Ecuador. The fact that Jewish males outnumber the Jewish female population is the primary factor making for intermarriage in the smaller communities.

All three community groups—Sephardic, East European, Central European—wish to retain the Orthodox spirit and practice in the synagogue in Latin America. They relish contact with Israel and with Jews and Jewish organizations in the United States and elsewhere. They are eager for Jewish literature, publications and information from abroad. With the destruction of the great spiritual and cultural centers of Jewish learning they look to America for rabbis, teachers and social welfare workers to fulfill their religious educational and welfare needs.

Contemporary Jewish life in Latin America, as everywhere else, has its share of problems and difficulties. But on the whole it is an increasing force among the remaining substantial Jewish communities in the world. The Jews of Latin America have done their part to aid their DP brothers overseas to reconstruct their lives, and in lending support to Israel. As affiliates of the World Jewish Congress, Latin-American Jews are not only keenly aware of the common problems of world Jewry, but are also links in the "Unity in Dispersion" chain which has again demonstrated the indestructible vitality of the Jewish people throughout the world.

A possible cloud on the horizon is represented by the influence of "Castroism" as an economic revolutionary and expropriation movement. The aggressive export of his ideas has exacerbated the class struggle in some Latin American countries, and stimulated riots, particularly in Caracas, Venezuela, against the Betancourt government and the propertied classes. Jewish businessmen who are primarily a middle-class bourgeois entrepreneur and social group have expressed concern for the future, although the Castro cloud is as yet no larger than the proverbial man's hand on the horizon. This is an economic rather than an anti-Semitic menace to Jewry in Latin America.

A serious incident in Havana saw Charles Shapiro, American owner of the important—now expropriated—department store, Los Precios Hijos, and members of his family, mauled in their own home. Mr. Shapiro, seventy-six years old, had lived in Cuba thirty-five years. The Castro regime insists this was an act of anti-Yankeeism, not anti-Semitism.

By the end of 1961 there were 2,000 refugee Jews from Cuba in the United States. Under Castro's confessed Marxist-Leninism the Jewish economic position will continue to deteriorate and further emigration may be expected.

CHAPTER SIX

AMERICAN JEWISH YOUTH: TWO GENERATIONS

by JACOB FREID

1. The Generation of the '30's and the Marxist Delusion

American Jewry's "lost generation" of the thirties is the suburbanite parent of today's youth and the grandparent of tomorrow's. The experience of the past generation, the present situation and the hopes and fears of the future generation, are central to the discussion of civil rights, Jewish education and the Diaspora-Israel dialogue.

Two tentative hypotheses are hazarded in considering whether or not American Jewish youth will refute the pessimism of the Israeli critics and negators of the Diaspora: first, that Jewish religious education and the institutions of the synagogue and the family failed to establish rapport with Jewish youth in the thirties; second, that Jewish secular and communal life, centers, movements, and organizations did not attract or involve Jewish youth intellectually or politically in the struggle for civil rights or Zionism, or creatively and culturally in Jewish literary or artistic expression.

Will Jewish education in America fail to meet the challenge of the sixties as it failed in the thirties? Will it meet the needs of Jewish youth and the Jewish community in this decade as it did not do then? Or will it limp along in a "River Platte rut"—a possibility so graphically presented by Uriah Zvi Engelman in his study. Can we benefit from the tragic experience and errors of thirty years ago? Why did they happen?

The 1930's were the questing days of the generation of the Depression, when conversion to communism was not uncommon for Jewish intellectuals. In the decade ended by the trauma of the Stalin-Hitler pact, many sincere, sensitive, high-minded young Jews were attracted to communism. It took the shocking revelation of the courtship of Nazism by the Kremlin, culminating in the agreement of the Soviet Union and Germany in 1939 to show that the God of the new revelation was a sham and a hoax no less false than the Golden Calf which had deluded their ancestors into idolatry.

Churning with the fire of idealism, they did not find the answers to their quest and their questions in the synagogue, the home, the community or in Judaism itself; nor, frankly, did a significant number even bother to look or inquire in those directions.

The central contribution to lessening prejudice and discrimination and combating anti-Semitism so that the burden of minority existence would be eased, had not yet been made. It was felt keenly by many young Jews, who, Jewishly myopic, saw the Communist party as the principal foe of injustice. They could not perceive that the vital onslaught in this struggle would be made by Jewish defense agencies in contrast to the opportunistic tactics of the party. Idealism and idealists were ready grist for the Communist mill.

Theirs was a compassionate perception of the temper of the time, and they reacted more keenly to both its frustrations and its idolatrous hopes. Unwilling to accept passivity and abnegation, their conversion to a new gospel according to Marx, Lenin, and Stalin, expressed in sharper form the views shared by those who felt Russia was the champion of the dispossessed. They so wanted to believe that the dictatorship of the proletariat in truth had arrived, that they gambled their faith on unrealized ideals instead of confining it prudently to commonplace loyalties. With a zeal compounded of idealistic spirit, they constituted themselves an advance guard spearheading the pathway to the better society. Those who flagged fell by the wayside; in the new theology momentary heresy could only be expiated by abject self-confession and a public *mea culpa* such as

Albert Maltz staged for the past generation's readers of the *New Masses;* others like Howard Fast were bitter-enders who had actually to touch the dead-end walls of their blind alley before they could make an ignominious about-face.

They saw the Communist faith as an answer to the hopes of man in their age, just as those before them had seen the French Revolution as "a vision of the Kingdom of God on Earth" and worth working for.[1] Somehow their rabbis, teachers, and parents could not overcome their secular-rationalist opposition to Jewish belief and practice. Their conflict with the immigrant generations, their rejection of the old tenets, the Depression's disintegration of the patriarchal father no longer able to fulfill his economic role as breadwinner (dramatized in *Awake and Sing, and Paradise Lost* by Clifford Odets), the Jewish anonymity and illiteracy of big city life, these and other elements caused a blind spot toward Judaism. The rabbis failed to convince them that *Malkah Shmayim*—the Kingdom of God—was a Jewish ideal and that they were the heirs to the prophetic concept that the advancement of human life and happiness was the only legitimate objective of society. Also, they were blocked off from communion with Zionism and the Zionist idea and its compatible relationship to the ideals of the Enlightenment and Emancipation. With the foresight to be premature anti-Fascists, they lacked the vision to be premature pro-Zionists before the Nazi holocaust and the miracle of Israel redeemed. Later a number of them were retroactively punished by McCarthyism for childish indiscretion, since repudiated.

Just as with the parents of Arthur A. Cohen, so many of their parents lacked "either the education or the opportunity, patience and time to transmit to their children their own understanding of Judaism."[2] The homes of the "Twicers" who attended synagogue only on the New Year and the Day of Atonement, were bereft of worship, liturgical knowledge, Hebrew and Jewish cultural or religious thought and problems.

---

[1] Richard Crossman, *The God that Failed,* (New York: Harper & Bros., 1949), p. 3.
[2] See his article "Why I Choose to Be a Jew," *Harper's* (April, 1959), and "conclusions" in Section IV.

In many Orthodox homes the social, psychological and irreligious dimensions of the nomadism of so much first and second generation Jewish youth during these depression years of the 1930's and the war years of the early 1940's, exposed a syndrome of Jewish family life and beliefs disrupted by and in contention with the attitudes and ambitions of the children. Rebels against the transplantation of old world folkways and pieties, the youth was antipodally receptive and ductile under the impact of American life and its secular-rational climate of opinion.

In many instances the result was a very real challenge to the resistance of Jewish homes as bulwarks against the devaluation of Jewish religious and cultural roots. Many parents were unable to hold the home lines of tradition, heritage and identification even though they resisted the insurgent skepticism of their "goldiner-medina"-bred children concerning the validity of Jewish identity, belief and practice. "Walkers-in-the-city" like Alfred Kazin were assimilated throughout the land.

At the same time the stress of economic necessity whittled away the time-consuming parental and grandparental observances demanded by piety and by ghetto-existence, with its reverent habits and mores rooted in the conformity and approval of community and home. The older generation's rationalization of this surrender was expressed as being a result of indoctrination of their progeny—for whom their love and hopes were so great but with whom their lines of communication were so tenuous—by a "free thinking" environment.

Buffeted by strange and intellectually hostile ideas brought in by the children from the outside, the practice of *kashrut* continued in the home, but holidays were often attenuated to gastronomics. Herman Wouk's parody of the *Seder* and *Bar Mitzvah* in *Marjorie Morningstar* are Breugelesque caricatures depicting the debasement of these occasions by "stomach" Judaism.

American education with its barrage on the concepts of piety, anthropomorphism, and "chosen people" ethnocentrism, as youthful jaundiced eyes saw it, demolished in young adult minds the traditional outlook on God, man, immortality and the Bible.

Many stopped there. Others of their contemporaries, as stated, traded the ethics of the fathers for the Marxist delusion. Still others intermarried. In this way during the troubled thirties did the youth of the depression turn away from Judaism. It was a generation in rebellion against its parents and its parents' world. It sought the opportunity to challenge the status quo, to work for a great cause, to sacrifice for a purposeful social goal. For Jewish intellectuals there appeared to be answers to Nazism superior to a "return" to Judaism; and there was the euphoric, evangelistic vision of the Soviet Internationale in which Stalin was the Moses of the new dispensation leading the proletariat everywhere to the future Canaan.[3] This would be the "scientific" climax of the Emancipation and Enlightenment. And it set its ardent followers among the generation of the thirties on the road to a social order where all national, ethnic and class differences would be fused into a universal humanity.

But many discovered, long before Howard Fast did, that the vision promoted by the Kremlin was only a mirage. The Moscow Trials, the betrayals of republican Spain, the Stalin-Hitler pact, not only revealed the promises of Soviet communism to be counterfeit; they taught that there could not be found in a temporal movement a salvation possible only out of time.[4] For these people, as Leslie Fiedler commented, the conscious beginnings of the "reach back" toward Judaism from discipleship to the most recent false Messiah, "did not depend upon the success of Hitler but on the failures of Stalin."[5]

It was another retreat from Moscow as ravaging to the soul as Napoleon's had been to the bodies of the Grand Army's soldiers. Many either never had possessed, or else had lost faith in Judaism, and despaired of Western and Jewish values and "bourgeois" liberties imperfectly known and misunderstood. They had bypassed Judaism and the synagogue to follow the Red banner. Their estrangement and lack of acquaintance with the civil defense agencies or Zionism, sidetracked them from the answer to their own doubts and inner struggles which might

[3] Leslie Fiedler, "Plight of the Jewish Intellectual," *Congress Weekly Overseas Edition*, (April, 1951).
[4] *Ibid.*
[5] *Ibid.*

have been inherent in involvement in a Jewish movement, with its similar comradeship of struggle and personal sacrifice for the ideal of human dignity and liberation from bondage.

2. The Generation of the '60's

Today the situation is considerably different from what it was in the thirties.

First the Communist illusion is unmasked and impotent.

Second, Hanson's law, that the grandson wishes to remember what the son wished to forget, appears to be operating in the suburbs, where "to be a Jew like one's father no longer means to be alien."[6] Uriah Engelman's attendance statistics of Jewish education, and those of synagogue affiliation accent this fact, in quantity if not in quality.

Third, the civil rights advances permit Jewish youth a greater peace of mind and educational and economic opportunity. By easing the onus of minority status they are making it easier for him to accept the religion and ethnic identity of his grand-father.

Fourth, the role of the community centers and university Hillels is more positive.

Most American Jewish youth of the thirties and early forties did not have a realm of discourse with the rabbi or Jewish educator to clarify the questions which troubled them and to give them insight into the conflict with their elders. Nor were the synagogues or community centers lyceums of youth or adult education, inquiry, and discussion where he could discover why, to become "truly American," he wished to shed the religious and cultural characteristics of his father.[7]

Troubled by doubts, groping for a personal *Weltanschauung*, beset by inner turbulence and outer frustration of opportunity in a time of economic debacle and despondency, the young Jew often turned away in rebellion from Judaism. The Jewish people, he believed according to Marxist anti-religionist opinion, had allowed themselves to be consigned to the dictates of a

[6] John Slawson, "Integration and Identity," The American Jewish Committee, (1959), p. 9.
[7] *Ibid.*

beneficent God, and if they did not understand the curious
incidence of His rewards it was because His ways are in-
scrutable. The post-World War I period of prosperity ended
in 1929, and in the years that followed, the idols of the market
place had fallen. And his search for a personal faith and public cause bypassed an understanding of Judaism's ethical qualities, principles and standards which might have fulfilled his
earnest quest.

In these years the YMHA centers were no more able to
transmit an intelligible, meaningful rationale for Jewish life
which integrated Western secular enlightenment with Judaism
than were the rabbis. In the forties the Jewish government
worker who joined the imposing "Y" at 16th and Q Streets in
Washington D. C., for example, could swim and play handball
to surfeit in the company of other Jewish young men. Its community center program was "bicep-tual"—providing exercise for
the biceps and muscles, not Jewish nourishment for the mind.

For a number of Jewish youth and incipient intellectuals, the
Hillel group, the university Jewish student society, and the college Zionist circle met the challenge of trial, ferment, change
and groping of these years before the outbreak of World War II.
Columbia University, for example, provided a cosmopolitan environment of graduate students from virtually every part of the
United States and from many countries throughout the world.
The ability to share vicariously the life experiences of students
from different cultures with their distinctive value systems, and
to debate the different frames of reference and world outlook
conditioned by diverse folkways, mores and national histories,
was a vital and enlightening aspect of a Columbia graduate
education.

Here also, Jewish students included refugees, concentration
camp survivors, and children of refugees from the lands of con-
tinental Europe. Israel and the lands of the Diaspora were also
represented together with every section of the United States
and Canada. They came from communities in America with too
few Jewish families to provide a *minyan*. The spectrum of
American-Jewish experience, economic and social status, education, knowledge and identification from virtually zero to zealot

orthodoxy was represented. Many were Jewishly illiterate, un-affiliated, anonymous. But though non-Gentiles, their vestige of identification made them feel less ill at ease in the atmosphere of the Jewish Graduate Society than in other student groups. They came primarily in response to the gregarious urge for socialization with other Jewish students, just as in the case of the move to the synagogue of the new suburbanites.

The Jewish chaplain at the university accepted these stu-dents on the basis of their social motivation.[8] He was also rabbi, counselor, discussion leader, adult education director and group worker, talents which he possessed to a remarkable de-gree. He provided a stimulating Jewish atmosphere in which the important social aspects of Jewish student camaraderie were intellectually and educationally environed. Able teachers and rabbis led discussion and study groups on Jewish social and religious thought, current events, issues and problems, the Bible, Zionism and Jewish history. The best minds of the faculty and the Jewish community—its intellectuals, scholars, writers and ar-tists—came to the Jewish Graduate Society to further the quest for truth and understanding by Jewish students in the free at-mosphere of a great university. The results were impressive. Students ignorant of, or out of rapport with talmudic and rab-binic Judaism, to whom Jewish scholarship was either arcane and unintelligible or unacceptably pietistic, had their skeptical and iconoclastic questions fielded expertly and perceptively by trenchant, knowledgeable, stimulating minds. These men had the indispensable ability to convey their insights, scholarship and wisdom in a manner that met the secular-rational-intellectual criteria of the university classroom to which the student gave an obeisance he would not vouchsafe the rabbi and the *beth hamidrash.*

The results were empirically observable. An impressive num-ber of Jewish students who openly confessed apathy, doubt, and antagonism, began to debate, discuss, inquire, read and study. Troublesome questions remained, but the need for Jew-ish knowledge and self-knowledge, identity and commitment

[8] Rabbi Isidor B. Hoffman, a man of conviction and ideals who under-stood youth and provided an excellant example of a modern *Tzadik* for it.

as preconditions of the search for their solution were acknowledged by many for the first time. The several hundred students
who made up the JGS membership changed its complexion
every few years, but its constituency was nevertheless a mature,
authentic community of responsive, knowledge-seeking Jews.

Return to Materialism

Those who are concerned about the lack of ideals of young
Jews should know that Jewish youth today, through accultura-
tion, is subjected to the same influences which have corrupted
the ideals and morals of young people throughout the world,
but, as with Jewish adults, is less addicted to delinquency. In
both the highly developed, industrial countries of the West, and
the under-developed, have-not countries of the East, nations in
Europe, America, Asia and Africa, are worried about the causes
and are seeking the solutions to the universal problems of youthful crime.[9]

The same goals of material affluence concerned both American-Jewish youth and German youth in 1960 despite entirely
different traditions and histories.[10] The motivations, the atmosphere, the prehensilities of the generation after World War II
are recapitulating the years following World War I. Then the
idealism of the Wilson era was in the past and the passion for
humanitarian reform was in the future. The twenties were
tedious, bourgeois and ruthless, its apothegm—"the business of
America is business." Disillusioned by the war that was to
have made the world safe for democracy, wearied by idealism
and frustrated evangelism, Americans devoted themselves to
making money with the same unabashed enthusiasm noted by
Alexis de Tocqueville a century before. Not even during the
turn of the century had Americans been so materialistic and so
servile to the ideals of the market place.

Again in the fifties there was a similar disillusionment about

[9] Gertrude Samuels, "World-Wide Story—Juvenile Delinquency," *Times
Magazine,* New York, February 14, 1960.
[10] Gerd Gaiser, *The Final Ball,* (New York: Pantheon, 1960), a novel
about post-World War II Germany and German youth. Compare with
the novels by Jerome Weidman and Myron Kaufman.

a global war and a similar domination of materialism and the status divinities of wealth, success, and dollar income. Not Marx but Mammon is the idol of the era of payola and the TV quiz scandal, and the easy though tainted buck.

World War II introduced youth to life as potential cannon fodder in an ante-bellum, World War III world of total insecurity. Scientific and technological genius had been the midwives of the nuclear age and the ICBM[11] fear. Man had achieved the beginning of the mastery over the flame of the universe; over the source of all life, heat, matter; of the prime energy of the cosmos; over the endless forces that light the sun and stars. The world appeared not to comprehend what had happened. Expectations, predictions, preparations for war went on as before. The world is haunted by the biblical admonition that where the leaders have no vision the people perish, and our leaders both East and West are puzzled by the remedy to the threat that war in our age may mean the end of man and transform his planet into a nova bereft of life. No social engineering has been devised to attain Isaiah's vision of *Pax Orbis* instead of international anarchy, balance of power and spheres of influence. Stymied by the East-West conflict, by the techniques of the game of power politics as old as civilization itself, and the fact that it has been played by patriots and politicians in all human experience in which people have identified themselves emotionally with national areas and their symbols, humanity had to endure the truth that, despite Billy Graham, there was no pat answer to the enigma "What shall I do to be saved?"

In such a world nihilism, existentialism, materialism, hedonism are guides for transient, ironic, incoherent and bleak human existence ruled and ruined by time and death. In the current plays of Samuel Beckett, Eugene Ionesco and Friedrich Duerrenmatt life is a grotesque, macabre joke. Nothingness is a positive force in the lives of Beckett's characters, who do not rebel against the misery and hopelessness of their environment. The atheistic existentialism of Jean-Paul Sartre and Albert Camus and their disciples reveals a debt to Nietzsche's assertion

---

[11] Intercontinental Ballistic Missiles.

that "God is dead"—an assertion repeated in a recent *Recon-structionist* essay.[12]

Just as the Dada art movement was congenial to a post-World War I world, so a philosophy of man as a finite and contingent being existing in a world devoid of purpose is congenial to the disordered and tragic nature of a planet whose inhabitants live in the shadow of nuclear fission, fusion and intercontinental ballistic missiles.

To protect itself in such a world today's youth seeks to be popular, to be liked by and to be one of the gang, and to conform to the gang's folkways. American Jewish youth today, as the former director of the Hillel Foundation, Arthur Lilyveld said, is a conforming not a reforming generation; and the youthful years are not a time of trial and error, of rebellion, of testing and of self-discovery. Now youth on the brink is concerned with comfort and fun in a nice, congenial society. A mad world which rebuffs attempts at reason with the response, "Don't interrupt me, can't you see I'm busy dying," does not deserve the idealism of the youth of the Oxford peace pledge and of fund-raising for the Spanish republic and Ethiopia—that was a quarter century ago when youth sought the opportunity to work for a great cause, a significant social goal. Today to be superficial, cellophane-wrapped, and foam-cushion insulated against troubling doubts is to be smart. The ends are those of a Veblenesque society with conspicuous consumption goals—not to change, not to create, but to use. Morality may be all right, but what about dividends?

The irony is that, as one of Willy Loman's sons says in Arthur Miller's *Death of a Salesman*, "It's what I always wanted. My own apartment, a car, and plenty of women. And still, . . . I'm lonely." In a thing-centered, acquisitive society this is the anguished cry of David Riesman's lonely crowd. John Osborne's *Look Back in Anger* vents the alienation of England's youth,

---

[12] Richard L. Rubenstein, "The Rabbi's Vocation," *The Reconstructionist*, November 27, 1959. "For Israel *galut* is ended and with it the *galut shekinta*, the exile of the Shekinah. Perhaps the death of the old father-God is prelude to the resurrection of the power of mother-earth in the soil so long barren of both fertility and her presence."

as John Braine's *Room at the Top* dramatizes a quick get-ahead prescription for success as devoid of morality as Theodore Drieser's *American Tragedy*. These also were the corrupted, alien Jews of Budd Schulberg's *What Makes Sammy Run,* Jerome Weidman's *I Can Get It For You Wholesale,* Myron Kaufman's *Remember Me to God*—an unattractive, unidentified, insecure breed.

Not only youth, but the entire Jewish community is affected by this corrosion of society and its goals.

Glenn Tinder says:

> Mass society is accompanied by a state of disintegration far more subtle, but no less painful and no less humanly destructive, than that which was manifest in conflict between classes. To differentiate it from the latter, that is, from *class* disintegration, it may be called *"mass* disintegration." This new challenge to human society is not manifest in picket lines, in poverty, or in the bitterness of one group against another. Indeed, it may be most profound where much is made of the camaraderie of the "team" or of the warmth of "togetherness."[13]

Franz Alexander, Karen Horney, David Riesman and Erich Fromm have written popular books concerned with the destruction of man's "organic relations" with his fellows and his world. The theme of estrangement is a *leitmotif* of the contemporary literary mind.

It is no wonder then that the synagogue has become the gravitational center of American Jewry, offering gregarious fellowship to the lonely and rootless Jewish crowd.

This is the challenge to the synagogue and the Jewish community. Their answer to Jewish youth can refute the negators of the Diaspora if it is a vital reply. It will not be so if wealth and philanthropy remain the foremost criteria of synagogue and communal prestige, power and leadership.

The action of the Council of Jewish Federations and Welfare Funds in setting up a cultural foundation is an auspicious and

[13] "1960: Failure of Political Imagination," *The Nation*, February 20, 1960.

hopeful start in this direction. The scholar, the creative artist, the intellectual are the rabbi's allies' in this formidable task. However, the intellectual, who is best able to establish rapport with youth, is the Jewish DP today. Since the intellectual's prime function is the discernment and communication of truth he is filled with questions to which the answers are difficult, and with arguments which ride roughshod over established attitudes and habits. He is critical and wants serious discussion and exchange of opinion. He accepts the plenary session pattern of the traditional sermon of the Sabbath, but he is opposed to homiletics in adult education where he wants the socratic exchange. He is seeking and wants to return. But who wants this smart-aleck who is an irritant, a source of disturbance and who doesn't even contribute to the building fund?

We are referring to those intellectuals of the past generation of Jewish youth who wish to return after the misadventure of their romance with dialectical materialism; and of the present generation who can contribute their insights and perceptions of the human predicament to the synagogue and the community for the health and growth of Judaism in the world today as a meaningful way of life, worthy of its past and capable of meeting the challenge of the present, morally and creatively.

Philo's "malicious critics" and intellectually uprooted educated "Jews" versed in the arts, sciences, humanities, and philosophy, but devoid of Jewish knowledge, training, conviction, or commitment, are not those we have in mind.[14] Rather is it the intellectual searching for, and wishing to engage in an intensive discussion of matters Jewish, both of secular-temporal concern and of faith and the quest for God, but out of step with social dance-hall Judaism.

The answer of American Jewry to Prof. Namier's "survival for

[14] These were the overwhelming number of the bright young men and women involved in the interesting symposium on "Jewishness and the Younger Intellectuals" in the April 1961 issue of *Commentary*. Ethically, morally, idealistically oriented as were their radical elders, these able, thoughtful prodigies nonetheless reflected, for the most part the same obtuseness and ignorance of Jewish history and social and religious thought, and the same elements of rejection, alienation, assimilation, hostility, and self-hatred.

what" query, and to its cynical critics in the continuing Diaspora-Israel dialogue, is being forged in the 1960's. The Jewish
scholar, teacher, rabbi, and intellectual must cooperate if Jewish
education is to be creative and have depth. In a world of disintegration, Judaism can be an integrating force, if its ranks
are filled by Jewish youths who are afforded the means to
become Jewish adults with convictions, knowledge, and commitment.

Difference and Sameness of Jewish Youth

There is less delinquency, divorce and drunkenness[15] among
American Jews, although the statistical chasm between them
and other groups in the United States, in the incidence of crime,
broken homes, and alcoholism is being narrowed by accul-
turation.

Today's Jewish children in suburbia are not too different from
their non-Jewish contemporaries. The hoary lament of the older
generation that the younger generation is going to the dogs, is
still reiterated, now embellished by the figures of increased juvenile delinquency. The family's dominance and discipline are
dwindling. Suburban America is child-centered, over-parented,
and car-pool-syndromed. The parents of the thirties who had
so little are accused of over-indulging their children who have
so much. Youth is charged with egotism, selfishness, limited
vision, and lack of family unity, obligation, and responsibility.

A survey asking young people to list the "worst" influence in
their lives, revealed that few teen-agers can bring themselves
to criticize their parents directly.[16] Ninety-one percent cited bad
companions or the evil example of adults outside their families.
But they do blame the parents of others for most juvenile delinquency. They consider parental love, interest, and understanding to be the best antidotes. Authority is not mentioned, and

[15] Rabbi Earl Stone of Denver, Colorado, complained that "Jewish social
drinking is getting out of hand." He fears the Jewish people will lose their
reputation for sobriety within another generation. He also pointed to a
growing divorce rate as evidenced by congregants coming to him for
counseling on this problem, and blamed gambling as a major cause.
[16] Eugene Gilbert, "Today's Teen-Agers," *Harper's Magazine*, November,
1959.

they don't give the parents much on the credit side. Only 20 percent of the group questioned listed their parents as "best influence." The majority chose good companions and inspiring, unrelated adults instead.[17]

Once again communion and understanding between the generations appears tenuous and hesitant. Conservatism and conformity are clearly on the increase, at least in the more tangible aspects of life. In 1946 a third of a large group of thirteen- to nineteen-year-olds said they would like to wear something different from their peers. In 1959 those who chose a leveling sameness totaled 95 percent.[18] This is the same imitative drive which covered the flaming youth of the twenties with yellow slickers—when F. Scott Fitzgerald's Princeton cheering section stood as one raccoon. It is just that the non-conformists—despite the oddball beatniks—are so scarce.

The Jewish teen-ager today will exert himself to obtain the grades he needs as his passkey to the doors of higher education. As for his Jewish education, he probably stopped going to religious school after his Bar Mitzvah.

For the American-Jewish parent in his late thirties, forties and fifties today, the two engulfing experiences were the great Depression and World War II. Hitler and the creation of the state of Israel were much less overwhelming in their impact. These parents are the heirs of these two events, whose norms and impressions have molded present views and thinking more than they realize. But to both the non-Jewish and the Jewish youth these are hazy and irrelevant periods.

"My, I'm tired of hearing about all those noble causes my mother worked for when she was in college," said a high school girl. "I don't believe they were all that noble. And who cares now, anyhow?"

The generations neither speak the same language, nor feel the same way about things. But it may be that today's youth is adapting to a unique situation never experienced before by any generation of adolescents. For the first time in its history, we emphasize, American youth has had to learn to live with total

[17] *Ibid.*
[18] Gilbert, *op. cit.*

insecurity in the world of intercontinental ballistic missiles, with atom and hydrogen bomb warheads. The technology of weaponry has made war irrational as an instrument of national policy, and has stripped the "peace" and "patriotism" slogans of a bygone idealism of their meaning. Not victory but survival is the problem facing the world and its youth. The hope is that if anybody can kill everybody, maybe nobody will want to kill anybody. But in such a world when a novel, *On the Beach,* is no longer fantasy fiction but a macabre possibility, to lose one's identity in the faceless mass and pattern of one's contemporaries, to join the other-directed ranks of organization men and the security of a weekly paycheck rather than to become a lone-wolf outsider, to desire tangible things above intangible principles—these may be the expression of the need for islands of protection, when, paradoxically, John Donne's phrase "no man is an island unto himself" has become prophecy, and there is no protection.

Like all youth, Jewish teen-agers are also affected by these apprehensive facts of life in a world of international anarchy and total insecurity. Jewish parents and religious and lay leaders, instead of viewing with alarm and lamenting the follies and oddities of youth, might do better to consider the Engleman-Dushkin report on Jewish education, and the contributions of Judaism and its principles to a sane and safe society in which children can grow up normally.

As elsewhere today, the responses of youth are mixed. Maurice Pekarsky, Hillel director of the University of Chicago, is worried by the heavy increase in intermarriage on the college campus, and the growing evidence he observes of the desire to intermarry among Jewish youth. As against our hopes for the positive influence of Hillels, he warns that university students are again flirting with escapism from Judaism, and there is a lack of the sense of the great Jewish tradition. While students have a warm Jewish feeling and wish to remain Jews, they have "no conviction, no commitment, no knowledge about Judaism."

On the other hand, Rabbi Jerome Davidson's recent survey for the Union of American Hebrew Congregations reveals an

interesting evolution of thought among Reform Jewish adolescents. This is the group considered to be least positively oriented to Judaism and Jewish concerns among religious Jewry
in the United States. These are the youth affiliated with the
religion of least inconvenience in contemporary Jewry according
to the biased view of Herman Wouk.[19] Yet Reform Jewish
teen-agers reject Namier's proposal for self-extinction. They
are concerned about Jewish survival, and, as heirs to the ben-
efits of the civil rights struggle, they are a more secure generation. Nor are they frightened by anti-Semitism or their Jewish identity. Though about 78 percent are not averse to dating
a non-Jew, the same percentage oppose intermarriage because
they believe it would prevent them from remaining Jews and
leading Jewish lives. These young people are not sitting for
a portrait of the vanishing Jew eager to implement the philosophy of the melting pot. Rather are they the identified,
secure Jews belonging to a socially accepted, intellectually
approved cultural pluralist America of many faiths and ethnic
groups.[20]

Yet Jewish youth today does not have too vital an understanding of its world, and its relationship to it as a Jew. Although the Jewish youth's father was misguided, he was an
idealist and fought for what he considered just and moral
causes. However, today's Jewish youth is not readying itself
for extraordinary effort in behalf of social and political ideals.
Like American youth in general, despite occasional picketing
forays in support of the Negro sit-ins in the South, he has shown
none of the political fervor and passion for liberty of Korean
and Turkish youth.

As for Jewish matters, the Jewish college student does not
generally appear to consider the Jews as an ethnic group, historically and nationally related, with distinctive common cultural characteristics that unite various Diaspora and Galut com-

[19] President Maurice Eisendrath of the UAHC rejects Wouk's description
as a canard.

[20] See Nathan Glazer, *American Judaism*, (Chicago: University of Chicago Press, 1957). This historical survey of the Jewish religion in America
is recommended reading for a review of Reform, Conservative, and Orthodox religious growth, development, and change in the United States.

munities. A large part of the reason why this is so is given by Dr. Engelman in his study. The Jewish college student's approval of the Zionist idea is not implemented by active membership in a Zionist organization.[21] From his American vantage point he commends the idea of a Jewish national state, takes pride in Israel's achievements, is earnestly interested in Israel's affairs, yet does not experience a direct relationship between Israel and his own Jewishness. The contemplation of Aliyah and permanent settlement in Israel has not occurred to him. It is this fact which so frustrates Golda Meier and David Ben Gurion as they clamor for American Jewish youth with their advanced training and technological know-how. This may explain the note sounded by the negators of the Galut, sounding their alarms to awaken American Jewry from what they warn is a somnambulism which will be shattered by the future's cruel reality, or dissipated by assimilation. These negators of the Galut (and the Diaspora which they equate with it), today echo the views of American sociologists of twenty years ago who expected the Jews to vanish into the melting pot of Americanization. But this view is no longer valid either demographically or sociologically. First, Jews are sharing in the population explosion of our times, and are past the dangers of possible extinction which existed in the last twenty years. Second, cultural pluralism, not the melting pot, is the fact of contemporary Jewish existence in America.

The great question of the sixties is whether the synagogues, as the paramount centers of the newly affiliated Jews of suburbia can, to a more rather than a lesser degree, achieve somewhat similar results amongst its youth and congregations as occurred at Columbia University in the Jewish Graduate Society. Otherwise the American Jewish revival will be no more than what Trude Weiss-Rosmarin terms a "renascence of Jewish institutionalism."[22]

[21] Dr. Leo A. Feldman, *The Personality of the Jewish College Student: A Portrait*, (New York, 1958), (mimeographed).
[22] "Is There an American Jewish Revival?", *The American Zionist*, December, 1959.

PART II

THE STRUGGLE FOR CIVIL RIGHTS

Legislation, if enforced, may be a sharp tool in the battle against discrimination; so, too, may court decisions that invalidate discriminatory legislation left over from the past. Legal action, however, has only an indirect bearing upon the reduction of personal prejudice. It cannot coerce thoughts or instill subjective tolerance. It says, in effect, "your attitudes and prejudices are yours alone, but you may not act them out to a point where they endanger the lives, livelihood, or peace of mind, of groups of American citizens." Law is intended only to control the outward expression of intolerance. But outward action, psychology knows, has an eventual effect upon inner habits of thought and feeling. And for this reason we list legislative action as one of the major methods of reducing, not only public discrimination, but private prejudice as well.

Certain recent developments lead us to believe that social science research in the field of ethnic relations may in the future play a larger part in the shaping of public legislative policy, and therefore indirectly in the reduction of group tensions.

. . . The argument for civil rights legislation rests on the fact that it can change the socio-cultural structure in the direction of improving opportunities for equal-status contact in the pursuit of common interests. For example, by outlawing restrictive covenants the Supreme Court makes it somewhat easier for Negroes to disperse themselves in a community and thus avoid the high congestion that leads to the perception of "threat." In the same way, all anti-discrimination legislation helps to dissolve the barriers that segregation imposes, and frees the forces of "equal-status" contact so that they may operate to reduce prejudice and tension.

Still other social science findings are germane to the problem of legislative remedies. Take the question whether prejudiced people will obey anti-discrimination statutes. . . . It is these findings of social science that led us to predict that anti-discrimination legislation will in principle be accepted and obeyed by the majority of American citizens even though preliminary protest is to be expected.

We need not elaborate the point further. We are saying merely: Social science tells us that if we wish to reduce prejudice in our society, attacks on segregation (legislative or otherwise) are scientifically sound and of high priority.

GORDON W. ALLPORT, *The Nature of Prejudice*

CHAPTER SEVEN

THE AMERICAN JEW AS CIVIL SERVANT

by JACOB FREID

The end of World War II saw bright young Jews mustered out of the armed forces and government service to become civil servants in the communal agencies of American Jewry. This was particularly true of the American Jewish Congress, the American Jewish Committee and the Anti-Defamation League of B'nai B'rith.

They came with a sense of commitment to a comprehensive program of positive Jewish life in a democratic society. Moved by the war experience, the Nazi catastrophe and the labor pangs which preceded the birth of the State of Israel, they wanted the opportunity to serve the Jewish community in a fiduciary capacity to the best of their talents, knowledge and professional training and experience. It was a time of ferment, innovation and creative experiment on the frontiers of social action, civil rights and intercommunity relations.

The men in the various departments of the American Jewish Congress, the American Jewish Committee and the Anti-Defamation League of B'nai B'rith had their fields of specialization, but they were not pigeonholed into separate compartments and made to devote themselves to parochial aims. They knew they were part of a great inquiry and experimentation into the nature of prejudice, group identity and belongingness, civil rights and Jewish survival.

This experiment in Jewish expertise was an affirmative answer to "knowledge for what?" It showed that Jewish understanding and social action need not be doctrinaire, and that

193

lawyers, social scientists, scholars, writers and community workers could make positive contributions to American democracy, Jewish self-understanding, and knowledge of Jewish history and contemporary problems. It gave both means and ends to minority groups in supplying a dynamic philosophy, program, and legal genius that revealed the possibilities of the United States Constitution. Implicit in each *amicus curiae* brief and court action was the enlistment of the legislatures and courts as democracy's allies in the struggle to break through the barriers to civil rights and educational, economic and social opportunity. Dedicated to the right of all groups to lead normal lives that offered fulfillment to aspirations, talents and personalities, rather than frustration, a program was developed not only for the Jews, but for all minority groups as well.

To these men the acknowledged function of the Jewish intellectual was to contribute his abilities as a bridge from the particular to the universal in understanding the world, how it functions and how to attach significance to those functions. Else the Jew was a sailor on uncharted seas, a fact which historically had exacted barbaric penalties, and his ability to mold the destiny in which he was involved would be dull or minimal in character. Legal scholars and lawyers grappled with the perplexities of civil rights, the separation of church and state, the defense of minorities, and the drafting and passage of legislation outlawing discrimination. Social scientists examined the roots of prejudice, intercommunity relations and group belongingness. Historians, scholars, authors and critics probed the problems of Diaspora, Galut, and their relation to Israel, Jewish life in other lands, population and economic trends, Jewish culture, art and literature.

There were frustrations and defeats, but there was also constant progress toward a meaningful horizon. Pledged to the service and freedom of man for full opportunity to "life, liberty and the pursuit of happiness," they allied the moral qualities and ethical principles of prophetic Judaism to those qualities of the Enlightenment and American life which have given this nation so much of its spiritual stature in civilization. And they implemented their insights in the spheres of public life: in the court chamber, the legislative hall and the executive office, in the market place, public accommodations and the halls of learning.

The American Jewish Congress (as the example best known to the editor), like the American Jewish Committee and Anti-Defamation League, was a union of lay leadership and professionals. Rabbi Stephen S. Wise was president. Like Franklin D. Roosevelt with the American people, Wise had a genius for winning the confidence and support of the Jewish masses, and in making his battles worth their fighting. A preacher of civic righteousness and prophetic utterance rather than a scholar or thinker, his instincts were completely democratic, and he could intuitively comprehend and dramatically champion a high course of action. Stephen Wise was politically astute, understood the art of leadership, had a talent for rhetoric, and perhaps the best platform voice in America. He used these abilities to champion a program at once bold and comprehensive to be devised and implemented by professional experts who shared his faith in the common people.

The entire context of Jewish social action in the United States was revolutionized by the Commission on Law and Social Action (CLSA) of the American Jewish Congress under the aegis of Alexander H. Pekelis. He formulated a Jewish community action approach to the social functions of law to combat anti Semitism and to achieve civil rights and first class citizenship in America for all. An appreciation of the import of Pekelis' law and social action thesis by Rabbis Stephen S. Wise, Irving Miller and Dr. David Petegorsky, combined with its incisive legal implementation by Will Maslow and Leo Pfeffer and their CLSA staff recruited from outstanding law school graduates, transformed the community defense responses of American Jewry to the attacks of Father Charles Coughlin, the Christian Front and their lunatic fringe allies, to a brilliantly conceived and executed strategic and tactical program solidly based upon American constitutional law.

The civil defense response was elevated during the decade after World War II from what Goodwin Watson in his essay "Action for Unity" (in the text), terms the exhortation techniques of advertising ballyhoo—with its car cards, billboards, posters, blotters, goodwill pledges—to a level of statesmanship and the discipleship of progressive democracy.

Pekelis was himself an authentic symbol of the Jew in *Goles*. As Max Ascoli, who knew him both in Italy and the United States, said, "He had an amazingly disturbing power to assimilate the culture of any country, to make himself into a citizen of every community. Therefore if the capacity of absorbing and dramatizing culture is, as I think, a Jewish trait, . . . [he was] thoroughly a Jew."

Those working with him shared his view that "one of the tasks that educators face today is to narrow the appalling chasm between those who, in schools and research centers, study our community, and those who in legislative committees and courts, shape its life."[1] Law was the binding force of man's relations with his fellows and of groups with other groups. It was too important in community life to be reduced to mere legalism and the concern of attorneys only. Rather must it enlist social science and its researches and conclusions in its proper function in a constitutional democracy. "Law without a knowledge of society is blind; sociology without a knowledge of law, powerless."[2]

Pekelis articulated a program of Jewish social action in America grounded upon Jewish existence and American law and society. The result was his historic memorandum to the American Jewish Congress in 1945.

He confronted American Jewry and its civil defense agencies with the need to determine its ends and the means necessary to attain them. He had no use for apologetics and anonymity in Jewish community relations. We must fight against injustice and discrimination not as anti-Semites, but as conscious self-respecting Jews, he said. It is not the robot equality of the subjects of a dictatorship we want, but the equality of free men in a free society.[3]

[1] Alexander H. Pekelis, *Law and Social Action*, selected essays, edited by Milton R. Konvitz (Cornell University Press, 1950), p. 14.
[2] *Ibid.*
[3] *Ibid.* See also, C. Bezalel Sherman, "Pioneer of Jewish Social Action," *Congress Weekly*, monthly overseas edition, (April, 1951).

The Bill of Rights and Minority Rights

Pekelis knew that cellmates in a prison also enjoy equality—but they do not have freedom. This was the significance of the Declaration of Independence and the Bill of Rights. That was why "the adoption of the first Ten Amendments, constituting our Bill of Rights, was indeed a vindication of the rights of the individual and was at least a partial return to the general philosophy of the Declaration of Independence."[4]

We seek freedom not only as individuals but as groups—as Americans and as Jews. Liberty was the price exacted by the Emancipation's blandishments of personal equality which enticed the Jews of Western Europe.

This is the caveat of the negators of the Galut in their entreaties and prophecies concerning the impossibility of creative Jewish survival with both freedom and equality in the Diaspora. But, as against Professor Namier's prescription for extinction, and the Jeremiads of leading contemporary Israeli intellectuals and officials that this was the inevitable fate of Diaspora existence, Pekelis, who was himself a leader of Poale Zion and a refugee product of the Galut, had posed a counter-thesis that this price need not be paid by the Jews in the United States. Indeed, he insisted that it must not be paid because it would close the way to American Jewish survival, and would mortally wound American democracy whose lifeblood would course only so long as the arteries of freedom did not harden against any religious and ethnic group.

It is easier for private, social, and business associations to deprive groups of their rights than it is for the official government, whose constitutional allegiance is to the Bill of Rights and to the decisions of the Supreme Court of the United States as the ultimate arbiter concerning the violation or affirmation of those rights.[5]

It is in these areas that American Jewry is most vulnerable to the charges and deprecations of the critics of Diaspora existence as being a half-life in a limbo of exile, for which *aliya* is the only cure. Local social equality, as John Slawson points

[4] *Ibid.*, p. 94.
[5] *Ibid.*, "Private Governments and the Federal Constitution," pp. 91-127.

out in his essay, is still often denied by disbarment from town
and country clubs, but walls of other private Jerichos have
been levelled. Restrictive covenants and gentlemen's agreements
in housing, with their American ghetto frame of reference are
decreasing; the restricted resort is atypical; state laws and
agencies offer recourse in instances of discrimination in public
accommodations, education and employment.

The social power of private associations still remains the
threat to American freedom. They still constitute an *imperium
in imperio*. In the Old World, discrimination was sponsored
and instituted by government; in the New World, where the
old deprivations gave way to new opportunities, the preponderantly native-born children and grandchildren of immigrant
Jews still joust with social discrimination. To C. Bezalel Sherman, combating anti-Semitism in the United States without
regulating or containing the power of these private organizations is "like pouring water in a sieve."[6]

> It is not the American government that enforces quotas
> against Jewish students in higher education, but the private
> universities. Economic discrimination against members of
> minority groups is not, as in Europe, a policy of federal
> government; it is a practice of private groups, like political
> parties, trade associations, professional agencies, craft un-
> ions, sport associations, etc. All restrictions on the power of
> governments written into the American Constitution are
> directed against the federal government. The state govern-
> ments are less restricted, while the "private governments"
> are largely free to do whatever they please.[7]

In the ten years since this was written, advances in this continuing battle have been scored. A study on admission of Jewish
students to college just recently completed registers a significant gain on this crucial front. Pekelis recalled his Odessa youth
when there was a law directly enacted by the Czar, establishing
a "healthy" proportion between Christians and Jews in any given
class.[8] "Today, my children here do not have to grow up under

[6] C. Bezalel Sherman, *op. cit.*
[7] *Ibid.*
[8] Pekelis, *op. cit.*, p. 102.

the humiliation of such a law. No matter what the factual situation, laws on the books have a reality of their own, and, believe me, the phrase 'all men are created equal' makes better reading and a better rearing for children than the circulars of a Russian or Prussian minister of education."[9]

The result of Pekelis' contribution to civil rights, sharpened and expertly refined by dedicated, brilliant men in the service of American Jewry, was to close the gap between the constitutional rights of Americans and the ability of some minority groups to utilize those rights. The CLSA, which he helped bring into being, gave an inservice education to the National Association for the Advancement of Colored People and other minority groups in the struggle against discrimination and prejudice. Today there is still argument on the scope of Congress, the American Jewish Committee and the Anti-Defamation League as Jewish civil defense organizations. Should their efforts be limited to problems of explicitly Jewish concern and interest, or should they subsume all problems affecting American democracy? To Pekelis it was as difficult to determine how to disassociate Jewish and American interests as to operate successfully on Siamese twins. The air of freedom was breathed by all. Contaminate it and all were affected. In a totalitarian land there was no freedom for Jews. Moshe Sharett, with an acute perception not shared by his Israeli colleagues, understands this difference between Jewish life in a democracy and a dictatorship. It is no wonder that throughout the two millennia of dispersion Jews were in the forefront of liberal thought and struggle as frontline soldiers in what Heinrich Heine called "the liberation war for humanity."

This is the basis of the close cooperation and support which American Jewry has given Negroes and other minorities. In virtually every important case the defense agencies include individual *amicus curiae* briefs. The aid of American Jewry in the struggle for desegregation has been of central significance.

The program which Pekelis presented for a revolution of Jewish community relations in America through law and social action included these cardinal principles:

[9] *Ibid.*

First, struggle for Jewish equality at home, equality in law, and equality in fact;

Second, protection of our civil liberties from the violent and fraudulent manipulations of neofascists and anti-Semites;

Third, active alliance with all progressive and minority groups engaged in the building of a better America;

Fourth, participation in the . . . attempt to protect the lives and secure the rights of what remains of the Jews all over the world; and

Last . . . action within the Jewish community aimed at communal self-knowledge, communal self-control, and communal revival.

This was a program worthy of allegiance. An older generation had seen, as the spearhead of such causes and programs of social betterment and equality of opportunity, only the Communist Party and its front groups. Even with the shock of discovery of their being duped they were unable to see Judaism, Jewish affiliation, and community identification and participation as a means of realizing the moral purposes and potentialities of American democracy for all peoples. For the wartime generation such a program existed. It coincided with the internal migration, the centrifugal push from the city centers to the suburbs with its proliferation of new synagogues and Jewish community centers, and community and social compulsions to affiliate.

This was a dynamic change from the dull programs which dared few actions and passions. It was a thinking, liberal program; it provided an opportunity to relate those prophetic ethical qualities and moral principles of Judaism to American life. For this reason, in the post-World War II years, outstanding sociologists, lawyers, scholars and thinkers became public men for the three major civil defense agencies, devoting their foremost talents to the betterment of Jewish and American life. It was a vital response to the Hitler holocaust and the independence of Israel. Those involved in its exhilarating vision and purposes could not accept the verdict of "negation" as pronounced in Israel.

The principles comprising this program appear to include:

The worth and dignity of the individual human being;

The fundamental equality of opportunity for all men for personal growth regardless of race, creed or national origin, and their right to lead normal, healthy American lives;

The hope of material security and independence for all and the prevention of discrimination as a bar to achieving that hope;

The general participation in the processes of government in every state in the union;

Separation of church and state and freedom of thought and conscience;

The rule by majority decision and the preservation of minority rights and cultural differences.

This was not a program for illiterate, anonymous, unaffiliated American Jews, those whom Abraham Duker calls "non-gentiles"—Jews who associated with Jews who didn't associate with Jews. It was a program for Jews with a sense of Jewish identity and belongingness, untroubled by charges of "dual loyalty." Jews with faith in the mind, reason and integrity of the American people, their Constitution and its political democracy as the instrument which would make the achievement of creative Jewish life possible in America.

Leo Pfeffer, scholar and authority on the doctrine of separation of church and state, in his essay here on the relationship of "Church and State in the United States—A Jewish Approach," shows how solidly grounded in these principles is that separation.[10] It is no wonder that Thomas Jefferson, who declared

---

[10] Indeed, when this editor learned that the "Lord's Prayer" was being recited in his local public school in the Lawrence-Woodmere, Long Island, New York school district, he and another Jewish parent as co-plaintiffs went through all necessary preliminary steps with the local school board to have the prayer discontinued as a violation of the separation of church and state. We then had Dr. Pfeffer institute court action. Before the matter came to the attention of the Supreme Court of New York and the Commissioner of Education of New York, the prayer was discontinued by the school board.

the independence of men from the tyranny of parliaments and kings, led the fight with James Madison for religious freedom.

Community relations programs today, more than ever before, under the aegis of the National Community Relations Advisory Council (NCRAC), the American Jewish Committee, the American Jewish Congress and the Anti-Defamation League of B'nai B'rith, are vehicles of adult education and forums of popular statesmanship. The gains on behalf of minority groups in general and the Negro in particular have been substantial. Pekelis' contributions to law and social action have been significantly adapted and employed by able civil servants of the Jewish community to enlarge democracy and to achieve its social, economic and political promise as against the special interest groups and private associations who would pervert that promise and frustrate its attainment. Sabbath sermons, community forums, adult education programs, periodical literature and books acknowledge that upon the people's insight into the vital issues of our time important social consequences depend, and that the community's representatives occupy a central position in the fight to break through to freedom and equality of opportunity by making accessible to all minority groups the information and understanding on which their choices and actions depend.

Prejudice and Discrimination

Our physical engineering and technology have achieved tremendous control over nature and man's environment. But social and psychological engineering in the realm of the minds of men and the foundations of human behavior is by comparison still in the Dark Ages in the degree of its mastery over man's irrational passions and prejudices, and the relationships between man and man, group and group, and nation and nation. This ability of civilized man to decipher the physical laws of the universe and to apply them to create scientific order out of the irrelevant disorder of uncultivated nature, has outdistanced the ability of society and social science to create the rational behavior on the part of men and nations which is so essential if physical science and technology are to be used for the welfare and not the atomization of mankind. The ominous result, as Gordon Allport said, is that "our deficit in social knowledge seems to void at every step our progress in physical knowledge."[11]

There is real hope, however, that civilization may yet win what H. G. Wells called the race between education and catastrophe. In the last sixteen years since World War II, in this area of prejudice and discrimination "there has been more solid and enlightening study . . . than in all previous centuries combined,"[12] and many men have come to believe that scientific intelligence may help solve the problem of prejudice. Among those who have spearheaded this development are Dr. Allport, Goodwin Watson, Otto Klineberg, Kurt Lewin, John Slawson and Benjamin Epstein. The American Jewish Committee in its monumental five volume *Studies in Prejudice,* the Anti-Defamation League in its *Freedom Pamphlets,* and the American Jewish Congress' *Jewish Affairs* series have made significant contributions to this problem which is so central to Judaism and the Jews. It is an ironical jest of history that the people who set forth the ethical guidelines for human conduct in the Ten Commandments have themselves been the foremost victims of prejudice through the centuries.

Dr. John Slawson in his essay, "The Unequal Treatment of Equals: The Social Club, Citadel of Discrimination," describes the American Jewish Committee's campaign against the barrier of social prejudice and discrimination. Human relations agencies such as his have played a considerable role in the achievement that "overt anti-Semitism is becoming relatively unfashionable in America."[13] But, as he cautions, "beneath the surface of conformity, the fires of group hostility smoulder and at times burn fiercely."[14] It is in this subsurface area that social discrimination perpetuates bigotry. And by remaining unchal-

[11] Gordon W. Allport, *The Nature of Prejudice* (Cambridge: Addison-Wesley, 1954), p. xiv.
[12] *Ibid.*
[13] John Slawson, "Social Discrimination: The Last Barrier," The American Jewish Committee, 1955, p. 7.
[14] *Ibid.*

lenged, it tacitly authorizes other discriminations, and implies the inferiority and undesirability of a person on the basis of his group identity, not his individual merit.[15]

In its new Institute of Human Relations, the American Jewish Committee is exerting its efforts to close the gap between man's physical conquests and his understanding of his fellow man.

"Action for Unity," by Professor Goodwin Watson of Columbia University, was a guide to the earnest citizen who found himself approached by numerous organizations which claimed to be doing important work in promoting "good will" and better race relations. With which should he cooperate? To what sort of agency should support be given? What activities promise the most return for the time and money invested? What techniques have proved the most effective in weaning people from prejudice?

"Action for Unity" offered the results of the first comprehensive attempt to give answers to these questions. It was based upon a nationwide survey. "Roots of Prejudice" was a companion study. Both essays consider the nature of prejudice and what to do about it. Other *Jewish Affairs* publications were concerned with Zionism and Israel, Jews in the Diaspora, Jewish art, Yiddish and Hebrew education, the extent of discrimination employment, housing education, religion in the public schools, economic and population trends among American Jews, displaced persons. Throughout the country adult education groups and religious schools used these studies in their discussion programs devoted to the problems of modern Jewry.

These *Jewish Affairs* essays were written for the Jew who was unaware of or had little inclination for the heavy, pedantic articles in scholarly journals. They attempted to be authoritative but also readable for the interested layman. Where necessary, those reprinted here, have been revised and brought up to date by their authors.[16]

---

[15] *Ibid.*

[16] Gideon Chagy established the Jewish Affairs series which was edited by him and the writer. David Petegorsky said: "The series made an extremely valuable contribution to Jewish information in this country. Several of the pamphlets have already become little classics in themselves and the

Gordon W. Allport and Bernard Kramer explore expressions of prejudice and trace them to their sources in "Roots of Prejudice." They found less than 11 percent of 437 Dartmouth, Harvard and Radcliffe undergraduates whom they tested declared themselves against legislative attempts—such as the Fair Employment Practices Act—to improve the opportunities of minority groups. But of these, seven-eighths were among the more prejudiced subjects. This is a significant finding. It is not only additional proof that prejudice is a reflection of a broader pattern of belief; it also strips the mask from those who say they oppose remedial legislation such as desegregation in the South, because "you can't legislate against prejudice," because "laws won't change human nature," because "you only make things worse by passing laws that won't be enforced." This evidence reveals that those who oppose legal remedies almost certainly do so because they themselves are bigots and defenders of bigotry, that opponents of FEPC and equality of education and housing legislation by such rationalizations reveal (to paraphrase La Rochefecauld), the hypocrisy which is the tribute prejudice pays to its public protestation of virtue.

It is the practice that breeds discrimination, then perpetuates it and habituates it. As William James said, "Habit is the flywheel of society"; and ingrained practice with the status of social mores is hard to break. Yet the law can blunt them and then break them, even though progress, as in Little Rock, Arkansas, is slow and uphill.

Allport and Kramer also focus sharp light on the formative influences of home, school and religion, and bare the shocking failure of parents, educators and religionists to inoculate the unprejudiced child against the environmentally acquired infection of prejudice. Another truth revealed is that prejudice generates itself (e.g., the famous case of Otto Weininger, a German-Jewish intellectual who committed suicide). *Hate breeds hate.*

entire series is regarded as one of the foremost that has been established in the pamphlet field, Jewish or non-Jewish, in many years. . . ." Mr. Chagy, who was an honor student in philosophy at Witwatersrand University in Johannesburg, is now Director of Public Information of the Fund for Adult Education of the Ford Foundation.

Self hatred among Jews is more evident in those who feel more victimized. What evidently happens is that the aggression of hostility built up as a result of persecution and discrimination is actually directed inwardly toward members of one's own group. That is why Arthur Koestler in *Thieves in the Night* called Jews the "ulcerated" race.

CHAPTER EIGHT

CHURCH AND STATE: A JEWISH APPROACH

by LEO PFEFFER

I wish to consider from a Jewish point of view, the constitutional and historical aspect of what has come to be the First Amendment of the Constitution. In a way this is rather paradoxical. I do not think there is a Jewish approach to the law of automobile accidents, or a Catholic approach to the law of real property, or a Protestant approach to the law of negotiable instruments—all of which are part of our civil law. But we do expect a Jewish approach to the equally legal question of the relationship of Church and State in the American democratic system.

Realistically, if not perhaps theoretically, I think this is valid. I do not think I am cynical when I point out that we do read into law, as into history, a good deal of what we would like to see in law and in history. And, in the best of faith, we interpret the events of history and the decisions of the courts in a light which is most satisfactory to our concept of what that history should have been and what those decisions should be. And so it is not suprising that there is a Protestant approach to the question of Church-State relationships in America which, I say again without cynicism, is remarkably sympathetic and attuned to what Protestantism considers the ideal solution to the problems of the interrelationship of Church and State. Nor is it surprising that the good Bishops of the Roman Catholic Church, when the decision of the United States Supreme Court was handed

down in the McCollum case in 1948, should express an interpretation of the Constitution which is considerably at variance
with the interpretation handed down by the Supreme Court,
but which was quite a happy one, if it had been accepted, for
the Roman Catholic Church and the Roman Catholic community in this country.

The approach I am going to suggest in respect to the relationship of Church and State is my own, a Jew's approach, perhaps,
rather than a Jewish approach. I can say that there are undoubtedly a number of Jews such as Will Herberg who disagree
strongly with my interpretation. Yet I think it is fair to say
that the overwhelming majority of Jewish spokesmen, representative of Jewish organizations and Jewish groups and Jewish thinkers who have written on this subject, would substantially agree with the approach I suggest here.

I think it is important to reiterate that this is a Jew's approach.
It is not, although unfortunately it has frequently been so called,
a secularist's approach. It reflects not merely the approach of
secular Jews in America, although secular Jewry certainly goes
along with it. It reflects the approach of religious Judaism in
America as well. And perhaps, with the exception of a very
small segment of the extreme right of Jewish Orthodoxy, I think
it reflects the approach of practically all of organized Jewry and
Judaism in America.

I would be less than frank, however, if I denied that the
approach which I am going to suggest, and which the Jewish
organizations and the Jewish groups have espoused, as the
Protestants have espoused their approach, the Roman Catholics
their own, I would be less than frank if I denied this approach
coincides very closely with the approach of secular humanism.
I believe it is practically identical with the approach of such
a non-religious secular organization as the American Civil Liberties Union, for example. It is, however, also identical with
the approach of at least left wing or liberal American Protestantism. Perhaps the term "liberal Protestantism is not the correct
one, because it includes a good deal of the Baptist Communion,
for which, in general, the term "liberal" would not be an accurate designation. It also represents the approach of the Uni-

tarians, the Universalists, the Friends, and a good deal, surprisingly enough, of low Episcopalianism. I would not call the Seventh Day Adventists liberal in the theological sense, but it is identical with their approach. Perhaps, it could best be said, that it represents at least one important segment of Protestant dissent.

It has been suggested that it is perhaps chauvinism which causes so many of us to identify the American pattern of Church-State relationships with America rather than with England whence it was derived; but chauvinism is not the exclusive possession of nationalists. Churches, and church adherents unfortunately share this failing, and Dr. Nichols* suggests that the American approach to the relationship of Church to State is a Protestant creation. He cites Mark Howe, who, while perhaps a gentle sceptic today, still has in him the blood of an ancient Calvinist tradition. And our brothers of the Roman Catholic persuasion likewise are not immune to this failing of chauvinism. They frequently point out, as Dr. Rommen** has, the sources of religious freedom in Roman Catholicism. For example, he mentioned Bishop Carroll. He might have mentioned the religious toleration act of Maryland as a great step in establishing religious freedom in America. Catholic writers are fond of pointing out that there was a time when Maryland was a Catholic colony. This, too, has amused me because I do not consider the Religious Toleration Act of Maryland a religious toleration act. I think a concept of religious freedom for those who are within the protected group, and death for those who are out of it, is hardly one consistent with religious freedom, as I view it.

Not to be outdone, we Jews—who make it our business to be the equal of everybody else, and perhaps a little more equal than others—we, too, have our chauvinism. It is a good American trait, and we are entitled to share it. And we, too, preach that, while Protestants say they created religious freedom under Cromwell and the levelers of the seventeenth century, and the

---

* James H. Nichols, Professor of Religious History, University of Chicago.
** Heinrich Rommen, Professor of Political Science, Georgetown University.

Roman Catholics say they created it out of Cardinal Bellarmine and Lord Baltimore's Maryland colony, we say we beat them to it by many, many centuries. We created religious freedom when the Maccabeans fought against the Seleucids in the second century before Christ. We, too, interpret our history not uninfluenced by chauvinistic motivations because, truthfully, the struggle of the Maccabeans was no more a struggle for religious freedom than was the Maryland statute of toleration or the principles and laws established by the Puritans in New England. The Maccabeans after their victory, went about forcibly circumcising all the Jewish Hellenists they could get hold of, and imposing upon them the restrictions in respect to freedom of worship which they had suffered under the Hellenists, just as our Calvinists in New England imposed such restrictions upon Quaker and other non-Calvinists, and just as a good deal of Roman Catholicism has imposed those restrictions on others.

There is nothing in ancient Jewish tradition which would indicate a sympathy either to separation of Church and State or to religious freedom. I do not think you could expect a concept of religious freedom from a people which gave to the world the idea of a jealous, monotheistic deity. Religious freedom is just not acceptable if you assume such a God. If you take "Thou shalt have no others gods before me" literally, you cannot acknowledge any rightness in religious freedom. Similarly, the very term theocracy, which we now use as a shorthand term for a close relationship between Church and State in which Church dominates State, was a term coined by Josephus to describe the priest-dominated, post-exilic second commonwealth of Israel when the secular powers were exercised by the priestly class. And of course Jewish history, after the Second Temple until the emancipation in the late eighteenth and nineteenth centuries, was a ghetto life in which the rabbi, as successor of the priest, exercised tremendous secular powers.

So I cannot in good conscience ascribe to Judaism the source, in any substantial extent, of the American principle of religious freedom and what we call the separation of Church and State. American Judaism, however, has embraced that principle passionately, loyally and faithfully. And it is not overly chauvinistic to say that American Judaism is perhaps the most vigorous, articulate, and the most unyielding champion of that principle of Separation of Church and State and religious freedom as spelled out by the United States Supreme Court. That, too, is understandable. Jews would be less than human, and we are not—or we would be more than human, we are not that either— if we did not feel a great debt of gratitude toward a system which, after almost two thousand years of persecution, has given Jews a real haven and a real equality. And it is, therefore, hardly surprising that we should accept that system as God-created and God-given and as the ideal of the good community.

What is that system? It is a system of complete religious freedom. It is a system which is enunciated in shorthand in the very first words of the Bill of Rights: "Congress shall make no law respecting an establishment of religion or prohibiting the free exercise thereof."

I suggest to you that of all the freedoms which Americans enjoy, of all the liberties which are part of our heritage, none exceeds in importance religious freedom. As a lawyer, I offer two *indicia*, two items of evidence to support this thesis. First, that religious freedom is the progenitor, at least in the American system, of all other freedoms. The Bill of Rights, which are the first ten amendments to the Constitution, contains a variety of liberties. The First Amendment says: "Congress shall make no law respecting an establishment of religion or prohibiting the free exercise thereof, or abridging the freedom of speech, or of the press, or of the right of the people peaceably to assemble and to petition for a just redress of grievances." Other liberties include the right to a fair trial, the right of one charged with a crime not to be compelled to incriminate himself, the right to know the nature of an offense with which one is charged, the right not to be put in double jeopardy, the right not to suffer cruel, inhuman punishment, and so on. I suggest that all these rights, and all these liberties, within our Anglo-American history, came about as a result of the successful struggle for religious freedom.

Take freedom of speech. Today we conceive of freedom of speech primarily as a right of the corner agitator, the radical, to get up and condemn the government, and demand that the rascals be thrown out, that we should have a revolution, and so on. In other words, we think of it primarily in terms of political speech. Historically, freedom of political speech came late on the scene. It came after freedom of religious speech was won. The battles for freedom of speech in England, from which we inherited our tradition, were initially battles for freedom to speak religiously, for freedom to speak in a manner deemed heretical by the established church. And after a good deal of suffering, persecution, and martyrdom, slowly the war for freedom of religious speech was won. By the time of the eighteenth century, after the Cromwellian revolution and the Restoration, the right of religious speech had been established as a natural right of Englishmen. And when those Englishmen came to these shores they followed what was happening in England. They, too, recognized it as a right of these Englishmen residing in the American colonies. Inevitably, it followed that if an Englishman had a natural right to speak freely on religious matters, he had a natural right to speak freely on non-religious matters. If he could speak freely on such important matters as eternal values and eternal truths, so important a matter as the sacred, obviously he has a right to speak on the less important matters of the secular and temporal. When the First Amendment came to be written, and it had been already established that Americans as former Englishmen had a natural right to speak freely on religious matters, it followed inevitably that they had a right to speak freely on political matters. Thus, freedom of speech was written into the Bill of Rights.

The same is true of freedom of the press. Freedom of the religious press was greatly restricted in England. Persons were even burned at the stake for printing the Bible—for printing it in the common tongue so that everyone could read it—and for printing religious tracts. It was the great glory of the Puritan revolution that it established a right freely to print religious books, tracts and documents. When that right was established, it followed that Englishmen and Americans had the equivalent right to print non-religious books and tracts, political books, tracts, documents, and

pamphlets. That, too, was written into the Constitution as part
of the Bill of Rights.

The same is true in respect to the right of assembly. We generally consider this to be a political right, and we think of it
in terms of the right to have a mass meeting to demand that
Tom Mooney be freed, or that we get out of China, or halt
nuclear bomb testing, or something of that type. We think of
it in terms of political assembly. Its origin in Anglo-American
tradition, however, was religious assembly, the right to assemble together to worship jointly in a manner not permitted by the
established churches. When the right of religious assembly was
won, inevitably the right of political assembly followed.

There are those rights which seem to be far removed from
religion, the rights incident to a fair trial, such as the right not
to incriminate oneself, or to confront one's accusers, or the
right not to be subject to double jeopardy or cruel and inhuman
punishment. All these rights, which are written into our Constitution, came out of the religious or heresy trials of the sixteenth and seventeenth centuries, in the Star Chamber in England. "Freeborn" John Lilburne, a Puritan leveler, religious dis-
senter, and heretic, was one of the heroes of the struggle for
fair trial. In his frequent encounters with the Star Chamber,
he continually asserted his rights as an Englishman, not to be
compelled to incriminate himself, to have counsel to help him
and not to be subjected to cruel and inhuman punishment.
He asserted these rights in these religious trials and one by one
they were accepted. Once they were accepted and became part
of a fair trial before an ecclesiastical court, it was inevitable
that they would be carried over into the secular courts and
that they would be considered rights of every Englishman and
every American. And so they, too, found their way into our
Constitution and our Bill of Rights.

Religious freedom is a progenitor of all our freedoms and
in that respect is the most important of them. When the state
was ready to grant religious freedom to its citizens, it was soon
ready to grant them other freedoms. Conversely, if a state is
prepared to deprive its citizens of their rights in matters of con-

science, it is inevitable that it will deprive them of all other rights.

There is a second item of evidence in support of the suggestion that religious freedom is the most important of all our rights. I do not suppose any statistics have ever been made on this nor do I believe that statistics could practicably be made. Yet, I suggest, that if at the time our Constitution was written—that is, during the last half of the eighteenth century—a statistical table could have been made of the causes for which throughout history men have shed the blood of other men—of the causes they fought over—topping this tragic list would be the cause of religion. Up to the latter part of the eighteenth century, it is probable that more blood had been shed allegedly for the greater glory of God or the gods, than for any other cause in history.

We still shed blood. We still have wars. Men still fight in battle with each other, and they still take up arms against each other. We fight for many things. We fight for political reasons, for economic reasons, for nationalistic reasons. But I think we have ended that horrible blasphemy that we fight wars because God wants us to do so—that we can promote God's will by picking up the sword and converting by force those in error and in darkness. I think we no longer commit that terrible sacrilege of saying "Thy will be done" when we drop an atomic bomb on a city.

Religious wars are happily a matter of ancient history. I suggest that a major cause for this turn of events was the launching of the American experiment of religious freedom and the separation of Church and State.

Dr. Rommen has pointed out that as long ago as 1830 the constitution of the Catholic country of Belgium incorporated a provision guaranteeing religious freedom. There is no nation today in the world that I know of which has a written constitution, which does not in that constitution at least pay lip service to the principle of religious freedom. We know that religious freedom is not absolutely secured everywhere, that there are restrictions and even persecutions in many countries. Yet, even in those countries where religious restrictions are most severe, if there is a written constitution, you will find a recognition of the right to freedom of worship. And that has resulted in the elimination and termination of the religious persecutions and religious wars which have plagued Europe for well nigh two thousand years.

I think America was the first nation to establish religious freedom as a binding principle of its organic law, the first nation to write it into its constitution. Almost all the nations in the world have emulated us in this respect. The experiment launched on these shores has been accepted and followed in nation after nation. It is for these two reasons: Religious freedom has brought forth other freedoms and has ended religious wars—that I suggest that the most important of all our freedoms is religious freedom.

My interpretation of religious freedom does not recognize any dichotomy between it and what we call separation of Church and State. The American experiment does not constitute two freedoms or two rights. Above all, it does not envisage one as major and the other as minor, one an end and the other a means. I find nothing in American history, nothing in the development of our principles which justifies the statement that separation of Church and State is a means and religious freedom an end, and that when separation of Church and State is inconsistent with religious freedom, separation must yield because religious freedom is the higher good. I do not believe that this can be historically justified on the American scene. I do not believe that those who established the American experiment conceived them as two different things, one a means and one the end. I do not believe that you can say that the head on a coin is the end and the tail is the means, or that my right hand is an end and my left hand a means. They are one and the same thing. Separation of Church and State, or what we have come to *call* separation of Church and State, and religious freedom were simply two ways of saying the same thing. When our Bill of Rights was written they were both put in—"no law respecting an establishment of religion or prohibiting the free exercise thereof"— because they were dual aspects of a single right.

If religious freedom were the end, and separation simply the means, there would be no reason whatsoever to spell out the means in respect to this end. Certainly in respect to no other freedom are the means put in as well as the end; the end alone is stated. I do not know what the particular means would be to freedom of speech, but the freedom of speech guaranteed in the Constitution does not have any means specified along with it. Indeed, it is not in the nature of a bill of rights to specify means.

Separation of Church and State and religious freedom in the American tradition are one and the same thing. This is because both rest on a dual assumption upon which our whole democracy rests. One is the assumption of voluntariness in matters of conscience and spirit, in matters of man in his relationship to God. I think that is as fundamental an aspect of American democracy as anything can be. Under no circumstances can democracy coerce a person in any way in respect to his relationship to his Maker, in respect to belief or lack of belief in God. And, if you accept the concept of voluntarism in matters of faith, religion, religious association and of worship, then I think you must inevitably come to the goal or ideal of absolute separation of Church and State.

Protestants perhaps understand this necessity better than our Roman Catholic friends and than we Jews do. American Protestantism interprets the struggle for religious freedom largely in terms of the struggle against taxes for religious purposes. Suppose the government does take some money out of the vast public treasury and pay it out to parochial schools or to churches. How does that affect your freedom? The amount so spent cannot exceed threepence of the money you pay as part of your whole tax burden. Nevertheless, Protestants recognize and we must too, that as Madison put it so eloquently in his Memorial and Remonstrance against the Virginia Assessment Bill, and Jefferson equally eloquently in the Virginia Statute for Religious Freedom, when you impose a tax for a religious purpose, you are exercising coercion and compulsion in the domain of the spirit, in the domain of the sacred. This is tyranny; it is despotism; it is a violation of the separation of Church and State. So, if you accept complete voluntarism in matters of faith,

I think you must come to the ideal of absolute separation of Church and State.

The second concept, which is equally fundamental to our democracy and which like voluntarism distinguishes democracy from totalitarian governments, is the concept that the state is the servant of the people, not its master. That as the creation of the people, it has only such powers as are delegated to it by the people, and if it seeks to exercise a power not delegated to it, it is guilty of tyranny and despotism. This is the second underlying premise of democracy: the concept of limited government. It is not so in a totalitarian state. The very name totalitarian indicates that the state controls and has jurisdiction over the totality of man's life.

And while at first glance it might seem surprising, on second thought, it is not surprising at all, that in those totalitarian states behind the Iron Curtain which are committed to the ultimate destruction of religion as an enemy of the people, religion is nevertheless subsidized by the government, it is taught in the public schools, and its teachers and priests receive state salaries. It might seem surprising that nations like Poland, Hungary, Czechoslovakia, and Romania, which are committed to the elimination of religion as the opiate of the people, to the Marxist concept that religion is a complete evil which must be destroyed, yet subsidize it, regulate it and grant it favors. It is paradoxical at first glance, but on second thought, it is quite natural and logical. If your state is totalitarian, then nothing which the people do is outside its control. Its powers encompass the evil as well as the good. So long as religion is an aspect of the people's lives, it is part of the powers and the jurisdictions of the totalitarian state. This is not so in a democracy—not so in American democracy, anyway. Our political government has only such powers as we give to it. This is the premise of the Declaration of Independence which expressly states that government has only those powers assigned to it by the people. This, too, is the premise of our constitution. Equally, the premise of both is that matters of religion, the area of the relationship of man to God, is not one which has been assigned the political government.

A view held widely within the Protestant community is that this concept is a Protestant creation. I think that is an over-simplification. I think, in the first place, it was not all of Protestantism, but left-wing or Protestant dissent that first espoused the principle. The concept of separation of Church and State and religious freedom, was accepted neither by the Anglican Church established in Virginia, nor by the Congregationalist Church established in New England. It was the creation of the dissenting sects, the popular and frontier sects, the nonconformists, the Baptists, Quakers, Moravians, Mennonites and, after some inner conflicts, the Presbyterians. The Memorial and Remonstrance of the Presbytery of Hanover presented to the Virginia Legislature considering a tax for religious purposes is one of the great documents in the struggle for religious freedom in America, and it is one which accepts completely the concept of what later came to be called by Jefferson the wall of separation between Church and State.

How did this come about within Protestantism? This was a religiously motivated development in Protestantism. Roger Williams, the founder, or one of the founders of the American Baptist Church, is perhaps most well known for his contribution. (Although his thinking started in England, we like to think of him as an American, and I think we can be permitted this little bit of chauvinism.) He developed it as a religious concept, not from the usually cited quotation from Matthew, "Render unto God that which is God's and unto Caesar that which is Caesar's," but from what he called the law of the two tables. He pointed out that the Ten Commandments, foundation of all religion, certainly all Christian and Jewish religion, were given by God on two tablets of stone, that on each tablet were five Commandments, and there was a line between them. On the one tablet you had the Commandments, using the Protestant and Catholic numbering, "Thou shalt have no other gods before me. Thou shalt make thee no graven image. Thou shalt not take the name of the Lord in vain. Thou shalt observe the Sabbath. Honor thy father and mother." On the other side you had, "Thou shalt not kill. Thou shalt not steal. Thou shalt not commit adultery. Thou shalt not bear false witness. Thou shalt not covet."

The five Commandments on the one side concern Man's relationship to God. They are of no concern to any other person. "It hurts not my neighbor," Jefferson said, "if I believe in one God, in twenty gods, or no gods at all." So, too, it hurts nobody if I take the Lord's name in vain, or if I rest weekly on Tuesday instead of Sunday. (Three hundred years ago Roger Williams strongly opposed compulsory Sunday laws, because he said this relates to man's relationship to God.) It hurts nobody if I make me a graven image. These obligations which relate to man's relationship to God belong to the tribunal of God, the tribunal of the spirit.

The Commandments on the other side, against killing, stealing, adultery and bearing false witness, affect man's relationship to his fellow man. By placing a line between these two tables, God expressed his intention to confer upon the tribunals of man, jurisdiction only of those transgressions which affect man's relationship to man. But any transgression in the scope of the first tablet, such as Sabbath observance, must be left to the tribunal of God, the tribunal of the conscience. And, said Roger Williams, if a tribunal of man, whether it be a court, a legislature, a governor or prince, seeks to control or regulate man's relationship to God, or punish for violation of any of the commandments on the first table, he is usurping—this is Roger Williams' term, and I think it is a tremendously significant term—he is usurping the prerogative of God. Indeed, he is playing God.

I think this was the influence that was so largely felt in Protestant dissent at the time our Constitution was written. But it would be unfair and inaccurate to say that this was the sole source of separation of Church and State in America. It was one of the two major sources. The other was secular humanism.

The latter part of the eighteenth century was a very secularistic period in American history. The rationalism which came from Locke, Voltaire, Rousseau, and the Encyclopedists permeated American thinking and culture. The molders of American political and intellectual thought in the latter part of the eighteenth century were not religious people, certainly not religious in the sense which we have come to accept that term today. It is a rewriting of history, (a practice which, I suppose, every nation engages in) to say, as I have heard it said so many times, that the men who framed our Constitution were religious people, that they were the friends of religion, that they would not have conceivably wanted to exclude religion from the public or official life of the nation, or in any other way act in a manner unfriendly to religion, and so on.

If "religion" is used in the sense of organized or institutionalized worship and practice—and this is indeed how it is generally used in this connection—the statement is in major part historically untrue. Most of the men who created our Constitution were not religious in that sense. They were humanistic and rationalist. They had a vague belief in some God who generally kept his hands off what was going on down here and to whom you satisfied your obligation by recognizing his existence and being good to your fellow man. Certainly they were in the main not adherents of institutionalized religion. It is not accidental that of the first seven Presidents of the United States not a single one was a member of any church upon his ascension to the presidency. The spirit of the intellectual leadership of the time was not a religious spirit. It was a spirit of rationalism and humanism. Next to the Bible, the most popular book in the last decade of the eighteenth century was Tom Paine's *Age of Reason.*

The principle underlying the philosophy of these people was the *Social Contract* of Locke and Rousseau, a concept which was incorporated into the Declaration of Independence and the Constitution. Governments, according to this theory, are formed by men to do for them what they themselves cannot do individually. Governments have only such powers and responsibilities as are conferred upon them by the people as part of the social contract. There are certain rights which are inherent and are not conferred, which are, in terms of the Declaration of Independence, inalienable; that is a legal term, meaning that which cannot be alienated or transferred.

First of these and above all others are rights of conscience, rights concerning man's relationship to God. It is something which cannot be transferred to government. Therefore, they believed, as did Protestant dissent, that the government which they were establishing would have no jurisdiction or control in the area of conscience, the domain of God, the arena of the sacred.

It is tremendously significant that this is not merely implicit, but indeed explicit, in the Constitution. It is the alpha and omega of our Constitution. Take alpha; the first part of our Constitution is the Preamble. It says: "We the people of the United States in order to form a more perfect union, establish justice, insure domestic tranquility, provide for the common defense, promote the general welfare, establish justice, and secure the blessings of liberty to ourselves and our posterity, do ordain and establish this Constitution for the United States of America." You will notice that this Preamble sets forth the purposes for which this Constitution is created, and for which powers were given to the government. Remark how very, very significant it is that among these expressly specified powers, any reference to a purpose of promoting religion or promoting God is conspicuously absent, that of all the purposes which were stated to be the purposes of the government for which powers were designated, there is not one mention of anything having to do with religion as a rightful purpose of this government. This is the alpha of the Constitution.

And consider the omega, which is the last, the very last clause of the Constitution. It says exactly the same thing. It says there shall never be a religious test for any public office in the United States government. The meaning and implications of this were well understood. The provision was argued, debated, approved and agreed to by everybody, that this meant that the Hindu, the infidel, the Jew, even a non-believer in God could be President of the United States, a congressman or a senator, or hold any other office. Why? For the same reason—and they said it explicitly—that man's relationship to God could not, and was not to be the concern of the government they were founding.

This was the alpha and this the omega of our Constitution.

How often do we hear it stated that we have prayers in Congress and "In God We Trust" on our coins. How often it is flaunted that "In God We Trust" is our national motto, that we have chaplains in Congress, and we acknowledge God every day in our public life. Yet, it is never said in the basic charter, the instrument from which all powers of government arise in America—that instrument is completely silent about God, does not mention God at all.

This, too, I assure you, was not an accident. It was a deliberate decision made by a people who wanted to confer upon their governors only secular powers, only powers relating to the temporal and nothing relating to the eternal.

This is what religious freedom means in our nation. This is what separation of Church and State entails within a democracy.

Let me finish on this one note. I started writing as a Jew. I want to finish writing as a Jew. This experiment, which I believe is an American experiment, was greatly beneficial to both state and religion, to both the people in their religious life and the people in their secular life. Whenever religion becomes entangled with the secular state, religion suffers, and so does the state. In II Kings, there is the story of Naaman, the leper, who was the chief of staff of the King of Syria and came to Elisha to be cured of his leprosy. When he left, he said he had always believed in the God, Jehovah, and would worship only God, Jehovah, but with this one exception, that when he accompanied his king into the temple of Rimmon, the Syrian idol, and the king bowed to Rimmon, he, too, would bow along with him. Would Elisha forgive him for this? Elisha said to him, "Go in peace." This is one of the illustrations of how a person's faith is corrupted because he combines it with his political function.

You will find another illustration in I Kings when Jeroboam revolted against the Davidic dynasty. What did he do? As far as the Bible shows, Jeroboam was a believer in Jehovah and was not an idol worshipper. Yet, in order to make sure that his people would not go to Jerusalem to worship Jehovah, he built two idols, two golden calves, and said to the Israelites "This is your God who brought you forth from the land of Egypt." He used religion in order to promote his political ends. The result was that idolatry was substituted for the Israelite religion. This has been the story of religion through its history whenever it ties up in any way with the secular state; it is corrupted.

Now as a Jew I want to say I am troubled for my own Jewish community. I think what has happened here is that American Jewry has finally achieved a position of equality. We speak about a Judeo-Christian civilization, a term which was unknown twenty years ago. When a Jewish synagogue was bombed in the South, the President of the United States immediately expressed his great shock and horror, although he apparently felt no need to express shock when schools were burned or the individual homes of Negroes were burned. As it was once fashionable to be anti-Semitic, it is now fashionable to be philo Semitic.

We Jews have arrived. We are now one of the inner circle. We are accepted. And I fear for this. I fear for this because, to reverse the Deuteronomist, Jeshurun has waxed fat, and is beginning to stop kicking. I fear for it because I am beginning to find among my rabbinic friends a somewhat lesser intensity in fighting for this absolute separation of religion and state, in protesting that the atheist has rights and that the non believer should not be put in the status of second class citizenship. We are now in the inner circle and we too talk about Judeo-Christian religion. If we can have Christmas in the schools, let us also have Hannukah. If there is to be Easter on television, so too should there be plays about Passover and the story of the Passover.

There is a great temptation to forget what to me is a basic concept of the American tradition: that there is no difference in the eyes of government between the believer and the nonbeliever, between the orthodox and the heretic, between the God-fearing and the atheist. There is but one Constitution which protects all. This is the American experiment.

CHAPTER NINE

IS AMERICAN JEWRY SECURE?

by WILL MASLOW

The security of American Jewry, the largest Jewish community in the world, is of concern not only to itself but to Jews everywhere. Jewish survival, in great measure, depends largely on the capacity of American Jewry to render material, political, and moral support to Jews in all lands. If Jews cannot achieve full equality in the United States, the freest society man has known, then Jews are not and cannot be secure anywhere outside of Israel.

How does one measure the security of American Jewry, or for that matter the security of any Jewish community which lives as a minority? Too frequently the status of a Jewish community is measured entirely by the extent of physical violence or discrimination directed against Jews. Such a measuring-rod, however, almost invariably yields a misleading and inaccurate result. Actually, at least the five following factors must be taken into account in evaluating the security of a Jewish community:

1. Do Jews enjoy full equality and equal protection under the law, and are the traditions of the country egalitarian?

2. Are Jews free to exist as a group, maintaining their own religious and cultural traditions?

3. Do Jews encounter discrimination or segregation from non-governmental sources in important human relationships?

4. Is any substantial proportion of the general population prejudiced against Jews?

5. What do Jews themselves think of their status and what are their inner resources?

Nor is it enough to apply these criteria mechanically, for it is their interrelationship that determines the nature of Jewish security. Formal equality under the law, for example, may have one meaning in a country whose traditions are egalitarian and whose basic momentum is toward an expansion of human rights, and an entirely different practical significance in lands with rooted traditions of persecution and anti-Semitism. Non-discrimination may help a Jewish community develop one character where it is permitted freedom as a group to develop its religious and cultural heritage, and another where that freedom is completely denied. Finally, the security of a Jewish community depends to a considerable degree on what Jews themselves think and feel. A Jewish community that is fearful in a free land may, for all practical purposes, be less secure than Jews in other lands, whose fortitude and sense of purpose impart dignity and self-respect to their lives as Jews.

Measured by these standards, how secure is American Jewry?

First and foremost is the fact that in no other country of the world does the structure and tradition of the law so completely and genuinely promote equality. The United States Constitution stands as a bulwark against any governmental discrimination against Jews. No law, federal or state, may or does subject the Jew, as such, to any disability or distinction. The Constitution itself forbids a religious test for public office. This protection, moreover, rests not on the current good will of a temporary majority in a legislature but is embedded in a constitution almost impossible to amend and whose pledge of equality is now more than 170 years old.

No other country in the world can boast such a legal shield.

But Jews are not secure unless they can exist as Jews without yielding any right for this privilege. Here, too, American Jewry enjoys unparalleled freedom. It is free, both in law and in fact, to observe the faith and ritual of its fathers, to preserve its cultural heritage, to build its educational institutions, to establish and maintain links with its fellow Jews throughout the world.

These privileges seem to be well guarded against encroachment because the First Amendment not only prevents any religion from being established as the "official" religion and any discrimination against a religion, but in fact, forbids government to aid any religion. Only in America, one of whose greatest contributions to the world was the separation of Church and State, is the right of Jewry to practice its religion without any disabilities so secure.

Nor is there any substantial social or economic pressure on the Jew to abandon his religion. On the contrary, Jews seem to gain respectability by religious affiliation. And Judaism itself is treated, at least on ceremonial occasions, as one of the three "major" faiths, although there are probably eight times as many Catholics in the United States as Jews.

But these constitutional bulwarks offer little consolation to the Jew refused private employment or the student denied admission to a college or a professional school because of his creed. Economic discrimination is a pervasive phenomenon in America today and the fact that it arises from non-governmental sources only makes it more difficult to combat. Who will deny that the chances of a Jewish job applicant or of a Jewish employee seeking promotion are substantially less than those of the non-Jew in almost every industry in which Jews do not predominate? In banking, insurance, chemistry, aviation, drugs, transportation, advertising, public utilities and heavy industry in general, it is only the exceptional Jew, the one who stands head and shoulders above his associates, who can make his way.

The extent of this job bias is difficult to assess in statistical terms because the census does not list the religious affiliations of those questioned. A recent study of job orders received by Chicago employment agencies showed that 20 percent barred Jews. A 1956 study reported that almost one-fifth of the employers in the major industries of the San Francisco Bay area admitted to researchers of the University of California a policy of discrimination against Jews. Other studies indicate that particularly at the executive or managerial level anti-Jewish discrimination continues unabated. Dr. John Slawson has estimated that in major American industries Jewish personnel constituted only one-half of one percent of managerial executives. The caseloads of the various state anti-discrimination commissions show no decline in the number of percentage of complaints filed by Jews.

The Jew has managed to adjust to his job-seeking difficulties by seeking his livelihood as a self-employer in trade or in the professions. The fact that often he has achieved more than he would have accomplished as a hired hand does not negate the fact that one who must shape his career according to the prejudice of others rather than his own aspirations is not wholly secure.

The problem of discrimination in education appears, on the other hand, to be considerably alleviated. Precise studies by the New York State Department of Education show that at least 50 percent of all the medical students in the ten medical schools of that state are Jewish—a far cry from the rigid quotas that prevailed in the thirties and forties. In most undergraduate schools, too, Jewish students, at least those with high grades, seem to encounter no greater difficulties in gaining admission than non-Jewish students.

But overt acts of discrimination are not the sole indication of anti-Semitic prejudice. To what extent are Americans infected with anti-Jewish stereotypes or prejudices which, though latent, may at some future time erupt into action? The public attitude polls are reassuring. When "open-ended" questions were asked such as "Which group do you think has too much political or economic power in the United States?" about 2½ percent spontaneously listed Jews, a sharp drop from polls taken ten or fifteen years ago. Yet 2½ precent of our population amounts to about 4½ million "self-igniting" anti-Semites, no mean figure. A January 1960 nation-wide poll revealed that 72 percent of those questioned stated that they had no objection to a Jew being President of the United States (only 68 percent had an objection to a Catholic for President). The fact is, that anti-Semitism is not considered respectable in the United States and no public officer ever avows any such attitude.

A minority group is secure if it is "accepted," and there are no more sensitive barometers of popular acceptance than the "exclusive" resort, suburb or social club. Judged by this gauge, the American Jews lack social standing. Barred from suburbs

of the Bronxville and Grosse Point type, from the snobbish resorts of Phoenix, Arizona, from the traditional metropolitan
social clubs, the American Jew is made to feel unwanted. A
golf club whose members are predominantly Christian that
admits Jews to membership is almost unheard of. Indeed, golf
clubs are a citadel of anti-Jewish restrictions untouched by the
changes around it. The crude legend "Christians Only" is no
longer seen in our resort advertisements, but certain "exclusive"
resorts still bar or seek to discourage Jewish patronage.

Nor can we shrug off these social slights because other
places of accommodation are available. What is involved is not
a question of discrimination but one of defamation and of social
unacceptability. In self-defense the Jews have organized Jewish
fraternities, Jewish golf clubs, Jewish Miami Beaches, segre-
gated substitutes for the social life they crave. But any ghetto,
no matter how gilded, indicates a people not yet emancipated.

Thus America today presents the picture of a society whose
law and tradition are strongly on the side of equality, in which
only a tiny percentage reveals anti-Semitic attitudes, and where
anti-Semitism as such is considered disreputable. Yet a persistent undercurrent of anti-Jewish attitudes and traditions is still
responsible for discrimination against the Jew in employment,
housing and the exclusive social or golf club. But it is also important to note the gathering strength of those forces in America
which seek, through governmental and public institutions, to
invoke the power of American law and tradition affirmatively
against any manifestation of racism.

What about the attitude of American Jewry itself? Does it
feel itself secure in its rights and status? This criterion is much
more difficult to apply with any degree of accuracy. It must be
assessed in qualitative rather than quantitative terms. For the
sense of security which a Jewish community feels is reflected
in the manner in which it conducts its communal affairs, the
forthrightness with which it is prepared to meet any challenge
to its security or impairment of the rights of its members, the
courage with which it takes a stand even on unpopular issues.

Here we encounter a strange paradox. Until recently, American Jewry, on the whole, did not reveal that inner sense of se-

curity and of belonging. And it was precisely the wealthiest, the self-styled "most assimilated and best integrated," and the most conservative groups in American Jewry which felt most insecure. These groups counselled the Jew against any action which would tend to make him too conspicuous; they urged the practice of "self-discipline" in conduct and behavior; and they made anticipated non-Jewish reaction the prime determinant of Jewish policy.

Yet even such groups have abandoned their anti-Zionist ideologies and take pride in their friendship toward and support for Israel. Organizations which insisted that Jews were only a religious group and not a people now organize Jewish international "consultative" bodies and cooperate with the World Jewish Congress. Nevertheless, the 265,000 Jews in the South feel constrained by fear of social and perhaps business ostracism to play no public part in the struggle against segregation. In many small communities where Jews are more visible than in metropolitan areas, flagrant and illegal intrusions of sectarian practices occur in the public schools while Jews and Jewish organizations remain silent lest they stir up hostile Christian reaction.

Within recent years, the balance of forces within the Jewish community has begun to shift. It is true that the counsels of fear are still heard in our midst—fears of charges of "dual loyalty" or of "aggressiveness" or harmful "public relations." More and more, however, the Jews have begun to think of the problem of their status in terms both of the forthright assertion of their equal rights as Americans and of their self-respect as Jews. That recognition has found expression in the leadership which Jewish groups are giving in the struggle for the extension of civil rights and the readiness to challenge even powerful religious and social groups when those rights are being impaired.

These changes are evidence of a deepening sense of security on the part of American Jews which enables them to live and think and act as full equals with their fellow-Americans. Despite economic and social barriers, despite a considerable degree of social unacceptability, American Jewry feels itself secure of the strength of the American tradition of equality and freedom.

Security and self-respect foster and reinforce each other. That is one of the most important facts of contemporary American Jewish life. For only a secure and self-respecting Jewish community can, on the one hand, make its full and creative contribution to America; and, on the other, discharge its responsibility in helping to assure the survival of the Jewish people.

CHAPTER TEN

ACTION FOR UNITY

by GOODWIN WATSON

It has proved easier to smash the atom than to smash the group and racial prejudices which abound in this country. The fight to achieve true brotherhood is as old as history. But that fight is far from won.

A visitor to the United States trying to study our methods of dealing with the problems of intolerance and group frictions will immediately be struck by the great number of organizations engaged in combatting prejudice. Hundreds of national agencies, including thousands of local committees, are working to improve relationships between Protestants and Catholics; between Negroes and whites; between Jews and non-Jews.

There are official bodies, such as mayors' and governors' committees, and private groups. There are sectarian organizations, devoted primarily to the interests of a single minority, and intergroup organizations drawing their membership from several groups. There are permanent coordinating bodies such as community councils or councils on race relations, and temporary groups to achieve effective action in specific situations. Also, a few research organizations dedicated exclusively to the study of prejudice and group relations have been established. And, in addition, many other bodies such as youth service agencies, labor unions and consumer groups have been drawn into the field of race relations when prejudice and discrimination disunited their own membership.

All these agencies have made some contribution to the cause of community cooperation. But there has been little attempt to assess the contribution each has made. The earnest, civic-minded citizen is likely to be approached by scores of groups who claim to be doing important work in promoting "good will" and better race relations. With which shall he cooperate? To what sort of agencies should support be given? What activities promise most return for the time invested? What techniques have proved the most effective in weaning people from prejudice?

This survey of the methods used by organizations engaged in translating the ideal of brotherhood into action charts popular pitfalls which can be avoided and points toward lines of action which seem to offer unusual promise.

The strategies, or working methods, of the agencies engaged in improving community interrelations, fall under seven convenient headings. These are: *Exhortation, Education, Participation, Revelation, Negotiation, Contention* and *Prevention*.

How are each of these applied in practice? What can we say of their relative effectiveness, and their greatest future value?

Exhortation

Exhortation is probably the simplest plan of action. Those who use it believe that its simplicity makes it effective. It consists in publicly urging Americans to practice cooperation and brotherhood because these ways of living are good. During Brotherhood Week, or Unity Week, or Good Will Week, the mayor, school superintendent, and representatives of various racial or cultural groups speak of the importance of cooperation. The citizen rides beneath car-cards and past bill boards which frame the good will theme in slogans. When a group of white and colored citizens organized the "Association for Tolerance in America" one of their first acts was to get out a bus poster reading "500,000 of these lads are fighting for you. Let them and theirs share in your democracy."

In the offices of almost every organization concerned with community relations will be found literature on the evils of intolerance and the desirability of practicing the idea that all men are created equal. A great deal of such literature has been distributed but its effects have seldom been tested. No organ-

ization seems to know how much of what it passes out is read
or how reading has influenced those it was intended to affect.

In Minneapolis, citizens were urged to pledge that "I will
never by rumor or careless conversation indict a whole race or
religious group by reasons of the delinquency of a few members." Despite the pledge, no Jew is admitted to the city's lunch-
eon clubs or the important civic boards, and even the almost
wholly commercialized Automobile Club boasts that it excludes
Jews. Sometimes pledges and exhortations of this sort have resulted in direct and effective action. In Detroit, the Council of
Social Agencies set forth a pledge of fair racial practices and
various member organizations did open up their clientele to
Negroes. But too frequently, exhortation wins only verbal support. While the Detroit Council adopted a code to eliminate
race segregation in its churches, it was agreed by all the individual signers there was little likelihood that practices in their
churches would be changed accordingly.

In general, thoughtful observers question whether the ceremonial declarations of faith in the ideal of brotherhood have
much positive effect upon community relations. Psychologists
point out that preachment has very little effect on conduct, and
that children who memorize a code of conduct by heart are no
less likely to violate it than other children. Who is not familiar
in life and in literature with the sanctimonious scoundrel? There
may have been cases where individuals have ceased to discriminate when they saw the discrepancy between their theory and
their practice. But they certainly are not numerous enough to
justify the tremendous volume of well-meaning effort put into
expressions of good will.

Researchers have shown, too, that exhortation is notoriously
apt to reach only those already converted. An occasional unity
meeting at which everyone is on his best behavior bolsters the
morale of those who are fighting prejudice but seldom reaches
serious offenders. Similarly, most "good will" literature is not
read by more than a fraction of those to whom it is distributed.
When it is read it is usually read by those who think they agree
with it; in the rare event that someone reads a pamphlet with

which he disagrees, the reaction is likely to be distaste and rejection.

Another limitation of the "good will" strategy is that it usually evades the real point of conflict. The feelings of the many who believe that Negroes are fine if kept in their place, or that Jews create trouble for themselves by being too clannish, or that white Gentile Americans consider themselves a master race and need to be deflated—these real attitudes do not come out in the brotherhood meetings or the high-sounding declarations of democratic faith. The "good will" strategy tends to praise what all find praiseworthy and damns what no one would defend.

The attempt to combat race prejudice by sweet reasonableness, exhortation and preachment, is strikingly revealed by an action of one unit of the National Conference of Christians and Jews. At a mass rally in a large city, numerous major civic and professional groups adopted a resolution condemning the city Board of Education for its exoneration of a teacher charged with preaching race hatred to her students, and expressing their grave concern over developments in the school system. Despite the fact that it had been listed as cooperating in the rally, the Conference of Christians and Jews felt itself compelled to repudiate any connection with the resolution. The Conference declared that it was not empowered by its membership to take action in controversial situations. The rally, it had been led to believe, was simply to discuss better human relations in the schools. Similar good will groups get themselves involved in the same contradictions. They will advocate general principles but shrink from their practical and specific application.

Some psychologists feel that exhortation is actually harmful. Expressions of "good will" serve to salve the American conscience. Taking a pledge or attending a "good will" meeting tends to become a cheap substitute for constructive action or a compensatory offering to make up for violations in practice. Sometimes the preaching is actually a cloak, as when notorious anti-Semites and reactionaries participate in "good will" programs to gain a reputation for Americanism.

Most agencies would be well advised to decrease the amount of time and effort now spent upon periodicals, posters, pamphlets, forums, radio programs, and public meetings which are devoted largely to expressions of the ideal of "good will." The expressions are debased by wide and easy circulation. Let exhortations be few, and resolutions be reserved for those occasions when, with specific choices in view and a full understanding of consequences, some individual or group or organization is determined to undertake more constructive policy.

But where the exhortation and the pledge can be combined with direct action, they assume new value as they crystallize the expression of the proper attitude toward community cooperation. They also give important public approval to those who are actively putting their preaching into practice.

There are, of course, publications and speeches which serve a clearly *educational* purpose. They belong to the strategy of education.

Education

Education serves, among other things, to clear away false conceptions and misunderstandings which are used to rationalize prejudices. The correction of a misconception may not end prejudice, but it will make it harder to communicate. Thus, a bigot who maintains that he hates the Jews because they murder Christian children at Passover will probably not become a believer in brotherhood when it is demonstrated that his belief is false. But a general dissemination of the true facts about Passover may prevent many people from being infected by that particular bigot.

In Chicago, an analysis of more than five hundred questions asked by pupils showed fifty recurrent fallacies about minority races and religions. The schools of a number of cities have begun to educate their students in the facts about minority groups and their culture, customs, and religion. One of the advantages of a public school project is that it involves many children who would not be reached by voluntary programs.

In Philadelphia, the school system prepared a course entitled "We Philadelphians" for use in junior high schools. Its object was to promote friendly relations among the several racial and religious groups in the city's population. In Springfield, Massachusetts, the high schools, working closely with religious leaders of the community, developed a course on "Religions of the World—Their Values to Democracy." Another course in anthropology had as its object the development of a democratic attitude toward ethnic and cultural differences.

Schools in many parts of the country favor the introduction of intercultural material in their curriculum. But a word should be said about the method of cooperation with school authorities. Some interested groups have had difficulty with school officials because they have neglected the obvious first rule, which is to become well informed on what the schools are already doing before coming in with new suggestions. Some groups sent deputations to ask that the "Springfield Plan" or some other specific program that has worked well in other schools be adopted. Experience has shown, however, that *educational programs must be integrally related to the particular local community*, growing out of its unique traditions, resources and special needs. Educational programs cannot be mass-produced for use all over the United States.

Any school program, to be effective in promoting good will, must begin by educating the teachers. Many teachers have been found to be victims of the very misconceptions which they were being asked to eliminate in their pupils. But whether or not teachers ought to be compelled to attend these courses on intercultural understanding is debatable. If attendance is voluntary, only the already converted attend. If it is compulsory, all are reached, but the program may be jeopardized. In Newark, New Jersey, for example, an attempt to obtain the greatest possible attendance at voluntary sessions led to the exertion of pressure upon individual teachers. These teachers aroused resentment against the entire program. On the other hand, similar programs for educating teachers in Springfield, Massachusetts, and New Rochelle, New York, incurred no such resentment. Teachers object less if all meetings are held on school time, and if they are freed from other duties in order to take part.

Some of the most important education goes on outside of schools and colleges. A flood of books, pamphlets and articles in

magazines and newspapers has further increased public understanding. Most of these reach only that small section of the
community which reads serious social discussions, but teachers,
ministers, club leaders, lawyers, etc., are influential because
others look to them for intellectual guidance. An interesting
development occurred in Detroit during World War II following several race riots of June, 1943. The Detroit library announced that the riots indicated the need for re-examining attitudes toward race differences and it undertook to prepare and
to distribute exhibits, reading lists for adults and children, and
leaflets on the subject of race attitudes. The object was not to
reach the hoodlum element that actually engaged in the rioting,
but to influence the allegedly intelligent, self-respecting citi-
zenry which assisted it unwittingly by spreading fanciful and
dangerous rumors.

Private agencies frequently conduct their own education programs through a variety of media. The Commission on Human
Relations of the Progressive Education Association, for example, has pieced together, from commercial films, shorts that
raise important educational issues. From the film, "Fury," scenes
leading up to a lynching were brought together in a fifteen-
minute short. The National Film Board of Canada has carried
the experiment further; they have added to documentary films
a brief "trailer" which turns the problem back to the audience
and raises the question for discussion in a useful and provocative form.

During the war, various efforts were made to publicize the
participation of minority groups, especially Negroes, Nisei and
Jews, in the war effort. The Jewish Welfare Board, for example,
published statistics on Jews in the Armed Forces. A Christian
draft board chairman wrote an article entitled "Jews Do Not
Evade Armed Service" which was reprinted and widely distributed. The thesis of the article was that not only did Jews
not seek deferment in the army in undue proportions, but they
actually supplied more men than their proportion in the general
population would lead one to expect. There are interesting problems in connection with this kind of literature: it may prompt
a "doth protest too much" kind of response; the implication that

the Jews are doing *more* than their share may reinforce the prejudices of those who dislike "the chosen people" complex attributed to Jews. Investigation should accompany any extension of such propaganda.

Labor unions offer an especially promising field for increased educational effort. The National Maritime Union reported that it found anti-Semitism a growing problem in its ranks. The union's position is emphatic and clear-cut, but not all union members feel the same way. The usual tactics of CIO leaders have included rebukes from officials at meetings and distribution of comic books and pamphlets. Quite possibly the situation calls for more wide-spread and more vigorous education. Study groups that emphasize that economic interests cut across race lines might be helpful if they could secure wider participation. Leaders should be trained in every shop (and in the case of the NMU, on every ship) to handle the common variety of "incident" for maximum educational value.

How effective is the strategy of education?

The judgment is favorable. Education in the facts frequently helps to sustain the confidence of minorities, to reinforce the vague good will of liberals and slowly to disintegrate the defense of the prejudiced. Myrdal, the Swedish sociologist, pointed out that the whites in the South no longer appeal as frequently as they did to biology or psychology to justify their treatment of the Negro. Segregation with unequal facilities may linger on for a time, but lacking the old intellectual justification, its defenders can only apologize and plead against over-hasty readjustments.

The value of the strategy of education is limited unless a special effort is made to reach individuals who will *act* on the basis of what they know. To educate policemen about some aspects of their job; to help bus drivers handle the routine conflicts of their daily work; to give real estate and housing officials facts on success of programs that do not discriminate—these are the educational endeavors that seem to promise the best results. For here information is brought in, not for its own sake, but as a guide to action.

Education frequently accomplishes more when it not only

informs the intellect but affects the emotions as well. When distinguished members of various ethnic groups appear before an audience, the impression their presence makes goes deeper oftentimes than do the ideas they present. The contributions, for example, which artists like Marian Anderson and Paul Robeson have made to the appreciation of talent regardless of race, are unmeasured but certainly large. The fact that Leonard Bernstein, Walter Damrosch, Ossip Gabrilowitsch, George Gershwin, Jerome Kern, Sergei Koussevitsky, Eugene Ormandy, Bruno Walter, are appreciated as conductors rather than as Jewish conductors may be regarded as wholesome. At the same time, it would do no harm for all American young people to be aware of their indebtedness to Jewish culture for producing an unusual proportion of musicians of extraordinary talent.

Education in the customs and religious rites of diverse cultural groups can be made a highly valuable experience. The danger here is that the quaint and the artistic are stressed at the expense of the less glamorous, and probably, more universal. The people of other cultures may be looked upon as museum pieces rather than as persons. It is, for example, one thing to idealize the ancient Greeks; quite another to include the Greeks of the neighborhood restaurants and candy stores in civic life.

Although it has been recognized that emotional education is important, there has not been sufficient investigation of the clinical aspects of prejudice. Prejudice serves different purposes in different personalities. It is not only important to know how a child or adult acquires prejudice—it is essential to know *why* prejudice is kept and used. The bigot will not release the false belief so long as it is emotionally needed. When the personality needs have been met, the prejudice can then be dropped because it is no longer indispensable. The important task of emotional re-training has not yet been adequately financed in any community. A step in this direction is, however, to be found in the strategy of participation.

Participation

The object of the strategy of patricipation is to get members of different groups to live together and work together in a common cause. Participation projects also educate the emotions and they have the reality, naturalness and solidity which emotionalized stories, films and special entertainments lack.

The first step is simply getting acquainted, and the programs of many agencies stop there. In Cleveland, and in other localities, visits are paid between white and Negro YMCA's and YWCA's. Dr. F. Tredwell Smith at Teachers College of Columbia University was able to show the modification of prejudice among his white students resulting simply from week-end contacts with Harlem professional and artistic groups.

Considerable research is still needed on the factors which facilitate getting acquainted. Does age, or sex, or degree of "class consciousness" make a difference? What type of person profits by the get-acquainted venture? Social scientists have begun to work on such questions in their investigation of group behavior.

A further step in participation is working together on common problems. The Kansas City Youth Round Table, originally a get-together for Negro and Jewish boys, has developed into a Negro-white social action group. The war has produced a host of examples of the diminution of prejudice following cooperation in the performance of common tasks. In the *Nation*, Eric Purden told the story of the submarine chaser, PC 1264, manned by a mixed crew among whom initial friction quickly disappeared. A Southern officer who had previously held all of the standard anti-Negro prejudices, was quoted as saying: "Half way through the trip I forgot they were black."

In Newark, New Jersey, a YMCA has not only sought members from all races, but has tried to make them active on committees. In many localities, the League of Women Voters has tried to do the same thing. Often, general community projects, rather than specifically interracial affairs, have afforded opportunities to bring different groups together. One important objective, therefore, is to try to increase the number of community activities in which different groups can focus their attention not on themselves, but on a common goal.

The third step in the strategy of participation is living together as friends and neighbors.

Experience has shown that it is more important to attack segregation than it is to attack prejudices. It has generally been assumed that discrimination grows out of prejudice. It is equally true that a good deal of prejudice arises from the fact that people observe discrimination as a normal fact in their own environment. If we try to change people's feelings while the caste barriers remain tacitly accepted, the habits built around those barriers would silently undo anything that is accomplished. On the other hand, persons with strong prejudices who have to live and work together soon experience human qualities and relationships which tend to break down prejudice. For example, white workers in factories who had been forced by the war, the FSPC, and CIO unions, to accept Negro co-workers, came to tolerate and eventually to like their new companions. Families who planned to move out of housing projects when Negroes came in, but who were delayed in moving, discovered that they liked their new neighbors and that they no longer cared to move.

It is often wise to establish non-segregation in fact *before* attempting to establish it in principle. In Washington, polls of white street car and bus operators indicated that if Negro operators were hired, the whites would refuse to work with them. But in fifteen cities where Negroes were put to work without previous notice or publicity, there was no trouble.

Revelation

Complacency is one of the chief obstacles to eliminating tension in disturbed areas of community interrelations. "Revelation"—not the religious experience, but the kind of shock that results from the sudden and dramatic disclosure of facts of which people were previously unaware—is the tried strategy against complacency. Frequently this disclosure has emotional overtones, similar to those aroused by an unexpected twist in the plot of a book or a motion picture.

Bringing the real facts vigorously and vividly before the community often takes courage, because the truth is often offensive, even to those who need it most. Organizations which are uncompromising in exposing racial and religious bias become storm centers in community life. They generate apprehension.

Their activities offend the fence-sitters who are more afraid of "bad publicity" than of injustice.

Liberal newspapers and organizations, for example, have used the techniques of revelation to expose organizations which foment race and religious antagonisms. In the midst of World War II there arose in New York a sinister figure known as the Black Hitler of Harlem. From his inappropriately named "Temple of Tranquility" he spread propaganda against the war and against the white race. He found many interested listeners among the resentful Negroes, until his connections with the Japanese were exposed. *Exposure exploded the project.*

In Chicago, Eugene R. Flitcraft's Gentile Cooperative Association, with plenty of funds from somewhere, was lining up anti-Semites. Plans were completed to sell ten thousand "Directories" at $12 apiece. The *Chicago Sun* played an important part in exposing this outfit and in getting the state to revoke its certificate of incorporation.

Many national organizations, such as the Friends of Democracy and the Anti-Defamation League of B'nai B'rith collect extensive information on native fascist developments and try to check undemocratic movements through public exposure.

The successful use of revelation, however, requires that those who use it refrain from going off half-cocked. The facts must be correct, and they must be sufficient to carry the weight of the charge. Careful surveys, bringing light to situations that require correction, are frequently prerequisites to exposure.

There are two possible objections to the use of revelation as a strategy. One is its obvious insufficiency. Finding out the facts does not by itself necessarily solve the problems. Obviously, facts, in most cases, have to be implemented by action. The second is that publication of the facts may, instead of correcting the situation, merely set a bad example to others elsewhere. It may put ideas in people's heads. But we must recognize that we do not eliminate problems by turning attention away from them. If there are enough right-thinking people in the community, shocking them out of their complacency may be wholesome. Allport, in founding Rumor Clinic, argued that rumors would travel despite the silence of liberals and that it would be better to make sure that a solid answer was ready at hand to refute them.

Before revelation can really become a major weapon, we shall have to know more than we do about the best methods of exposing unpleasant situations so that they become a matter of immediate personal concern to the largest number of citizens. We need careful research, too, to tell us how much publicity is a good thing and in what situation it is better to resort to negotiation.

Negotiation

When prominent citizens get wind of difficulties somewhere, their first inclination is to try to smooth things over and to keep it out of the newspapers. Then they reach for a telephone to call up a few influential people with whom they can talk on a confidential basis. They are happiest when this method succeeds in "fixing things up," straightening them out, or at least giving an appearance of having everything fixed up and straightened out. This is the strategy we term negotiation. Most of the official agencies—mayors' committees, governors' committees, and the like—operate on this pattern.

The influence of the mediators and negotiators may sometimes be very great. Their behavior usually follows the cultural pattern of the dominant business and political leaders. They are "men you can trust," people with "fair minds and cool heads"; they are not "radicals"; they don't "go off half-cocked." Negotiators do frequently seem to exercise great influence. Protest groups may try for a long time to get certain offensive advertising discontinued when one man of prestige can arrange to have this done by calling a friend whom he knows by his first name and with whom he often has lunch.

An extreme instance of the confidence that some wealthy laymen have in their ability to handle any difficulty that may arise was found in one Jewish leader in a mid-western city. He liked to "take care" of anything that came up. When a committee of citizens was appointed to deal with an issue he felt this to be very unwise and attempted to substitute one skilled negotiator on the "inside," instead of this dangerous meddling. He wanted no committees and no public discussions. His remarkably frank analysis of the most serious problem facing the Jews of this community was: "To find someone to replace me when I die."

The persistent danger with individuals and organizations who seek to be useful only as "fixers" is that they seldom take a stand as a matter of principle. Compromise tends to be regarded as good in itself, regardless of the principles and interests at stake. Negotiators tend to become merely an expression of balance of forces. They themselves, then, are not a force. More often than not the driving pressure groups, pro and con, determine the dynamics of the situation, and the negotiator becomes only the mouthpiece which makes the score official. And, finally, what is perhaps a more serious objection to "fixing" is that it hides the issue and the facts from the public and stifles any long-range community-backed solution to race problems.

On the other hand, negotiation and compromise may sometimes make a significant contribution by cutting through one impasse and freeing progressive forces to prepare for struggles to come. But it is important to distinguish between compromise with reactionaries, which constitutes a form of dangerous appeasement, and constructive compromise which takes the community one step forward.

When compromise threatens to weaken the forces of cooperation it frequently becomes necessary to resort to contention.

Contention

There are groups who are dissatisfied with the first five strategies, even though each of the five often brings constructive steps. They demand less talk, less promises, and more action.

Experience has shown that while inflexible people can be very unpleasant they do often get results. It is especially true that when a community places a high premium upon good will and harmony, groups which threaten disturbances get a lot of attention and a great many concessions.

A man who had retired after several years of work as head of an active mayors' committee in a large city was asked what had been the biggest contribution to improving the interracial and inter-faith relations in his community. "Well," he said, "it caused us a lot of headaches and it is probably full of potential dynamite for the Negroes themselves, but I would have to admit that it was aggressive, militant, uncompromising demands of the National Association for the Advancement of Colored People that made us move further than anything else. They cause us a lot of trouble but they get attention."

The demands for which groups have been found ready to fight fall in four categories: defending differences, equalizing opportunities, removing barriers which express segregation, and defeating political anti-Semitism.

The assumption that all should become alike (like the white, Protestant, Anglo-Saxon middle-class) was implicit in the "Americanization" programs a generation ago. Immigrants were urged to give up old-country ways and to fit into the uniform pattern of the dominant ethnic group. "Well, why not?" it is frequently asked. "Isn't it the easiest solution of our problems of race and religious conflicts? Amalgamation into one race with one culture is the inevitable and desirable outcome."

Today, however, there is general recognition that we live in a pluralistic society and that both America and the world will suffer if the various cultural groups who make up our population are not encouraged to develop their distinctive contributions. Clearly, the right to maintain certain differences is something for which democratic Americans would, if necessary, be prepared to fight. There can be no possible dispute over the desirability of defending the right of all groups to live and worship in peace and security. Volunteer groups should receive more training in the techniques of protecting legal rights. But militancy of defense extends beyond the enforcement of legal protection. In includes the use of economic pressure and pressure of public opinion against violators. This is an area in which liberals need to become more competent. A crude generalization would be that "liberals" rely too much on good will and are too afraid to offend; that "radicals" are so convinced that everyone can be pressured that they overdo the tough stuff and make unnecessary enemies. One of the big tasks of social research is to discover when the cooperative approach should be used and when to get tough.

In communities where segregation is still too firmly established to be budged, the goal for immediate struggle is achievement of equal opportunity. This is the goal of those who are fighting for a permanent FEPC. Many groups are now asking for legislative action to prevent discrimination against Jews, Negroes, Italians, and Nisei in colleges and graduate schools.

Active groups have won victories against unequal recreational and social opportunities. Equality, for example, has forced the opening of public restaurants to Negroes by the device of entering a restaurant in mixed groups, and insisting quietly but firmly on the legal right to be served. In one northern city, the National Association for the Advancement of Colored People forced all the downtown movie theatres to admit Negroes on the basis of substantial equality. As an indication of the resistance that even such a small step will arouse, and the necessity of maintaining a militant spirit to make the strategy of contention work, it should be noted that this fight was won only after several years of picketing, publicity and litigation. Real estate developments are another area where something can be done to improve conditions without breaking down segregation.

Today, the bus boycott and the sit-in strike have also become tactics against segregation, as are the trips by the Freedom Riders.

Here is the heart of the struggle in American communities. Negro resentment against army and navy treatment was more against segregation policies than against inequality of privileges.

In private housing, "incidents" turn up continuously, revealing the difficulties Negro families have in finding the kind of homes they want. Attractive neighborhoods are closed off by restrictive covenants to prevent lease or sale to non-whites. The Urban League and other NAACP organizations spring into action against any move in a northern community to enforce separation along race lines. Interracial schools with interracial teaching staff; interracial hospitals with interracial staff of doctors and nurses; interracial housing projects; full access to community recreational facilities—these are the goals for which some individuals and groups are constantly struggling.

Employment has been an area of conflict over participation by minority groups and bids fair to be worse now than when the war was over. The AFL-CIO and the FEPC have been major factors in the fight to get employers and fellow workers to accept competent Negroes as employees along with whites. An attempt has been made by the League of Women Shoppers to use economic pressure to get department stores to employ more Negro clerks. The petitions they circulated included the statement, "We prefer to shop at those stores which practice this policy of *equal* opportunity for work and advancement." The department stores which do employ Negroes were commended.

The fight to prevent segregation and discrimination is being most effectively waged in certain unions. The National Maritime Union has developed tactics which are worthy of careful analysis because they have been unusually successful. The NMU's task is not an easy one. They are asking men of different races not merely to work in the same shop, but to live together in the crowded quarters of a ship. It should be remembered, too, that seamen are not as docile as a church sewing circle.

Leaders on board each ship are trained by the union to deal with the problems that commonly arise. In the matter of race relations, these rank and file leaders (not ship's officers) are given both an *ideology* and a *methodology*. Ideologically they fight prejudice as a boss's trick to divide and weaken the labor movement. The methodology is described in the following passage, taken from a sheet in a training course entitled "What To Do When a Seaman Refuses To Sail with a Negro Brother":

1. The first step to take is to call a meeting of the entire crew, except those who are needed for the safe navigation of the ship.

2. At this meeting you state the problem that some brothers refuse to accept the Negro brother. Then you ask the brothers who object to the Negro to stand up. Have each brother who objects to the Negro brother state his reasons.

3. His arguments are to be answered point by point. His arguments are invariably fallacious and easy to expose.

4. In the event that these men refuse to accept logic, or to discuss it with a view to settling it, then invoke the Constitution of the NMU. Ask those men if they believe in the NMU Constitution. They will invariably say yes. Ask them if they believe in all of the Constitution; not in parts of it. They will again say yes. Then, ask them if they believe in the clause that states that there will be no discrimination. If they say no, then obviously they do not believe in all the Constitution. If they say yes, then what the hell are we fighting about?

5. If that is not successful, then tell the brothers that they are not obligated to sail with a Negro, so they can get off the ship. And, in order to save a lot of inconvenience, they can leave their Union books because their books will be no good to them.

Reference has already been made to the importance of removing discrimination as a first step toward the breakdown of prejudice.

The discussion of legal measures brings us to a major field of contention—the political struggle against those who use anti-Semitism as part of a program of native fascism. The truly serious danger to democracy in America lies in the susceptibility to demagogues who seek to capitalize on any crisis in order to extend their power.

The usual reaction to agitators like Joe McWilliams and Gerald L. K. Smith, is to laugh them off or to shrug the shoulders. The failure to have that reaction in Germany needs to be more clearly appreciated. Today, George Lincoln Rockwell is having no greater success than his predecessors.

Among active approaches, there is the fact-gathering and publicizing technique discussed under the strategy of revelation. Several organizations have made intensive investigations of the more prominent anti-democratic agitators. But unfortunately, organizational policies have sometimes interfered with full and free use of the data collected. Differences of opinion concerning the wisdom of "stirring up trouble" have hampered effective attack.

When the proposed action attempted to appeal to libel laws or to deny to these agitators the use of auditorium or radio or press facilities, the issue of free speech was raised and the liberals were divided. Much clearer thinking about the problem of free speech is necessary.

One of the most difficult problems in the fight against native fascism is that of reaching the people most apt to be influenced by it. The numerous agencies of adult education have not been successful in reaching the majority of Americans with only a grade school education or less. The many commentators and columnists reach only the educated minority. No one has yet found out how to reach the masses in the United States with any program of socially significant education. The National Citizens' Political Action Committee of the old CIO demonstrated more success in reaching the rank and file than has any other movement in the country. To be sure, they hadn't tried to do more than get out the vote. It has become imperative that experiments be undertaken to find methods which will arouse interest among the low-education, low-income, non-reading adults who compose the majority of the American people.

Prevention

Some of the most constructive work in the whole field of intercultural activity has been directed to meeting problems before they become acute.

The simplest methods involve predicting areas of potential conflict. In Detroit this is done with considerable accuracy: the police commissioner compiles each week the reports regularly reaching him from public and private observers listing all incidents involving conflict. By week-to-week comparison, the commissioner can tell which areas of the city are becoming most troublesome, and can chart the rise in tension. Other means to the same end involve charts showing population shifts and public opinion polls. All of these methods indicate that areas inhabited by the least educated persons, who are likely also to be the most complacent, are the areas of greatest tension. Frustration, ignorance, and anxiety continue to be the richest soil for race and religious hatred.

When the areas of danger are identified, prophylactic measures must be applied. One which has been used is the training
of public officials to meet the threat of conflict. The bias of
public officials, particularly police officers, has often been a
basic cause of rioting. In Detroit, the police commissioner,
formerly a social worker, takes disciplinary action against any
officer found to act unfairly. Police training in race relations
is firmly established in Boston, Washington, San Francisco, and
a number of other American cities. Much more work should be
done in training other groups of officials who are in a position to
aid or hinder the harmonious cooperation of racial and religious
groups.

Frequently, the suggestion is put forth by members of the
dominant as well as by members of minority groups, that efforts
should be made to control behavior which allegedly occasions
prejudice. Certain groups are making efforts in this direction.
The New Jersey Federation of Women's Clubs, for whom a
course was conducted by the Council for Democracy, asked,
typically enough, why Jews did not behave themselves better,
so that it would be easy for Gentiles to like them. There are at
least four ways of answering such a question. One is to cite
the efforts of various Jewish organizations to work out methods
of self-discipline. A second is to reject completely the notion
of group social characteristics, and to cite the notion as one
form of racist thinking. A third is to reject the stereotype, but
to express the conviction that Jewish organizations and groups
are one avenue for reaching Jews with methods of making
them better Americans. Still another method is to defend such
possible group characteristics as inaccurately accented speech,
methods of dress, special predilections, as positive contributions
to the patchwork design of American life. Which of these is the
best answer no one knows yet.

Among more militant groups those minority members who
attempt to raise the standards of behavior are subjected to piti-
less criticism. Such people are disliked for what seems a Phar-
isaic attitude of assumed superiority to their fellows, and for
the objective reason that they give aid and comfort to those

whose attacks upon minority groups bear little relation to the realities of minority group behavior.

Finally, an effective program of prevention must attack the whole life of the community. It must be more sweeping than any activity in the field of community interrelations has ever been heretofore. Since scapegoating arises from frustration, anything which makes life more livable may contribute to reducing hostility toward minorities. Thus efforts to get social security, higher minimum wage, family allowances, birth control, community play-grounds, etc., all contribute indirectly. Giving groups constructive activity and a democratic experience will substantially reduce racial and religious intolerance. No aspect of community relations activity needs to be emphasized more than the need for the positive programs of those groups and leaders who are themselves sources of prejudices and friction. And these efforts must be based on much more complete information on the nature of the psychology of prejudice than we have presently available.

Are there certain kinds of frustration which are especially likely to lead to scapegoating? If we can discover that virulent anti-Semitism is likely to spring from certain identifiable disorders of community life, we can concentrate the strategy of prevention on those disorders so that it will achieve its highest efficiency. We can hope that scientific research will shed true light on this problem.

The Need for Knowledge

Our study indicated the major area in which each method can be employed, and the general type of questions which must be answered in order to raise the efficiency of the use of each method to its highest level.

The field for improvement in intercultural relations is almost limitless. But the time for improving them may be short. This means that effort must be concentrated where it can accomplish most, and that the effort must continue even while it is being evaluated. Even while the struggle for brotherhood continues, the effectiveness of its strategies and weapons must be studied. The war indicated that the battlefield itself was the best laboratory for testing weapons. From the continuing struggle for brotherhood, a continuing flow of knowledge must be derived. In the light of this new knowledge, some strategies must be dropped, others revised, new ones developed. The process must be continuous and unflagging if we are to be vouchsafed an encouraging glimpse of brotherhood in our time.

CHAPTER ELEVEN

ROOTS OF PREJUDICE

by GORDON W. ALLPORT
and BERNARD M. KRAMER

Why is it that so large a majority of people in our society displays religious and racial prejudice? Psychologists agree that these attitudes of animosity or distrust are not inborn; they are not hereditary like the color of one's skin or the shape of one's eyes. Prejudices are acquired in growth and it is important to find out just what it is in our society and culture that produces them. While it is possible to fight prejudices without knowing how they originate, any victories so gained are usually of a temporary character only. The necessity to tackle symptoms is frequently urgent and unavoidable. But only if we learn *how* an individual or group comes to have certain attitudes toward other individuals and groups will we be able to control the spread of that disease effectively.

The present study is an attempt to apply scientific methods and techniques to certain common prejudices. Our results, added to those of other investigators will, we hope, eventually yield a comprehensive analysis of the causes of prejudice. Once we have this knowledge we can plan intelligent and effective programs of action to eradicate them.

It would seem a safe estimate that at least four-fifths of the American population bear feelings of hostility toward some group or other. This estimate, necessarily rough, is based on various types of evidence such as the following: (a) In a hundred typical life-histories obtained from college students, 80 percent contained admissions of group prejudice; (b) certain unpublished research of the Commission of Community Interrelations

253

of the American Jewish Congress shows that in a random sample of population drawn from Times Square, New York, pedestrians, only 17 percent gave virtually unprejudiced replies to questions formulated to gauge anti-Semitism; (c) only 22 percent of the Harvard and Radcliffe students in this very study reported that they did not feel uncongenial toward any group at all.

It is more difficult to estimate the proportion of our population so virulently infected that with slight provocation it would join other "scapegoat addicts" and engage in acts of violence. Yet we do know that some bigots in our country today advocate Hitler's savage policy of extermination of certain minorities. We know also that tendencies to loot and to lynch lie close to the surface in many apparently sane and respected citizens.

But it is neither the benevolent minds of the unprejudiced fifth of the population nor the pathology of the rioter that interests us in the present investigation. We are concerned rather with prejudice in a rank-and-file group of college students as it was revealed with the aid of a fairly long questionnaire.

Our subjects were 437 college undergraduates; 214 from Dartmouth, 166 from Harvard, and 57 at Radcliffe. All were enrolled in elementary courses in psychology. While there is reason to suppose that college students (perhaps especially those studying psychology) are disposed to give less prejudiced responses than a more unselected group, still there is no ground for believing their life-experiences, with which the questionnaire deals, to be in any sufficient way atypical.

One of the most important findings of social psychology in recent years is that prejudice (or lack of prejudice) is a *general state of mind*. The person who is anti-Semitic is usually anti-Negro, anti-Catholic, anti-everything and everyone outside his own particular group. For this reason it is possible accurately to measure prejudice with a simple general scale consisting of a few questions on attitudes toward each of the groups against whom prejudice is most frequently directed. We applied such a general prejudice scale to our students, then divided them into two approximately equal groups, one *more prejudiced* and the other *less prejudiced,* according to their scores on the scale.

The more prejudiced students differ from the less prejudiced in a host of ways other than prejudice. The following pages describe and explain these differences. Through the analysis of differences between prejudiced and unprejudiced individuals the hope is eventually to lay bare the roots of prejudice.

Are Parents Guilty?

Parents exert the earliest and probably the strongest influence on the development of prejudice. Each of our students was asked to report the extent to which he thought his attitudes toward minority groups had been influenced by those of his parents. The table shows the results.

Thus, 69 percent of our students acknowledged that their attitudes toward minority groups reflect parents' views in some degree. Six percent have reacted against these views, and 25 percent claim to have been uninfluenced by them.

The answers of this last group, however, are highly suspect. So many studies have demonstrated the deep and lasting effect of parental attitudes on those of their children that it is scarcely conceivable the attitudes of these particular individuals were not influenced by the parental model. It is more likely the influence was there but not recognized.

The curious fact is that these subjects who do not admit such influence are precisely the subjects whose attitudes are most prejudiced. Sixty-one percent of them fall into the more preju- diced half of the general distribution, and 39 into the less prej- udiced half. We shall demonstrate more fully in later pages that this lack of insight, this failure to understand the influences that shaped his present attitudes are fundamental characteris- tics of the bigot.

Those students who took over their parents' attitudes without

Students Reporting Various Degrees of Parental Influence

Taken over parents attitudes	18%
Taken them over in a modified way	51%
Reacted against them	6%
Not been influenced by them	25%
Total	100%

change are slightly more prejudiced than the average. In a recent study, Frenkel-Brunswik and Sanford report similarly that anti-Semitic college girls tend to take their political and social convictions directly from their parents and report less "ideological friction" with their parents than do students who are not anti-Semitic.

Least prejudiced are the small number of students who have reacted against their parents' views. In rejecting the parental attitudes, they seem to have developed liberal-rebellious, equalitarian attitudes with which all college teachers are familiar.

Are Schools Fighting Prejudice?

"Do you feel," the subjects were asked, "that you have been influenced by your teachers or your school experiences with respect to your attitudes toward minority groups? If so, state briefly how."

We found that our less prejudiced students tend to report school experiences favorable toward minority groups. Those more prejudiced tend either to recall unfavorable school experience or to deny that school had any influence at all upon them. There are three points to be noted in these results:

(a) Only 31 percent report exclusively favorable memories of their school in respect to lessons of tolerance and understanding. The remainder recall unfavorable or mixed influences or none at all.

(b) As in the case of other early memories, the past situation, as it is recalled, tends to conform with present attitudes. We cannot, therefore, say unequivocally from our results that favorable school training leads to less prejudice and that unfortunate school experience leads to the reverse. The subject may be rationalizing his present attitudes in ascribing the credit, or blame, to the school.

(c) In the case of the more prejudiced we again find evidence of unawareness, or lack of insight. Those who say the school had no influence upon them are preponderantly prejudiced. It was so, too, with those who said their parents had no influence upon them. Again it seems that bigots are peculiarly

Number of Students Reporting Various Types of School Influence

	Less Prejudiced	More Prejudiced
Scientific facts about race	22	9
Favorable in general	123	75
Unfavorable in general	4	30
Mixed	31	60
No Influence reported	13	20
Total	193	194

insensitive to the origin and nature of their own attitudes. Apparently smug and satisfied with their narrow views of the world, they seem to regard them as "natural" to themselves and not acquired from specific sources.

The table above summarizes the results obtained from the question, "What do you consider to be the most important thing that you have learned in school about minority groups?"

Two facts in the above table stand out: (a) Children apparently do learn something in school that decidedly affects their ethnic attitudes (even allowing for a certain amount of *ex post facto* rationalizing), but what it is they are seldom able, in later years, to tell. Vivid teaching seems to be rare. (b) The only specific teaching the subjects recall (in sufficient numbers to be reported) concerns "scientific facts about race." Where this lesson is reported the students fall preponderantly in the less prejudiced half. But only 8 percent report having learned scientific facts about race. Apparently, this useful lesson is neglected in our school curricula.

Age and Prejudice

Our next table shows the percentages of subjects at successive ages who are more prejudiced.

The young child undoubtedly starts life without prejudice and during pre-school years seems almost incapable of directing hostility toward any group as a whole. The great bulk of prejudiced attitudes originates in the school years, and the acquisition of prejudice continues throughout the age range we studied.

The relative freedom from hostility of sixteen and seventeen

Prejudiced Students at Successive Ages

16-17 years	36% more prejudiced
18-19 years	55% more prejudiced
20-21 years	55% more prejudiced
22 and over	59% more prejudiced

year-olds in our study may be due to the fact that this younger group has had the benefit of training in schools where the principles of tolerance and inter-group understanding have received more stress in recent years. Or the result may be accounted for by the fact that brighter pupils (who are usually also the younger students in any class) avoid the traps of prejudice. Our research unfortunately provided no opportunity to correlate prejudice scores with tests of intelligence or college grades.

Does Familiarity Breed Trust?

Does contact with minority groups enhance or diminish prejudice? The answer to this question is still in a confused state. On the one hand, it is obvious that certain contacts lead to friction. Riots, we know, break out where contact is close, involuntary and provocative—chiefly at intersections of ethnic residential districts or in parks and recreational areas where antagonistic groups mingle with and insult one another. People low on the economic scale who live or work beside members of other ethnic groups are often likely to tangle with them. Sheer proximity does not necessarily produce neighborliness and trust.

On the other hand, certain types of contact clearly make for a reduction of prejudice. World travelers, students of other cultures, international societies of scientists, democratic organizations of all types, demonstrate that close association with members of other ethnic groups may engender understanding and feelings of fellowship.

One task for the future is to distinguish types of contact that have beneficial results from those that worsen inter-group relationships. The complexity of the subject can be seen from the evidence concerning American service men abroad. In some particulars their contact with foreign populations reduced prejudice, in other respects enhanced it.

By way of hypothesis, we suggest that genuine contact between members of groups having the same, or nearly the same, economic and social status improves friendly relations between them. Conversely, contact between members of groups holding very different economic and social status (or between members of groups equally deprived of status) intensifies rivalry and the desire to establish status at the expense of one another.

Although our results are not adequate for testing this hypothesis completely, they supply evidence in support of it.

Striking results come from a question asking whether the subject has associated with many members of various minority groups in school, at work, in recreation, as neighbors, or as friends. It was found that the more numerous the equal-status contacts, the less the prejudice. Thus, for example, anti-Semitism was much less prevalent among non-Jews who reported many equal-status contacts with Jews than among those who cited few or no such contacts. Results with reference to Negroes again showed that equal-status contacts had markedly beneficial effects.

Considerable contact of *any kind* with Negroes seems, among our college students, to be associated with less prejudice against Negroes. Equal-status contacts, however, are particularly favorable to the reduction of prejudice. Additional support for this conclusion comes from analysis of the question which asks, "Have you ever known a Negro with about the same education as you have?" Only 14 percent of our sample answered, "No." But of these cases, 69 percent appeared in the more prejudiced half of the general distribution.

So far as contact with Jews is concerned, we find that "considerable contact" of an unspecified order does not make for the reduction of prejudice. In fact, a large percentage of anti-Semites claim "considerable" contact with Jews. But when the kind of contact is limited to equality of relationship (neighbors, schoolmates, friends), the results are very favorable.

Our results, then, show clearly that equal-status contact is a good thing. They also indicate that merely casual, or unspecified, contact, however frequent, is not so beneficial.

There is sound psychological reason why equal-status contact should lessen prejudice. A person who has no knowledge or only causal knowledge of a minority group becomes easy prey to second-hand generalizations. If I do not personally know energetic and cultivated Negroes, I find it easy to accept such labels as "lazy and shiftless," "all right in their place," and the like. If I do not know neighborly and public-spirited Jews, I may accept the legend that they are "self-centered," "skin-flints," "materialistic," etc.

What About Religion?

"To what degree has religion been an influence in your upbringing?"

Replies to this question are instructive to persons who claim that religious training is virtually a thing of the past. Our students report religious influence in the following degrees: very marked, 28 percent; moderate, 41; slight, 21; and none at all, 10 percent.

Lumping together the individuals who claim religion as a marked or moderate factor in their training, we find more cases in the higher prejudice group than in the lower.

This finding, distressing as it must be to religious leaders, is confirmed by other studies. For example, Frenkel-Brunswik and Sanford report their anti-Semitic girl students to be moralistic, puritanical, and conventionally religious. They are also nationalistic. This pattern, they explain, is a generalized hostility toward minority groups which seems to serve "as a source of support that could substitute for genuine effort and achievement." In short, the highly prejudiced person has been brought up to lean on external, institutionalized sanctions which imply hostility toward groups who do not subscribe to the same institutional pattern.

A different light on the subject is obtained from the question, "How, if at all, do you think your religious training, either in church or at home, has influenced you with respect to your attitudes toward, and opinions of, minority groups?" When the replies are classified as "positive," "negative," "neutral," or "mixed" we find that 51 percent of the cases fall into the "positive" group; that is, they report that religion tended to reduce or to allay prejudice. Of course, 57 percent appear in the less prejudiced half and 43 in the more prejudiced half of the general distribution. We note that Frenkel-Brunswik and Sanford likewise report a strong religious factor in the cases of many girls free from anti-Semitism. Contrasting these cases with the conventional religious belief of the anti-Semites, they write that those who are low on the anti-Semitism scale are by no means generally irreligious, but religion takes another form.

Our results, while not entirely conclusive, indicate that the mere exposure of an individual to a religious upbringing does not incline him toward tolerance. If anything, it disposes him toward prejudice. But if, in retrospect, he reports that religion has had a positive influence on his attitudes, he does indeed show a higher degree of tolerance toward minority groups. If, in retrospect, he claims that religion had an unfavorable, neutral, or mixed effect on him, his prejudice scores tend to be higher.

In short, tolerance may grow from certain types of religious training, but not from mere exposure to religion in the home or at church.

Taking the attitudes of various groups toward Negroes only, we discover that Catholics lead the list in anti-Negro bias, followed by the Protestants. By comparison, Jews and persons lacking any religious affiliation are markedly free from prejudice.

Hate Breeds Hate

There is a theory that want, persecution or frustration produce hostility and aggressive impulses in their victims. Taken at its face value this theory would lead us to expect that victims of prejudice would themselves be more inclined than the average person to show hostility toward other groups (both toward their persecutors and, by virtue of "displaced aggression," toward other minority groups). At least one study has indicated that Jewish students who feel themselves victims of prejudice do tend to be more prejudiced against the Negro than those Jewish students who do not feel themselves to be victimized.

In an effort to test this hypothesis, we designed the following question: "To what extent do you feel that you yourself have been a victim of prejudice because of your membership in a minority group? (a) to a great extent; (b) more than average; (c) average; (d) less than average; (e) not at all."

The largest minority groups in the present study are Catholics, numbering 110, and Jews, totalling 63; and our analysis of the effects of victimization will be in terms of these two. Their responses to the question are shown below.

Further breakdown of these responses provides certain supporting evidence for the frustration-aggression interpretation of scapegoat tendencies. The Catholic students were divided into two groups with respect to their responses to the victimization question, i.e., the more victimized and the less victimized. The results indicate that the greater the feelings of victimization the greater is the tendency to be prejudiced against the Negroes. The more victimized Catholics, the results show, also tended to be more anti-Semitic.

A curious, if similar, result is the finding that the Jewish subjects who felt more victimized tended to be more anti-Semitic than those who said they were less victimized. What seems to happen is that the aggression or hostility which is built up as a result of being the object of persecution and discrimination is actually directed toward certain members of one's own group, perhaps because of fear of reprisals that would follow should the resentment be directed again the Gentile persecutors.

Yet, this interpretation is by no means complete. Most of us know cases in which members of minority groups develop sympathy for other persecuted minorities as a result of persecution and discrimination that they themselves have suffered. Our data concerning the feelings of our Jewish subjects toward Negroes

Jews and Catholics Who Acknowledge Various Degrees of Feeling of Victimization

	Jews	Catholics
Great extent	9%	2%
More than average	16%	4%
Average	29%	16%
Less than average	43%	28%
Not at all	3%	50%
Total	100%	100%

More and Less Victimized Jews with Various Degrees of Anti-Negro Feeling

	Least Anti-Negro	Somewhat Anti-Negro	Most Anti-Negro	Total
More victimized Jews	29%	44%	27%	100%
Less victimized Jews	10%	72%	17%	100%

tend to corroborate this bit of common knowledge. The table above shows distribution of the more and less victimized Jews with respect to their anti-Negro feelings.

The more victimized Jews show a greater tendency than the less victimized Jews to be found in either the strongly pro-Negro or strongly anti-Negro camp. In short, the feeling the Jewish subjects have of being victims of prejudice may lead either to sympathy or to antipathy toward the Negro group.

In addition to the evidence just cited, we recall that in our group Jewish subjects are the least prejudiced of all, though they are the most frequent victims of prejudice.

We conclude that a marked tendency exists for victims of prejudice to turn on other groups—or occasionally their own—with feelings of hostility and hate, just as the frustration-aggression hypothesis predicts. At the same time, however, some victims of prejudice tend to sympathize with other unfortunates.

Prejudices and the Sexes

The following table shows the distribution of prejudice in our three college groups.

It appears that at the time our study was made either the Dartmouth atmosphere, or else its process of selecting students, engendered higher prejudice scores. In estimating sex differences in prejudice, the safest basis for judgment lies in com-

Prejudice in Different Colleges

	Less Prejudiced	More Prejudiced
Radcliffe	67%	33%
Harvard	61%	39%
Dartmouth	34%	66%

paring Harvard and Radcliffe students, since the standards of selection are similar in the two institutions.

Does the Bigot Know His Victim?

Twenty slides, each showing the photograph of a male college student, were presented to our Harvard and Radcliffe subjects. They were asked, after seeing each photograph, to report whether they thought it was of a Jew or non-Jew. They were permitted also to say "Don't know." The pictures were selected from a five-year-old edition of the Harvard Senior Class Album. An equal number of Jews and non-Jews were included in the series, although the subjects did not know how many of each were presented. An effort was made to select faces that varied widely in cast. The order of the presentation on the screen was random.

Three findings were significant. (a) The average student correctly identified eleven faces out of twenty—in other words, he was wrong about as often as he was right. (b) Students with higher total prejudice scores judged more faces to be Jewish than did students with lower scores. In other words, they were more suspicious of the identity of the persons photographed. (c) Students with higher anti-Semitic prejudice scores were slightly more successful in identifying the Jewish and non-Jewish faces than students with lower scores. Their success was probably dependent on an ability to pick out the small number of Jewish faces which fitted the popular stereotype of how a Jew looks.

We are dealing here with an interesting instance of "social perception." People who are unprejudiced are less sensitive to the identity of those with whom they deal. The story is told of Tommy (white) aged six, who asked his mother if he might bring Sammy home to lunch someday from school. The mother, knowing that Tommy attended a "mixed" school, asked if Sammy was white or colored. Said Tommy, "I don't know, but I'll look next time I see him and tell you."

An age-comparison study of rumor transmission found that while 85 percent of adult subjects specified the racial membership of characters in a series of pictures, only 43 percent of grammar school children did so. As a rule, race is less important to children.

Many people, free from anti-Semitism, have felt bewildered and uncertain when someone asks if a friend whom they may have known for years is Jewish or not. Often the reply is, "Why, I don't know—I never thought about it." The question of the racial identity of other people is of small importance to the person free from prejudice. Yet it is of considerable importance to the bigot, and for this reason the bigot can more swiftly spot his "enemy"—if the "enemy" fits the picture which the bigot has built up of him.

Educated Parents: Tolerant Children

The analysis of students' prejudice scores reveals that they bear an appreciable relation to the educational level of their parents.

We already know that higher educational achievement on the part of an individual tends to be associated with a lesser number of hostile attitudes.

The novelty of the present finding consists in the demonstration that the favorable association between educational level and freedom from prejudice reaches back into the preceding generation: the more educated the parent the more free is the child from prejudice.

Early Memories

One of our questions asked each subject to write about the earliest memories of his experiences with minority groups he now disliked.

We found that with an increase in prejudice there is a steady and consistent rise in negative memories. We found, too, that anti-Jewish memories are far more common than anti-Negro memories among our college students.

Concerning the progressive increase of unfavorable memories with rising prejudice, two interpretations are possible: (a) Those who are more prejudiced actually have had more early distasteful experiences. (b) The selectivity of memory conforms to the pattern of current attitudes. Thus, the person who today is anti-Semitic, when asked to report some early memory concerning Jews, will select (or invent) an unfavorable incident.

It is very unlikely that the proportion of actual negative early experiences should follow so precise a relation with present prejudice. For this reason the second interpretation of our results is more justified than the first, although both may be correct. One recalls (or invents) early unfavorable experiences in order to justify one's current hostility.

Science Students Less Prejudiced

An analysis of major programs of study indicates that students specializing in natural sciences tend to be most free from prejudices. The trend is not conclusive, but so far as it goes suggests that social science is not doing its educative work well enough.

The Bigot's World

Many writers, including especially psychiatrists and psychoanalysts, have regarded prejudice as a pattern of life, claiming that the threads of hostility are lock-stitched into the fabric of personality. They argue that it is not enough to isolate single factors which seem positively to have caused prejudice, and to attempt to reinforce this or that particular factor in action programs. Rather, they say, remedial work requires therapy for the individual as a whole, a modification of his total outlook, a recasting of his style of life.

In accordance with this view, certain questions in our series were designed to tap the relationship between prejudice and the broader systems of belief held by our subjects.

We first asked the question, "To what extent would you agree with the following proposition: The world is a hazardous place in which men are basically evil and dangerous?" The results show that those who regard the world as a jungle are distinctly more prejudiced than those who do not.

Another question attempted to discover whether an authoritarian outlook entails group prejudice. It was found that those who feel that we do not have enough discipline in our "American way of life" tend to be more prejudiced.

Another of the broad questions endeavored to tap the temperamental factor of tendermindedness or sympathy. Those who say that they are "particularly prone to sympathize with any underdog" are much less prejudiced than those who say they are not so inclined.

A similar question read: "Often when I meet a Negro I am slightly ashamed of the fact that I think of him as a Negro, and not simply as another person. Yes——, No——." Those who admit such shame appear significantly more often in the less prejudiced half. We are reminded of the description of the American dilemma by Myrdal, the famous Swedish sociologist. Each American is susceptible to sharp conflict when his prejudices clash with his American creed. Those who are aware of the conflict and who suffer guilt feelings from it are closer to freedom from prejudice than are those who repress their shame and suffer no conscious discomfort. Shame is thus one step toward emancipation from bigotry.

This point is further fortified by the results obtained from the question which read: "Which of the following refers to you? (a) I don't think I'm prejudiced at all. (b) I know I have prejudices and regard them as natural and unavoidable. (c) I know I have prejudices and am somewhat ashamed of the fact." Of those who say that they think they have prejudices but regard them as "natural and unavoidable," 74 percent fall into the more prejudiced half of the general distribution. Of those who say they are ashamed of the prejudices they hold, 60 percent fall in the less prejudiced half.

Turning to another aspect of the "world outlook" of bigots and non-bigots, we are able to explore a theory advanced by Ichheiser. This writer suggests that anti-Semites may be individuals who, for some reason or other, are apprehensive of swindlers and attach this fear, because of traditional generalizations, to the Jewish minority. Answering the question, "If I were to express a greater fear of one of the following types of criminals I would say that I am more afraid of (a) gangsters, (b) swindlers," those who acknowledge greater fear of swindlers also revealed a tendency to be more anti-Semitic.

It turns out, however, that those who are more afraid of swindlers also have higher prejudice scores in general. Those who are more afraid of gangsters (may we not say, a more natural and normal fear?) are less prejudiced. Ichheiser's hypothesis is not, therefore, borne out precisely as he intended it. We find rather that people who are suspicious of being tricked in ordinary dealings are more prejudiced in general. Those who do not fear crafty dealings so much as direct physical attack (by gangsters) are less likely to be hostile toward minority groups. The suspicious philosophy of life engenders bigotry.

One other question serves to show likewise that prejudice is a reflection of a broader system of belief. The individual who disapproves of legislative attempts to improve the opportunities of minority groups such as the Fair Employment Practices Act is very likely to be prejudiced. Less than 11 percent of our subjects did, in fact, declare themselves against such legislative attempts, but of these, seven-eighths fell into the more prejudiced half of the general distribution.

The last finding points a finger at those who say they oppose remedial legislation because "you can't legislate against prejudice," because "laws won't change human nature," or because "you only make things worse by passing laws that won't be enforced." The fact is, that those who oppose legal remedies almost certainly do so because they themselves are bigots.

The findings reported in this section are clear proof that prejudiced responses are not dissociated from the total pattern of personal life. The person who views the world as a jungle, where the traveler must choose to become "the diner or else the dinner," who is prone to fear swindlers as a menace to his safety, who is authoritarian in outlook, who has no sympathy for the underdog, who rejects legislative attempts to protect minority groups, who feels no shame at his own prejudices—such a person includes prejudice in his style of life.

Why People Scapegoat

Man has a propensity to prejudice. This propensity lies in his normal and natural tendency to form generalizations, concepts, categories, whose content represents an oversimplification of his world of experience. His rational categories keep close to first-hand experience, but he is able to form irrational categories just as readily. In these, even a kernel of truth may be lacking, for they can be composed wholly of hearsay evidence, emotional projections, and fantasy.

One type of categorization that predisposes us especially to make unwarranted prejudgments is our personal values. These values, the basis of all human existence, lead easily to love-prejudices. Hate-prejudices are secondary developments, but they may, and often do, arise as a reflex of positive values.

Prejudice, if not acted out, if kept to oneself, does no great social harm. It merely stultifies the mind that possesses it. But prejudice expressed leads to discrimination. Generally, discrimination is based not on an individual's intrinsic qualities, but on "label" branding the individual as a member of a discredited group. It means separating forcibly and unjustly from our vocation, our neighborhood, our country, a person against whom we are prejudiced because he bears an unsavory label. Scapegoating differs from discrimination chiefly in the amount of aggression shown. It is when conditions are ripe—if frustration, ignorance, and propaganda combine in proper proportions—that discrimination breaks over into scapegoating.

These are the motivations behind discrimination and scapegoating.

Thwarting and Deprivation

People are often deprived of what they want or what they have. Such deprivation frequently results in anxiety and then in aggression. In scapegoating, such aggression is directed not against the *source* of the thwarting or deprivation, but against *any* object that happens to be convenient. Sometimes this scapegoat is at least partially to blame. But as a rule the scapegoat is made to pay not only for the deprivations in which he may have played some minor part, but also for frustrations of long standing, most of which have nothing whatever to do with the scapegoat. The cat sharpening her claws on the rug may annoy one, but after a bad day at the office, the kick one directs at the cat is likely to be more vicious than usual.

In times of social crisis our deprivations are multiplied many times: prices are high, so, too, are taxes; war threatens, we grow fearful. There is no direct action we may take to do away with these deprivations and threats, therefore we respond to our frustrations by scapegoating the government, the Negro, Labor, the "Reactionary," or the "Communist," or the foreigner, or the religion of some other fellow.

Guilt Evasion

Guilt feelings arise from the omission or commission of certain deeds. Such feelings may be relieved by blaming others for one's own sins. This projection of guilt onto others is the classic form of scapegoating. The goat carries our burden of sin. Hitler, the archscapegoater, blamed the Jews for precisely those crimes against morality and decency of which he himself was eminently guilty: conspiracy, war-making, demoralizing the social life of the community, sex perversion. It made Hitler feel innocent to heap his sins and those of his countrymen on the heads of an innocent group.

Such guilt projection is common. All of us are prone to this weakness. We never feel so innocent as when we "see" and criticize our own sins in other people.

Fear and Anxiety

1. Fear is an acute feeling that some specific danger threatens us. It may be reduced or dispelled by a preventive attack on what is considered to be the threat. Often in times of fear, we do not distinguish between real and pseudo-threats.

Our fear of spies and saboteurs in wartime led us to be unduly suspicious of foreigners and of innocent minority groups. For many months all of the Pacific Coast Japanese-Americans were held in internment camps, although few, if any at all, were really spies.

2. Anxiety is a vaguer anticipation of danger. Like fear, it represents a feeling of insecurity. It can be alleviated by rationalizations which take the form of verbal scapegoating.

In times of social strain, like the present, we may not actually intern a minority group. But it helps "explain" our vague anxieties to ourselves if we talk about the disloyalty, conspiracies, or threat of other groups. With all these menaces around us, why shouldn't we feel jittery and anxious? We talk and lie, and lie and talk, about such "dangerous" groups, hoping thereby to relieve our anxiety—or at least to justify it to ourselves.

Self-Enhancement

1. Feelings of *inferiority* may lead to scapegoating, in order that the individual may convince himself of his own value and strength.

The physically weak child, by verbally scapegoating another child, affirms his own strength. Or he may bully a still weaker child in compensation for his own feelings of inferiority.

2. The individual who feels *insecure* may obtain comfort by allying himself with a distinctive ("better" and "different") group, and thus bolster his ego.

It is no accident that hate groups take on the insignia of pomp and ritual. Nor is it strange that the mumbo-jumbo of the Ku Klux Klan, and of the Columbians, and of similar organizations should attract the insecure, the negligible, the nobodies of our society. An inflation of the ego results from joining with others who declare themselves better than some scapegoated group (of darker complexion, foreign origin, or different faith).

3. Very important as a factor in scapegoating is the demagogue's *desire for power*. Scapegoating is a useful tool of his attempt to gain power, for it helps to achieve unity among supporters. He tells them that the group they hate is in fact responsible for their troubles, and that by rallying around him, the leader, they can most effectively defeat their enemy. The demagogue creates a bogey in order to solidify his own leadership.

Conformity

Conformity makes for security. If everyone around us is given to scapegoating, and particularly those we value highly, then only by imitating their actions can we be fully accepted in the group whose approval we desire. Many Germans scapegoated the Jews to establish themselves as acceptable Nazis and thus avoid persecution for themselves. In our own society most people will agree with a bigot rather than contradict him to his face and thus lose caste in the bigot's eyes.

Conformity may be less deliberate than mentioned in the above case. An individual may conform to the current pattern of prejudice and persecution simply because he habitually imitates the prevailing folkways. He is scarcely aware that he is an imitator.

Children, as we shall see, are especially inclined to take over parental prejudices uncritically. They will unquestioningly accept their parents' assurance that Negroes are people with whom one just doesn't have social contacts.

Tabloid Thinking

Periods of social strain bring out vividly the helplessness every individual feels in the face of worldwide forces. He must seek to simplify the issues in order to make possible some understanding of this social chaos. It is less trouble to think of "the bankers," or the army "brass hats" as responsible for war, than to figure out its complex economic and cultural causes. Simplification of issues provides for economy of energy: if a person feels hostile and aggressive, it is more economical for him to attack one single obstacle in his path than to diffuse his attack upon the many true but not fully understood causes of his difficulties.

The psychological reason for tabloid thinking is well expressed by Thouless:

> The most finely developed mind reaches at some point the limit of the complexity it can grasp. With the majority of men, this limit is reached rather early. Long before it is reached a certain mental idleness steps in, making us tend to accept mental food well below the limits of our digestion.

An issue seems nicely simplified if we blame a group or class of people rather than the complex course of social and historical forces.

It is much easier to blame the Democrats or the Republicans

in Congress for some policy of which we disapprove than to look up the voting records of individuals and find out who is really to blame (undoubtedly a mixture of Republicans and Democrats).

In all cases we have discussed, we note that our aggression is "displaced." The group we blame is wholly, or largely innocent. Why is it that aggression is seldom directed against the *true* cause of the deprivation, fear, guilt?

Among the factors which may prevent the expression of aggression against the true provocator are the following:

1. We may be afraid that the party who is really to blame will retaliate and make it worse for us. When you are really angry at your boss, you cannot confront so powerful a being with your wrath, and so may turn on your secretary who is helpless against you.

2. We may be afraid that some other party will punish us for too direct an attack.

In some regions of the world, if a white man violates your interests in some way, you would certainly be punished for taking the law into your own hands, but you may store up your wrath and without fear of punishment take it out on some defenseless colored person who has the misfortune to cross your path.

3. We may have strong internal inhibitions against attacking the provocator. In our society, one may not hit a woman even if one has good reason to. One may, however, bottle up one's rage until an unprotected scapegoat appears.

4. Often, of course, the provocator isn't accessible: he cannot be reached because of external rather than internal obstacles. The schoolboy who ate up his pal's candy-bar is absent, so the deprived boy becomes irritable and aggressive toward some classmate immediately present.

5. Most important of all, when we are unable to understand the roots of our discomfort, we may turn to a preexisting prejudice to supply the "cause" and receive the wrath.

If a marginal worker loses his job, this economic frustration is no easier to bear simply because the worker is ignorant of its causes. Having a pre-existing prejudice against foreigners, or Negroes, this prejudice is allowed to grow into violence because it seems vaguely related to the complex issue which the worker does not understand. "Displacement" thus results from an illogical association of ideas.

6. Once in a while the respect or love we feel for the provocator may make it impossible to believe that he may be guilty.

In her eagerness to defend her son from an accusation, the mother may accuse the little boy down the street.

Top management in an industrial firm is remote and endowed with great prestige. Hence, it sometimes happens that a disgruntled worker fails to blame these policy-makers for the conditions that offend him but directs his venom instead at the foreman or even at his fellow workers.

Self-Knowledge

The cognitive processes of prejudiced people are *in general* different from the cognitive processes of tolerant people. In other words, a person's prejudice is unlikely to be merely a specific attitude toward a specific group; it is more likely to be a reflection of his whole habit of thinking about the world he lives in.

For one thing, research shows that the prejudiced person is given to two-valued judgments *in general*. He dichotomizes when he thinks of nature, of law, of morals, of men and women, as well as when he thinks of ethnic groups.

For another, he is uncomfortable with differentiated categories; he prefers them to be monopolistic. Thus, his habits of thought are rigid. He does not change his mental set easily, but persists in old ways of reasoning—whether or not this reasoning has anything to do with human groups. He has a marked need for definiteness; he cannot tolerate ambiguity in his plans. When he forms categories he does not seek out and emphasize the true "defining" attributes, but admits many "noisy" attributes to equal prominence.

Impressions that are similar, or that occur together, or that are spoken of together, especially if a label is attached, tend to cohere into categories (generalizations, concepts).

All categories engender meaning upon the world. Like paths in a forest, they give order to our life-space.

While they are often modified through experience when they no longer serve our purposes, still the principle of least effort inclines us to hold to coarse and early-formed generalizations as long as they can possibly be made to serve our purposes.

Categories normally assimilate as much as possible into their unitary structure.

They tend to resist change. The device of admitting "exceptions" serves to preserve the category (re-fencing).

Categories help us to identify a new object or person, and to expect from it (him) a certain kind of behavior to accord with our preconceptions.

Since categories may comprise a blend of knowledge (kernel of truth) as well as false ideas and emotional tone, they may reflect both directed and autistic thinking.

When evidence conflicts with categories, it may be distorted (through selection, accentuation, interpretation) so as to seem to confirm the category.

A rational category is built around the essential or defining attributes of the object. But nonessential and "noisy" attributes often enter into the category, lessening its correspondence to outer reality.

An ethnic prejudice is a category concerning a group of people, not based on defining attributes primarily, but including various "noisy" attributes, and leading to disparagement of the group as a whole.

When we think about causation, especially about causes for our own frustrations and ills, we tend to think anthropomorphically, i.e., we blame a human agency, often minority groups.

Categories that are two-valued, especially those that declare objects within a category to be all good or all bad, are easily formed, and readily control our thinking about ethnic groups.

It is characteristic of the prejudiced mentality that it forms in all areas of experience categories that are monopolistic, undifferentiated, two-valued, and rigid. In general, the opposite tendencies seem to mark the cognitive processes of tolerant people.

An important ingredient in a person's philosophy of life is his insight. Does the highly prejudiced person know that he is prejudiced? Does he know what forces are playing upon him? Does he know his underlying motives? Is he familiar with his own inner life?

Our subjects were asked to rate themselves on the extent of their own prejudice. The following table shows the relation of these self-ratings to *actual* prejudice as measured by objective scores on our prejudice scale.

Thus, the more prejudiced person has far poorer insight that the less prejudiced person. The latter knows how he stands in relation to the population at large; most of the former think (falsely) that they are only "average" or "less than average" in their prejudice.

Deficiency in insight on the part of the bigots is demonstrated in yet other ways. For example, we have already noted that those who say they were "not influenced" by their parents are, in the majority of cases, high in prejudice. The same is true of those who say they were "not influenced" in their schooling. Apparently the bigot does not know what it is in his environment that has influenced him, or indeed that he has been influenced.

The dull, unaware quality of the prejudiced mind is likewise demonstrated by Frenkel-Brunswik and Sanford who, in their work on anti-Semitism among college girls, employed methods quite different from ours. These authors, in characterizing anti-Semitic students, speak of them as "conventionally decorous," having "little familiarity with their inner lives," showing a "generally externalized orientation," expressing "devotion and obedience toward parents, and toward authority in general," and being "unaware of their underlying motives." In their explanations of events these anti-Semites stress externalized and physical causation and admire power and authority. They are suspicious of "plots hatched in secret by politicians."

By contrast those who are free from prejudice are given to "self-blame" and to admiring "humanitarians, artists and scientists." They possess varied interests and are "able to make critical appraisals of their parents." Girls low in prejudice likewise show less social anxiety and less superstition than do girls high in prejudice.

From all these results we conclude that prejudice is woven into the very fabric of personality. A style of life is adopted. It proceeds by rule of thumb. Categories of good and evil are taken over ready-made from the environment and projected upon the outer world, where they are endowed with attributes of power (authority to be obeyed, or menace to be feared). Self-criticism, self-knowledge, self-blame play little or no part in this categorical style of life.

A personality relatively free from prejudice, on the contrary, is apt to discriminate items within the environment, assigning praise or blame, sometimes here, and sometimes there, according to prevailing circumstances but not according to rigid rules. Alertness, flexibility, relaxation, characterize one's relations to the environment. And in the process of adjusting, self-blame and self-knowledge tend to play a prominent part.

There are important ethical implications in these remarks. We are saying that prejudice will be prevented only if the philosophical mold of one's life is sound. A sound mold requires a basic trust of mankind, freedom from the jungle outlook, from rigid categories, from the paranoid inability to take blame upon oneself or to adopt the point of view of the other fellow. A sound mould requires one to know the extent of one's own hostile attitudes, to feel some shame in having them, and to understand their probable roots in home environment, in school, as well as in one's own temperament.

It follows that schools, artists, and leaders of opinion should strive to interpret the environment in an articulated way. They

Self-Ratings on Prejudice

	Percentages of Actually Less Prejudiced	Percentages of Actually More Prejudiced
More prejudiced than average	3%	22%
Average	13%	38%
Less prejudiced than average	84%	40%
Total	100%	100%

should expose the fallacy of stereotypes, of ethnic generalizations, and prevent the settling down of the philosophy of the
jungle. At every step individualizing, discriminating, factual
judgments should be called for. Such influences, especially if
strengthened by a reasonable degree of social and personal
security, ought in time to lead our population to such surroundings that out-groups and in-groups will view one another with
less alarm, and with growing fellow-feeling.

America, on the whole, has been a staunch defender of the
right to be the same or different, although it has fallen short
in many of its practices. The question before us is whether
progress toward tolerance will continue, or whether, as in many
regions of the world, a fatal retrogression will set in. The whole
world watches to see whether the democratic ideal in human
relationships is viable. Can citizens learn to seek their own welfare and growth, not at the expense of their fellow men, but
in concert with them? The human family does not yet know the
answer, but hopes it will be affirmative.

CHAPTER TWELVE

FREEDOM OF SPEECH AND
FREEDOM OF THE AIR[1]

by ALEXANDER H. PEKELIS

No other aspect of the present controversy is of greater concern to the American Jewish Congress than the question of the consistency between its position in this proceeding and its unwavering attachment to the basic principles of the First Amendment. We wish to state at the outset that we are submitting the evidence we have gathered to the Commission[2] because we are fully satisfied that the acceptance of the theory upon which we have proceeded will result in a fuller protection of the basic aims of free speech and free press.

Our legitimate interest in the elimination of anti-Semitic discrimination and antiminority prejudice has never been conceived by us either as possessing an ideological autonomy or as having a possibility of achievement in a framework other than that of a free society. Our aims are full equality but we know that there can be no genuine equality where there is no freedom. Any short-range "gains" in the protection of minorities would be futile if they undermined the constitutional guarantees upon which the institutions of a free people are built. American minorities have no other weapon and no other hope than American freedom. The American Jewish Congress is no special-interest group and has never sought to achieve any illu-

[1] This is part of a pioneer brief in the use of law in the struggle for minority civil rights. It is an example of the creative and vigorous use of law and social action against bias and hostility shown to minority groups that was to score important gains in the succeeding years.—Ed.
[2] Federal Communications Commission.

sory "advantage" for the group it represents at the expense of
the general community. Jews, it has been said, are like other
people—only more so. Our special interest, if any, in this case,
lies in the fact that we are twice interested as Americans and
as Jews, in the preservation of our common and basic freedom,
freedom of speech, freedom of the press, and freedom of the air.

Free Speech: Competition and Monopoly

There are many mansions in the house of freedom. Freedom
of speech from a soapbox and freedom in a courtroom, freedom
of fair political comment and freedom of teaching, and freedom
on a picket line and freedom before a microphone are not necessarily coextensive in either scope or intensity.

To realize in what form the general principle of freedom of
expression can manifest itself concretely as the freedom of the
air, we must keep in mind the specific origin of at least one
of the prevailing conceptions of free speech. This conception
is indeed only one of the manifestations of the philosophy
of a great century which found another expression in the theory of the free market. Holmes' classic formula, "the ultimate
good desired is better reached by free trade in ideas—the best
test of truth is the power of the thought to get itself accepted
in the competition of the market" (Abrams v. United States),
still bears the clear indication of its connection with the doctrine of laissez faire and the underlying assumption that, in a
free struggle, the fittest will survive and the best idea triumph.
Just as free competition in the economic field will achieve economic equilibrium, social and political equilibrium will be
achieved by free trade in ideas.

Once adopted, however, the free market analogy must be
fully pursued. No advocate of economic laissez faire has ever
suggested that the theories of free competition and free play
of the laws of supply and demand should be left untrammeled
where no free market exists and where such free play is physically impossible. Adam Smith himself emphatically excepted
natural monopolies from the purview of a doctrine which identified economic freedom with freedom from governmental interference. Where monopolistic power threatens the helpless or

unwary consumer, the preservation of ideological symmetry and of a uniform definition of freedom will sacrifice the substance of liberty to its form. Faced with the fact of a natural monopoly and with the dangers of economic or intellectual exploitation, society, jealous of the substance of its liberty, will choose freedom through, not freedom from, its government. Laissez faire means let the market alone, but has never meant let the monopoly alone.

Freedom of the Air

For broadcasting purposes, the air is a natural monopoly or at best a natural oligopoly. The maxims calling for the "market test of truth," for laissez faire, or for "free trade in ideas" sound ironical when applied to a medium of communication whose very existence would be, in fact, destroyed if the basic condition of free trade—"free access to the market"— were preserved. The competitive test of truth has no meaning in a forum in which not even one thousandth of one percent of the total population is permitted to own a voice of its own.

These hard facts of radio life have long been recognized by our courts and commissions. The United States has already experimented with total "freedom" of broadcasting from governmental regulation. "The result was confusion and chaos. With everybody on the air, nobody could be heard" (National Broadcasting Co. v. United States). "The plight into which radio fell prior to 1927 was attributable to certain basic facts about radio as a means of communication. Its facilities are limited; they are not available to all who may wish to use them; the radio spectrum is not large enough to accommodate everyone." "Unless Congress had exercised its power over interstate commerce to bring about allocation of available frequencies the result would have been an impairment of the effective use of these facilities by anyone" (Commission v. Sanders).

The truth of the matter is that the regulation of broadcasting must be predicated on and related to not only the congressional power over interstate commerce, but also its power to protect freedom of speech as well. The freedom to listen is indeed the indispensable counterpart of the freedom to speak (Martin v.

Struthers and Marsh *v.* State of Alabama). The freedom to use the air for purposes of communication between those who speak and those who listen would be totally destroyed by unreasonable governmental inaction which, under certain circumstances, may become as grave an impairment of constitutional freedoms as affirmative action. "In enacting the Radio Act of 1927, the first comprehensive scheme of control over radio communication, Congress acted upon the knowledge that if the potentialities of radio were not to be wasted, regulation was essential" (National Broadcasting Company *v.* United States), which means that if no regulation had taken place, the radio potentialities would have been wasted and freedom of the air denied to the country. A federal statute dealing mainly with economic matters, the Sherman Act, has been construed on at least one occasion as aiming at the protection of "free trade of ideas" as well. A *fortiori,* the standard of "public interest, convenience or necessity" contained in an act dealing with communications only must be construed as aiming at the protection of interests "akin to, if not identical with those protected by the First Amendment" (Learned Hand, J., in United States *v.* Associated Press).

In the field of radio communications, just as in any other field of human interchange of ideas, the basic aims and purposes of the First Amendment must be preserved. On the air, as elsewhere, communication must give the people adequate knowledge of public issues; enable them to make a free (that is to say uncoerced, informed, and enlightened) choice between various opinions and courses of action; elevate their cultural, aesthetic, and moral level; and enable them to exercise their political rights intelligently and to fulfill their political duties and responsibilities. The aims remain the same and the substance of liberty remains identical. But the achievement of those aims in the field of broadcasting can be assured only through and with the help of governmental action and cannot be brought about by the simpler device of governmental abstention. Therein lies the great difficulty with which a government is faced when it is determined neither to usurp the ultimate choice which must rest with the people nor to abdicate its duty to protect that people from a similar, and less warranted, usurpation by monopolistic private licensees and their customers, who have received no popular mandate and bear no political responsibility to anyone.

Private Trustees of Public Interest

In facing this difficulty, the choice must be made between an affirmative or negative prior control, or censorship, of the specific content of the programs and the grant of a wide discretion to the licensees in the exercise of the public trust with which they have been vested. Congress has chosen the latter alternative and proscribed all censorship of specific programs by the Commission. The primary, the basic responsibility, the gravemen of the public trust, has been left not with the Commission but with the private licensee. The Commission has consistently recognized this special position of the station owner and has never attempted to substitute its own criteria of operation for those of the broadcaster: "Under the American system of broadcasting, it is clear that responsibility for the conduct of a broadcast station must rest initially with the broadcaster" (In re Mayflower Broadcasting Co.). The only form in which public regulation can manifest itself in the United States is the setting up of general criteria of performance and the selection of licensees who can be expected to live up to these criteria and be worthy of the widely discretionary public trust they are seeking from the Commission.

In this sense the Federal Communications Commission has much less power than other administrative regulatory agencies. The Interstate Commerce Commission may, for instance, prescribe not only the rates but the forms of service it expects from the operators. The routes, the schedules, the number of cars, the frequency of the stops, the type of freight, the extension or the abandonment of branch lines, and even the treatment of personnel are under the direct supervision of that agency. The Federal Communications Commission has no comparable powers. Once a license is granted, the licensee remains practically free in his operations. The Federal Communications Commission regulatory requirements and standards are general in form and the Commission has only a very limited power, if any, to issue specific directives to the licensee with respect to his program, be they affirmative in nature or couched in a cease and desist order. The Commission's only real possibility of assuring broadcasting in the public interest and of enforcing respect for its general standards of operation is to perform its paramount duty and function, that of selection of trustworthy licensees, with utmost care and on the basis of a thoroughgoing inquiry into the ability of the licensee to serve the First Amendment's basic aims of information, discussion, and enlightenment.

The United States has adopted a unique system of radio regulations unparalleled in other countries. It is a most daring experiment, substantially based on the belief that a properly selected set of private licensees prompted by the profit motive is capable of performing a delicate public duty and serving public interest, convenience, and necessity in an area as vital for the political and cultural life of a country as that of formation of public opinion and public taste through the medium of mass communications. The success or failure of this experiment based on a great confidence in responsible private enterprise will obviously depend on whether or not the Federal Communications Commission will succeed or fail in establishing minimum ethical and cultural standards of performance and in selecting licensees who can reasonably be expected to live up to such standards and thus serve the public interest. Where there is no genuine competition tending to control standards, the task of creating standards and checking the monopolistic power of the franchise holder falls upon the regulatory agency. To be able to select only those licensees from whom adherence to such standards can be reasonably expected, the Commission must inquire into the specific communications background of the applicants and examine their past performances, particularly in the areas of public information, education of public taste, and enlightenment of public opinion. The evidence introduced by the AJC bearing on the character of newspaper activity of one of the applicants, the *Daily News,* is an illustration of the inquiries which must precede an informed and successful selection.

A "Momentous Issue"

The *Daily News* has objected, however, to the introduction of such evidence and has claimed that it is inconsistent with the provisions of the First Amendment and hence inadmissible.

The objection of the *Daily News* cannot possibly mean that to deny it an FM license is to deprive it of free speech. Whenever there are more applicants than available channels, some of them will inevitably be "deprived of free speech." In the present proceeding, for instance, there are seventeen applicants for the available five channels; hence, there must be twelve denials of freedom to broadcast. Our evidence only tends to show that it is more proper to classify the *Daily News* with the rejected twelve than with the privileged five.

Since the *Daily News* claims no special privileges under the Constitution, its objection must deal not with the purpose for which our evidence has been introduced, but with its nature; not with the possibility of denial of a license, but with the reasons adduced for it. From the oral argument of its counsel it is apparent that the *Daily News* challenges the power of the Federal Communications Commission (a) to predicate its decision on the content of the broadcasts which may be expected from the applicants; (b) to take into account the applicants' past performances in the communications field, and more especially their activities as publishers or owners of newspapers.

This challenge goes, therefore, to what we have shown to be the very heart of the regulatory power of the Federal Communications Commission. By challenging the power to select applicants with a view to their capacity to serve the public need for genuine and unbiased information and debate, the challenge threatens the prime condition on which the American experiment in radio regulation hinges. Therefore, without raising the question as to whether or not the *Daily News* has, as a corporation, the right to invoke the protection of the First Amendment, we shall examine the merits of what the *Daily News* counsel correctly describes as a "momentous issue."

The Choice among Competing Applicants

We believe that the preceding discussion of the nature of the free speech doctrine and of the essential constitutional and political purposes of the Federal Communications Act are sufficient to show the socially dangerous and logically untenable character of the *Daily News* argument. We shall, at this point, add only the proof of their inconsistency with settled constitutional principles.

The United States Supreme Court has expressly stated that the Federal Communications Commission has broad regulatory powers: While Congress did not give the Commission unfettered discretion to regulate all phases of the radio industry, it did not frustrate the purposes for which the Communications Act of 1934 was brought into being by attempting an itemized catalogue of the specific manifestations of the general problems for the solution of which it was establishing a regulatory agency (National Broadcasting Company *v.* United States).

"The touchstone provided by Congress was the 'public interest, convenience, or necessity,' a criterion which 'is as concrete as the complicated factors for judgment in such a field of delegated authority permits'" (National Broadcasting Company *v.* United States).

The Supreme Court has also expressly repudiated the fallacious notion that the Commission is permitted to pass on the technological and financial qualifications of the applicants but not on their moral and intellectual competence; or that it may set up strict engineering standards of service, but no standards pertaining to the content and quality of service.

The Act itself establishes that the Commission's powers are not limited to the engineering and technical aspects of regulation of radio communication. Yet, we are asked to regard the Commission as a kind of traffic officer, policing the wave lengths to prevent stations from interfering with each other. But the Act does not restrict the Commission merely to supervision of the traffic. It puts upon the Commission the burden

of determining the composition of that traffic. The facilities of
radio are not large enough to accommodate all who wish to
use them. Methods must be devised for choosing from among
the many who apply (National Broadcasting Company v.
United States).

The Court thinks, in other words, that if it has to make a
choice, it may as well make an intelligent one. And no intelligent choice would be possible if, in the selection of prospective
trustees of a mass communication service, their intellectual and
moral qualifications were barred from the consideration of the
selecting agency. It is just because the Commission may not
directly control the veracity of the individual statements before they are broadcasted from a station (this would be censorship) that "caution must be exercised to grant station licenses
only to those persons whose statements are trustworthy" (In re
Western Gateway Corp.).

The Commission has often asserted its power to go beyond
the merely technical and financial qualifications. Its report,
Public Service Responsibility of Broadcast Licenses (March 7,
1946), contains a complete collection of legislative, administrative, and judicial authority on this point and it would serve
no useful purpose to set them forth again. From the Commission's first Annual Report (1928, p. 161) to the express statements of congressional leaders who, in introducing the 1934
Communications Act, called upon the Commission "to take the
steps it ought to take to see to it that a larger use is made of
radio facilities for education and religious purposes" (78 Cong.
Rec. 8843); from the discussions of the Commission and federal
courts calling for examination of the "nature and character of
the program service rendered" and asserting the "duty" of the
Commission "to take notice of the (applicant's) conduct" (Trin-
ity Methodist Church v. F.C.C.), to such rhetorical questions
asked by the Supreme Court as "how could the Commission
choose between two applicants" equally qualified from the financial and technical viewpoint "if the criterion of public interest were limited to such matters"? the authorities represent
one unbroken line tending to make sure that the Federal Communications Commission is put in the position of being able

to select licensees from whom service in the public interest can be expected.

It is noteworthy that the radio industry itself has not doubted the power of the Commission to take into account program service. In testifying before the House Committee on Interstate Commerce, the National Association of Broadcasters stated:

> It is the manifest duty of the licensing authority, in passing upon applications for licenses or the renewal thereof, to determine whether or not the applicant is rendering or can render an adequate public service. Such service necessarily includes broadcasting of a considerable proportion of programs devoted to educational, religion, labor, agricultural and similar activities concerned with human betterment (Hearings on H.R. 8301, 73rd Cong., p. 117).

The *Daily News* itself has not doubted the relevance of its broadcasting policies and has made ample representation as to the type of programs it intends to broadcast and as to the general civic policy it intends to follow. It was not until the credibility of the *Daily News* allegations, representations, and promises was challenged by our petition to intervene that the *Daily News* advanced the claim of inadmissibility of the policy and character questions it had itself put in issue.

Original Grants and Prior Conduct

We have thus seen not only that the constitutional objection raised by the *Daily News* cannot be directed against the mere fact of denial of a license to broadcast, but also that it cannot be directed against the examination of the content of the prospective service by the applicants.

It is equally obvious, however, that the *Daily News* cannot object to an inquiry into past conduct in order to test the qualifications of the applicants and the degree of reliance that can be placed on their promises. If a judgment about the future performance is to be made, past conduct must be considered. There can be, of course, no evidence of future conduct except that based on inferences drawn from the past. The exclusion of past conduct from the Commission's consideration would necessarily reduce the whole proceeding to a perfunctory finding that the applicant does now make certain allegations and promises, all investigation of the performance of past promises being strictly irrelevant!

This conclusion being obviously absurd, we must now examine the possibility that the original broad constitutional objection of the *Daily News* can be construed as contending only the inadmissibility of evidence of past conduct in fields other than broadcasting.

This contention, is, however, untenable mainly because it would of necessity limit the Commission's power of informed and intelligent selection to the renewal application, excluding it from the all-important field of original grants. The theory would violate the Act itself, which does not distinguish between grant and renewal and certainly does not limit the requirement of "public interest, convenience and necessity" to renewals. The counsel for the *Daily News* has put it very well when he says: "The Act says that the same principles shall apply on renewal as apply on original grants." He will not disagree with us when we say, conversely, that the same principles shall apply on original grants as apply on renewals: the applicant's past conduct must be taken into account in order to determine his willingness and ability to serve the public interest.

The broadcasting industry has also expressly asserted that no distinction can be made between renewals and original grants. In the already quoted passage of its statement to the House Committee on Interstate Commerce, the National Association of Broadcasters said:

> It is the manifest duty of the licensing authority, in passing upon applications for licenses or renewal thereof, to determine whether or not the applicant is rendering or can render adequate public service. Such service necessarily includes broadcasting . . . devoted to . . . human betterment (Hearings on H.R. 8301, 73rd Cong., p. 117).

If the capacity of a new applicant who has no broadcasting record to render public service by adequately informing the public and promoting cultural and moral human betterment is to be tested, how can it be done except by examining his conduct in fields other than broadcasting?

The Renewal Inertia

It will certainly not do to give every new applicant a chance to operate the station and then judge him by his performance. First of all, the problem of who should get that "chance," the *Daily News* or another applicant, would still have to be solved. Second, it would be wasteful and dangerous to make first grants indiscriminately and then try to remedy the situation by refusals to renew. Finally, the lack of discrimination in original grants would in itself lower the general level of performance, and the natural desire not to upset existing patterns too radically by frequent refusals to renew and not to destroy important financial investment would tend to perpetuate lower standards. The inevitable tendency in a renewal proceeding is to ascertain whether or not the license holder has abused its grant, not whether or not he is the best possible licensee available. The radio industry has done its level best to further that tendency. In the words of the American Civil Liberties Union, "The opposition of the industry is evidently based not so much on fear of censorship, as its spokesmen allege, as on the idea that radio licensees alone should have control, except in cases of flagrant misuse of their privileges" (Radio Programs in the Public Interest, American Civil Liberties Union, July, 1946). While obviously this approach must be opposed, it would be unrealistic not to count on the existence of a natural renewal inertia, and neglect the strongest and most direct means to assure service in the public interest, i.e., the selection of original grantees whose capacity for public service is beyond reasonable doubt.

Special Privilege for the Fourth Estate?

Having shown that it is impossible and legally unsound to limit examination of the applicants' qualifications to their past use of radio licenses, we are now faced with the minimum residual meaning of the *Daily News'* sweeping challenge, i.e., with the contention that the examination of the editorial policies or patterns of news selections of newspaper applicants for radio stations is a violation of their constitutional immunity from censorship.

If this contention were accepted by the Commission it would create the paradoxical situation that newspapers alone, among all applicants, would be exempted from the obligation to show that they are intellectually and morally qualified to become the holders of an important public trust. We are not here concerned with the desirability of concentrating in the same hands several major media of communication. It may or may not be desirable that a newspaper should own and control AM, FM, and television and facsimile channels. But it is certainly inconceivable that the position of power which newspapers hold in the field of public information and formation of public taste and opinion should be used as an argument for their exemption from an inquiry to which all other applicants would be subjected. After all, the First Amendment applies not only to newspapers. All citizens—and aliens as well, for that matter—enjoy the right of voicing their opinions and exchanging news and ideas. No one can be deprived of that freedom except in the case of a "clear and present danger of substantive evil." But everyone's use of that freedom can be examined when a selection must be made and a public trust confided to those who have given evidence of higher standards of accuracy, veracity, and objectivity. Newspapers have applied for and obtained a growing number of available radio channels. The whole system of inquiry into the intellectual and moral qualifications of original grantees would break down if so important a segment of licensees as the newspapers were granted an exemption. Newspapers—and the rest of us as well—may have a constitutional right to be prejudiced, biased, unfair, inaccurate, and, within limits, even mendacious. But none of us—not even newspapers—have a constitutional right to obtain a public trust despite such prejudice, bias, unfairness, inaccuracy, and mendacity. As Justice Holmes has put it once—and in a much more questionable case—"He has a constitutional right to talk politics, but he has no constitutional right to be a policeman" (McAuliffe v. Mayor of New Bedford).

A man may have a constitutional right to try to misinform, mislead, and miseducate the public as long as he operates in a competitive field open to anyone who wishes to pursue a different policy. But he has no constitutional right to be preferred in his demand for a monopolistic or oligopolistic public franchise in a field of a restricted communications media.

"Our Policy Will Carry Over"

Quite aside from the general principle of relevancy of newspaper policies, the *Daily News* has made the examination of its policies inevitable in the present proceeding. By the manner in which it has tried to support its application, it has, here again, put its newspaper activities and performances in issue and cannot now escape their examination. This is not, as counsel for the *Daily News* thought, a "technical question of cross-examination." It goes to the very heart of the *Daily News* direct case which is based on its newspaper performances and which must fail if evidence of these performances is withdrawn or if they are shown to fall below certain minimum standards. Section 8 of *Daily News* Exhibit 2 opens with the following solemn statement: "We consider the right to operate a broadcast station as a responsibility as well as an opportunity. Our policy on the *News* has been that we are a medium for public welfare and community interest, as well as a dispenser of news. This policy will carry over to the radio station."

The *Daily News* sought to persuade the Commission that its service as a newspaper justified the granting of an FM license. Since the *Daily News* relies upon such service as justification for the granting of the permit, and since it promises that "This policy will carry over to the radio station," it is eminently appropriate to examine its record to determine whether it has the qualifications justifying the granting of a construction permit. The presiding officer, in overruling the *Daily News'* constitutional objection, thus summarized the situation:

> I can only say, gentlemen, that the applicant, News Syndicate Co., Inc., has presented a case, a substantial portion of which does deal with the circulation of the *Daily News* through the country, the *Daily News* in public service, and

it has introduced evidence of its participation in many worthwhile and worthy causes. A good portion of the direct case constituted a presentation of material designed to show why the News Syndicate Co., Inc., would be qualified to run a radio station. It seems to me that it is perfectly appropriate to examine into what the applicant, who is a newspaper, does with his newspaper.

On cross-examination the *Daily News* executives made it clear that they would be responsible for carrying out the policies of the television and FM stations if those licenses were granted.

In answer to a specific question, F. M. Flynn, the general manager of the *Daily News,* stated that the *News* "undoubtedly would set the broad policies" of the FM station and has also, in substance, agreed that it expects to achieve there "the same standards of truthfulness and accuracy and freedom from bias" achieved in the *Daily News'* newspaper activity.

The examination of Carl Warren, the *Daily News* "broadcast editor" responsible for the WNEW copy, has thrown further light on the chain of continuity that links the *Daily News* to the WNEW newscasts and would link the latter to the FM station. In response to a question from the presiding officer, Mr. Warren testified that a news story originating in the Washington office of the *Daily News* is put on a "leased wire" in Washington and that it comes "right to (our) broadcast room in the *Daily News* building"; that "it arrives over a teletypewriter machine . . . and is available to the broadcast desk as well as to the telegraph desk and other desks which handle it." It is thus clear that the WNEW newscasts are fed from the general newspaper sources of the *Daily News.* In its turn, the staff of the WNEW newscast is destined to service the *Daily News'* FM station. "The same men who now service WNEW would service the newscast portion of the FM station, if the *Daily News* ever gets one." Mr. Warren who now "assumes responsibility for the copy on the WNEW newscasts" expects "to achieve the same high standards of accuracy and freedom from bias in the operation of the newscasts on the FM."

The record is replete with similar statements showing the close connection, asserted by the *Daily News* itself, between its past and present newspaper patterns, performances, standards, and policies and the future policies of the prospective FM station. It would serve no useful purpose to quote them all; they are but illustrations of the basic confession made by the *News* itself: "This policy will carry over to the radio station." Can it be seriously maintained that, before letting that policy "carry over," the Commission is entitled to find out what that policy is and to decide whether it is consistent with certain minimum standards of service in the public interest?

Drawing the Line: An Unreal Issue

What are then, finally, these minimum standards of public service to which the applicant for a franchise must be expected to adhere? We are fully aware that it is on this issue that the line must be drawn between an odious political or partisan censorship leading to the domination of the air by an oligarchic government-sponsored group, on the one hand, and an honest and impartial effort to assure genuine freedom of the air despite the technologically inevitable oligopolistic structure of the broadcasting industry, on the other.

The difficulty of drawing the line pursues every student of law from his first classes in Torts, where he tries to master the law of negligence, through the quicksands of equity to the problems of due process. At times the difficulties in drawing the line and the fear of arbitrariness by administrators, jurors, or judges are such that society is tempted to do nothing rather than do something imperfectly or crudely; to choose the legal certainty of inaction rather than risk an intervention based on discretion. Judges and administrators feel this escapist temptation frequently, but yield to it only rarely—and even more rarely with good results. In no case, at any rate, could the results of an "escape into the certainties of inaction" be more disastrous than in the field of minimum fair broadcasting standards. The inevitable result would be that a broadcasting of business, by business, and for business would take over a task entrusted by Congress to a responsible public agency.

Moreover, the hue and cry of people who do not know where to draw the line often refers to wholly imaginary difficulties which arise only in a few borderline cases, while the bulk can be adjudged without difficulty. It is clear, for instance, that the Commission would violate the First Amendent if it made the grant of a license dependent on whether or not a newspaper has supported a Republican or Democratic candidate or been for or against the New Deal. But is it not equally clear that the First Amendment is not violated if the grant of a public trust is made dependent on whether or not a newspaper is trustworthy, truthful, devoted to public welfare, and free from racial or religious bias? The fact that difficult borderline cases may arise here, as elsewhere, in the future is certainly no reason to deny a clear answer in the clear "polar" case.

Ex ore Tuo te judico

That this is a "polar" case is made fully apparent by the fact that the Commission could accept, without hesitation, the minimum fair standards and policies of decent broadcasting set forth by the *Daily News* itself. We certainly would be ready to stipulate that its past performances be judged exclusively on the basis of the criteria of its own making.

Whatever the difficulties of hypothetical cases, the *Daily News* can have no avowed reason to oppose an investigation based on criteria, the promised adherence to which has been set forth by the *Daily News* itself as the compelling reason in support of an application for a radio station. *Ex ore tuo te judico*, we say to the *Daily News:* we judge you by your own words.

The *Daily News* used effective language in its application when it said that "the important position of a radio station in the life of the community with its power to entertain, instruct and inform, necessitates a policy of operation that is progressive, instructive, entertaining, without bias and always in good taste." It has also listed the following pertinent "Basic Program Policies":

1. The name and word of God must be used with reverence.

2. Treat all races, colors and creeds fairly, without prejudice or ridicule.

3. Bar all profanity and salacious material from all productions.

4. Avoid detail of murder or suicide.

5. Avoid all forms of misrepresentation and false and misleading statements.

We accept these standards and submit that our evidence will show that in its past newspaper performances the *Daily News* has failed to live up to them, and that it, as a newspaper, has (a) indulged in inaccurate, malicious, and biased misrepresentations of the role of ethnic minorities in American life, and (b) has printed about them more unfavorable and less favorable news than the other New York City morning newspapers. We believe that these facts, if proved, would show a clear violation of the second and fifth principles stated by the *Daily News*, being respectively fair treatment of all races, colors, and creeds and avoidance of false or misleading statements. Therefore, and since the *Daily News* has promised, or rather threatened, that its policy "will carry over to the radio station," the grant of a franchise would not be, on the strength of the *News'* own standards, in the "public interest, convenience and necessity," and should therefore be denied.

Past Performances and Present Beliefs

We must, finally, call the attention of the Commission to the fact that our evidence deals not only with past performances of the *Daily News*, against which the objection of inadmissibility has been raised, but tends also to point out some of the present beliefs and conceptions of the *Daily News* executives with respect to what constitutes proper standards of radio performance. These beliefs and conceptions, admitted and confessed by the *Daily News* representatives themselves, are concededly admissible and relevant evidence. To the extent to which they contradict the initial assurances and representations of the *Daily News*, they are in themselves sufficient to show the lack of necessary qualifications and, because of their gross departure from the generally accepted standards of fairness, must inevitably lead to the denial of the *Daily News* application.

CHAPTER THIRTEEN

THE UNEQUAL TREATMENT OF EQUALS

THE SOCIAL CLUB ... CITADEL OF DISCRIMINATION[1]

by JOHN SLAWSON

Social discrimination is central to the problem of anti-Semitism, producing harmful results which go far beyond personal affronts and embarrassment.

Social discrimination can be a symptom of deep and dangerous hostility, temporarily suppressed or modified to fit the temper of the time, but nevertheless potentially explosive; it serves to perpetuate the infection of bigotry; it implies the inferiority and undesirability of an entire group of Americans; and these far-reaching implications and consequences require our particular attention.[2]

We in the American Jewish Committee have noted that the public temper showed, relatively speaking, a readiness for social change in the direction of reducing this seemingly polite form of anti-Semitism. Naturally the phrase "relatively speaking" is important. The national atmosphere created a likelihood of receptivity. We cautioned that this undertaking was delicate indeed and had to be pursued with full awareness of the pitfalls and

[1] An example of the American Jewish Committee's approach to prejudice and discrimination—one of the last barriers.—Ed.
[2] John Slawson, *Social Discrimination: The Last Barrier*, American Jewish Committee, 1955.

with much circumspection; but we viewed the malady as more dangerous than the treatment.

The Status Drive

We define social discrimination as "group conduct which excludes a person from social association solely because of ethnic origin, religion or race." There is another definition, very much to my liking, in the *Encyclopaedia of the Social Sciences:*

> "The unequal treatment of equals." The Encyclopaedia goes on to say that social discrimination involves "the alteration in competitive power of those presumed to possess a competitive status."

This view highlights a facet of our subject whose importance we perceive more clearly today than we did at first. I mean the striving for status, which we have come to recognize as a prime motivating force behind the urge to discriminate. To climb the social ladder, one steps on someone; to be one of the select group, one must exclude others. Their personal qualities, whether superior or inferior, are immaterial. In fact, quality affords virtually no protection against discrimination in the social sphere.

Yet, it is awkward to reject individuals who clearly meet all the qualifications of membership. It is much easier to exclude a whole group as a matter of policy; and Jews are readily an identifiable group and convenient victims.

Of course, not all barriers arise from this competitive status drive. In many instances, they do not necessarily signify hostility. Some may persist more out of habit or custom than because of bigotry.

Let us now see what has happened to social restrictions since 1955, when our program in this field was initiated.

The First Five Years

During this period, we have pursued a number of activities, both local and national. Virtually every chapter has discussed the problem. Many have produced important data on their communities as part of our study program. Some have taken first steps by "nudging the conscience of the elite leaders of the community." A few have taken definite steps.

The matters dealt with have included restrictive housing, service and fraternal organizations, resort advertising, college and high school fraternities. Two chapters have concerned themselves with programs in business and industry. Three chapters have made a start among the social clubs, one with notable success. There have been reports of encouraging changes—a softening of hostile attitudes toward social association with Jews.

In most communities, the number of exclusive neighborhoods has decreased; yet some bad pockets still remain, such as those in Bronxville, New York, and in fourteen or more neighborhoods in the District of Columbia and its suburbs. As Irving Engel pointed out about a year ago, in testifying at the New York hearings of the United States Commission on Civil Rights, officials occupying high posts in all branches of our government make their homes in Washington's restricted areas, thus knowingly or unwittingly sanctioning un-American practices. This situation has been the subject of several meetings between our Washington Chapter leaders and the Commissioners' Council on Human Relations of the District of Columbia. Let us hope these discussions will inspire vigorous steps to eliminate for all time this blot on America. For the capital city is the mirror of our country to the outside world.

Discrimination against Jewish students in college fraternities has now largely passed into history. Currently only two national fraternities out of sixty-one still have anti-Jewish restrictions, as compared with twenty-five about fifteen years ago. I report these figures with great satisfaction, for the attitudes and behavior patterns which fraternity members carry with them as they take their places in adult life ultimately help shape the dominant social patterns of our society.

The Trophy was a national television program dramatizing this problem, for which AJC received an award. You also know that improvement in the fraternity situation was greatly accelerated by the work of the National Committee on Fraternities in Education, with which we closely cooperated.

We should note, however, that the general lowering of barriers will not automatically open the door to the "executive suite." I am referring, of course, to the absence of Jews in top managerial, supervisory and policy-forming positions in the large corporations which are increasingly the pivotal centers of American business and industry. Although some progress has been made—as in one of New York's major banks—we still have a long way to go. For example, in a city which can be considered one of the main industrial centers of America, there is almost a complete absence of Jews in executive positions in the major companies—including two which do their recruiting from two eastern universities where 40 percent of the students are Jewish.

To gain a firmer grasp on the "executive suite" problem, which remains one of the most serious direct consequences of social discrimination, we are planning a number of studies. The first, to be conducted at one of the best-known graduate schools of business administration, will examine the recruiting practices of large corporations and the selection of industrial careers by students. Through this and similar undertakings, we hope to be able to penetrate the hard shell of corporate discrimination and reach the core of the exclusionary practice itself.

Considering the complexity of the issues and the understandable reluctance to plunge into such a sensitive field, I believe we have accomplished as much as could have been expected during this initial period. With clearer understanding, and aided by the improved national climate, we can now move forward on firmer ground, so that five years hence we may look back on our achievement with satisfaction.

The Primary Citadel

There is one area in which reluctance to act has been most pronounced—mainly, I believe, because the issues are beclouded with a great amount of misunderstanding. I refer to the social club. This subject burst into the headlines only recently with the reported unwillingness of the West Side Tennis Club in Forest Hills, New York, to admit the son of Ralph Bunche, Negro official of the United Nations and a distinguished winner of the Nobel Peace Prize.

The incident created a stir in the national conscience. An

editorial in the Mt. Kisco *Patent Trader,* read by residents in two of the wealthiest and most conservative counties in the United States—vigorously condemned exclusionary practices and suggested that the various country clubs in those two counties, all of which are exclusionary, should re-examine their admission policies.

A study of social discrimination in a northeastern city which we have called Alton, conducted for us by Vance Packard, author of *The Status Seekers,* contains some pertinent information. He says that in spite of discouraging stereotypes entertained by the "elite," nine out of eleven influential persons under sixty years of age, such as the chairman of the bank, the chairman of the university board of trustees, the top industrialist and the leading lawyer, could be characterized as "possible sword carriers in a discrete battle against discrimination."

Discussion by one of our own staff members with the president of one of the top clubs in New York also yielded encouraging responses that should, in the not too distant future, produce desirable results.

Yes, there is a certain amount of readiness for change even in this primary and most sensitive citadel of social discrimination. Nevertheless, it is still a citadel. While our chapter cities report non-exclusionary admission practices in at least half of their city clubs and about one-fifth of their suburban clubs, the most important clubs, both city and suburban, are almost all exclusionary. For example, among the twenty-eight university clubs throughout the country, only two have any Jewish members. In New York City, out of the top ten social clubs, only one has Jewish members. A leading member of that club, on learning that some of his fellow members had been selected on the basis of intellectual eminence, is said to have observed disdainfully, "Now isn't that a helluva way to run a club!"

Interestingly enough, our AJC membership has consistently rated the social-club problem low in importance. We have had similar reactions from certain of the Jewish community relations councils in different cities. And, recently, upon reading a paper before a convention of Jewish community relations workers, I met with the same response—that social-club practices are relatively unimportant. In my opinon, all of these low ratings simply reflect the fact that neither the nature of the problem, nor its significance, nor the treatment it requires, have been fully grasped.

No Question of "Rights"

Let me state unequivocally that the social club is an extension of the living room. It is private. Exclusion from a social club in no way violates the civil rights of any person—perhaps no more than exclusion from someone's living room would do so.

What we are challenging is not the right of free association, but simply the freezing of ethnic, religious or racial groups into a "caste" system. The practices implicit in such a system actually restrict the excluder as well as the one excluded. Reducing the opportunity for meaningful and enjoyable contacts narrows the social horizons of both alike. Insofar as the Jew is concerned, the imputation of group inferiority carries with it many detrimental and far-reaching connotations, not alone for him, but for his children and for those yet unborn.

We are talking about social responsibility and not legal rights. We maintain that congeniality is the *only* criterion that should govern social association. But congeniality depends on what a person is—his character, his social amenities, his intelligence, his cultural and other interests, his recreational skills—and not on the way he worships his God, the place where his father was born, or the color of his skin.

Assessments of personal worth and quality are certainly relevant to the criterion of congeniality. Impersonal blanket judgments are definitely irrelevant. Their meaning, in effect, is this:

> We have never met you. We don't know you. In fact we don't care what manner of man you are, what graces you possess, what distinction you have attained in your business or profession, in civic affairs, in the arts, in sports. It's enough to know you are a Jew. We don't want to associate with you.

Social equality will never be achieved if we are satisfied with tolerance on the basis of sympathy, or even justice on the basis of an alleged civil right. This is no task for the social philanthropist, nor for the lawyer as a lawyer, nor for the judge as a judge. It is not even in the province of a civil rights committee. It is a task for the social psychologist, the educator, the persuader. It means activating the fashion molder, the community pace-setter, to influence others in his social circle —to affect attitudes resulting in action, or action ultimately modifying attitudes.

The point, in short, is that improvement in this realm of social discrimination must come about through purely voluntary changes. Only when religious and ethnic differences among the American people are fully accepted as normal and no longer equated with either superiority or inferiority, and when each person is judged on the basis of his own worth, can social discrimination be ultimately effaced.

Acceptance of Religio-Ethnic Differences

During the past five years, we have made certain studies of the history of social discrimination not alone in the United States, but also in England and France, and comparative studies of social discrimination leveled at ethnic groups in the United States. The experience of the Irish in America is of particular interest.

Remember how the image of the Irish Catholic immigrant changed during the past half-century? Starting as the underdog, the "wild Irishman," the "comic Irishman," the "political-boss Irishman," he is able today to reach the highest pinnacle of the social ladder. The Irish have gradually become part of the folklore of America.

Today the Jews also are becoming part of America's folklore. Witness A Majority of One,[3] Only in America, The Goldbergs on television, the entry of Jewish colloquialisms into the American language. To be sure, Jews as an ethnic type are further removed than the Irish from the Anglo-Saxon majority. Moreover, the Irish, who started with peasant skills, rose much more slowly than the Jews in the business and industrial world,

[3] A 1959-1960 hit play by Leonard Spiegelglass about an American Jewish widow in Japan.

and therefore drew down upon themselves less hostility from their Anglo-Saxon competitors.

The contributions of religio-ethnic groups are increasingly regarded as part of the American pattern. An excellent example is Brandeis University—its faculty, its student body and its extra-curricular activities. Equally important, the Judeo-Christian tradition is increasingly accepted as part of the American heritage. I believe that, generally speaking, the social discriminator is not aiming at Judaism itself; it is largely at the point of contact—social, industrial and economic—that the Jew is rejected.

The "Upper Crust"

One of our chapters reports that "exclusionary discrimination against Jews in non-Jewish clubs appears to gain in rigidity in direct proportion to the financial, industrial and social eminence of its membership." In this connection, it is interesting to note the answers to the question we have asked in our public opinion polls, year in and year out, to measure social distance: "Suppose a Jewish family were going to move next door to you, how would you feel about it?" Usually, eight to nine out of ten say it would make "no difference." But when we separate out the upper income group, the proportion of "no difference" falls to six out of ten.

However, the so-called "upper crust" in the United States is probably still insecure in its social status—certainly when compared with its counterpart in England. Dr. Howard Brotz points out in his *Survey of the Position of the Jews in England* (1957) that while the upper middle classes may refuse to accept Jews in their country clubs, the traditionally aristocratic London clubs have no such restrictions.

One of the earmarks of American life today is the direct and immediate relation between the social club and the "executive suite." The president of one of the most important chemical concerns in the country, on hearing the remark that Jewish executives were not to be found in his corporation, replied that members of his executive family were also members of *the* country club. That was all he said. The chairman of the board of a bank, questioned in one of our studies, said bluntly: "An active banker belongs to every damn club in town. It is part of the game."

We have repeatedly heard that the club is the "business-man's castle." Some time ago, *Life* magazine pointed out that 73 percent of major corporations paid all or part of their key executives' club expenses.

The corporation itself is becoming a primary institution for the attainment of social status. In certain instances it is beginning to take over the position now occupied by the top club, setting in motion a reverse progression—from the "executive suite" to the "elite club." Attacking the problem of the "executive suite" directly, as we are now contemplating through research studies and related activities, should prove fruitful in providing new insight into the social club issue itself.

Suggested Treatment

From our experiences in communities where direct handling of the problem was attempted, we have learned that the only approach having a reasonable chance of effectiveness consists of informal, non-aggressive moves with one or two club leaders, who themselves will take the initiative in pressing for changes in policy. Pressure tactics, far from yielding fruitful results, will in all probability boomerang.

This was well illustrated in one of our chapters where the president of the State Bar Association took the initiative in reforming his club's practices. He told the chairman of our chapter that if there had been any publicity or legal action or outside interference, the proposal to accept Jews as members would have been defeated by united opposition instead of being approved.

The approach used by Dr. Bunche at the West Side Tennis Club is rarely successful. It was a great achievement, but should not be ventured except in a comparable situation, where the individual taking the initiative is a person of exceptional distinction and the club is of a quasi-public nature.

Of course, joining a social club does not always mean full acceptance. Despite admission, one can be very lonely. Jews cannot expect to be comfortable with Christian members if they have not come to know one another first through informal home entertaining and friendly intermingling in community affairs. Personal friendships appear to be a more powerful motive than any abstract sense of justice in getting barriers removed.

We must recognize the deep insecurity which lies behind the urge to exclude, and we must anticipate the likelihood that our opposition may be a highly educated "upper class" group, articulate and persuasive in rationalizing individual rejections. In whatever manner we decide to handle the subject, we must be sure it is broached by attacking discrimination itself, not the discriminator.

We should also be willing to embrace the concept of gradualism and to accept as a practice, not as a policy, the "benign approach"—that is, the gradual admission of a small number at a time. Repugnant as this may be in principle, it can be very effective in practice. It must not, of course, be used as a stopgap. Providing the effort is honest, progress may be indicated if just a crack is opened and not the entire door in the beginning.

Our staff specialist, who has had more to do with these matters than perhaps anyone else in the AJC, puts it very precisely:

> The kind of "force" to be employed is more properly a matter of chemistry, requiring a catalyst to accelerate internal movement by Gentiles, rather than physics, characterized by the pressure of external force.

These barriers are not coming down overnight. They will give way gradually, very gradually indeed. When, after a prolonged record of exclusion, there is a willingness to accept at least one or two Jewish members on merit, we would be wise to err on the side of generosity in evaluating the motives that inspired such a move.

An important detail often comes up: "What do I do when invited as a guest to an exclusionary club?" There is no definite answer, for much depends on the circumstances in each particular case. In general, however, experience indicates that a distinction should be made between an invitation from a friend or acquaintance to come as his personal guest, and an impersonal call to attend a civic function of some kind.

A social invitation from an individual usually indicates a wavering of restrictions, an inclination toward acceptance of Jews which should by all means be encouraged. Until recently, for instance, members of an exclusive club in an Eastern seaboard state hardly ever had Jews as guests—simply because Jews were not considered acceptable, even as guests. Now they have begun to invite Jews quite often. It is our feeling that the breaking down of at least one barrier, and the frequent presence of Jews, will eventually help bring about further change. Under appropriate conditions, depending on the relationship with his host, the guest might even mention that Jews are not eligible for membership—simply to throw a pebble which may set off some ripples.

But when an organizational meeting or civic function is arranged at an exclusionary club, a different issue is presented—quite different from the case of the individual host extending hospitality toward an individual guest. An invitation to a meeting is no token of cordiality. It simply says: "For these special, non-social purposes we don't mind having you in the crowd since we open our facilities to the general public on such occasions."

In responding to this impersonal gesture, one might well find opportunity for clarifying the situation in an unmistakable way—perhaps in a letter that read something like this:

> If you will change the place of the meeting from a club to which members of my faith are not admitted, I shall be very glad to attend.

To repeat: neither this advice nor any other can apply to every situation. There are many possibilities for effective action—all depending on the circumstances and the personalities involved in each particular instance.

Practices of Jewish Clubs

If we are to deal seriously with social discrimination, we must become concerned with the reverse side of the picture—exclusion by the Jewish club of non-Jews.

We can no longer shut our eyes to this phenomenon. It has

recently provoked a number of controversies. I do not mean to imply that if Jewish clubs open their doors, the Christian clubs will do likewise. But I do believe our action will have influence in the long run. Furthermore, we can hardly pursue our goals on any consistent or justifiable basis if we persist in keeping up our own bars. This problem persists in Jewish fraternities. While, as I said before, very few restrictions remain in the general fraternities, there are many in Jewish fraternities.

There is an assumption that failure to admit non-Jews cannot be termed exclusionary, since it is simply the result of their lack of interest in seeking to join. However, a genuine probe in most situations would disclose that an informal policy of barring non-Jews exists. This happened in two clubs on the West Coast, where the issue came up because applications were received from Christians. In both instances the problem was clarified and eventually solved.

Another club on the Coast has adopted an explicit open membership policy; some twelve Christian members are now in the club.

In a Southern city, at a chapter meeting on social discrimination, one of our AJC leaders stated that the leading Jewish club had a restrictive policy, as evidenced by its refusal several years ago to accept a Gentile who was in every respect eligible for admission. In that city, as a matter of fact, most country and city clubs are either 100 percent Gentile or 100 percent Jewish.

What are the reasons for this behavior on the part of Jewish clubs? Of course, it may have started because of the practices in Gentile clubs. But, should this condition persist? Can it be defended on any grounds, such as congeniality, group survival, fear of intermarriage? Certainly it is incompatible with Jewish integration into American life to claim a right to privacy in this regard. We have already dealt with this claim on the part of Christian clubs. The same degree of social responsibility must be expected of us. Insofar as group survival is concerned—intermarriage and related considerations—we should recognize by now that we cannot preserve the Jewish group by walling in its members—certainly not in a free and open society.

We also have discussed elsewhere[4] the necessity to take risks in the interest of preserving freedom; likewise the need to create for young and old within the Jewish group the kind of situation that will cause a Jew to be one—not involuntarily, not because of hostiles from without or coercions from within, but because he wants to.

Changing the policy of Jewish clubs may not of itself assure immediate changes in other private clubs, but it would remove one basis for rationalizing anti-Jewish restrictions. In the long run, the elimination of barriers by Jewish clubs would prove very helpful in reducing all forms of social discrimination.

A Task for AJC

Now, in conclusion, I trust that what I am about to say will not be misunderstood. The social-club aspect of social discrimination—and, as a matter of fact, practically all of the problems in this area that do not relate to liberty, but perhaps more to fraternity—should not be handled as civil right matters, nor through the processes of campaign, legal procedure, or external coercion. Certainly, no "official" approach should be utilized.

In all modesty, may I say that the AJC is very well adapted by virtue of its membership and staff to pursue our goals in this delicate area. It is an undertaking that requires long-range, affirmative, persuasive actions. Our leadership has the requisite contacts and personal friendships in various communities in this country to initiate actions discreetly and tactfully with those referred to as the "upper crust."

What is now required is for us to be willing to risk the inconvenience of trying to do something about the problem, for the sake of eliminating the problem itself. Let us here and now resolve to dedicate our efforts to overcome this deceptively unobtrusive form of anti-Semitism, lest in the long run it prove our Achilles heel.

[4] *Trends in the American Jewish Community.* Second printing, February 1960, p. 23; *Integration and Identity.* March 1960, p. 0f.

CHAPTER FOURTEEN

THE JEWS IN MIDDLETOWN[1]

by N. C. BELTH

Lancaster, Pennsylvania, had its equanimity upset during Brotherhood Week. A handful of civic leaders, Jews among them, refused to attend a reception for the town's guest of honor at the town's leading club which, controlled by the social elite, discriminates against Jews. Mrs. Eleanor Roosevelt, the guest of honor, also absented herself. The socially elite, their gesture of *noblesse oblige* in dropping the bars of discrimination at their club for a few hours thus rejected, felt outraged and angered.

They should not have been surprised. What happened in Lancaster happens often in Middletown, U. S. A.—although not always under such spectacular circumstances. Jews who take a lead in community and civic affairs frequently turn their backs on social invitations to the "restricted places." They do so as an act of resentment against the norm of community life that prevails in a particular kind of middle-sized American town.

What these norms are—and particularly what the status of Jews is in the Middletowns of America—is revealed to some extent in recent studies of a Cornell University intergroup relations project financed partly by the Anti-Defamation League.

Define Middletown as having a population of 25,000 to 100,000

[1] The Anti-Defamation League of B'nai B'rith is the third major group contributing significantly to the struggle for civil rights. It has made numerous invaluable studies such as the following important examination of the effect of discrimination on the ways of life in an average middle-sized community.

The assessment of its executive director, Benjamin Epstein, of the current status of anti-Semitism in the United States should be compared with the views of Will Maslow, executive director of the American Jewish Congress in his essay "Is American Jewry Secure?"—Ed.)

and a Jewish population of from one to three percent of the total. What happens to Jews in such towns? To what extent do they live to themselves and how wide is their participation in the life of the city? Are they accepted by non-Jews? To what degree and in what areas?

Jews form a separate community in Middletown in that they have a shared culture and heritage, a sense of psychological unity and an established organizational and leadership structure of their own. (Not true for all Jews, of course. Many have only a blurred sense of the culture and little of the unity.) This does *not* mean a separate community in the physical sense—that is, within one part of town. Nor do Jews differ in that other prerequisite of "community"—its economic structure.

Middletown's Jews are in a sound economic position. They are predominantly in the middle and upper classes and, in almost all instances, are better off than a cross-section of families in the community at large. There are relatively few areas of economic life from which Jews are excluded.

But once this has been said, the exceptions can be noted. If the town's economic power rests in the hands of an historically entrenched old guard, Jewish participation is almost nonexistent in prominent locally-owned industries and in local banking, finance, and law firms which draw their business from these industries. There are also few Jews in the labor force and, therefore, few in labor union leadership. Jewish concentration thus comes in commercial enterprises and the professions —the self-employed occupations not subject to employer discrimination.

Middletown Jews play a minor role in local politics. One sample of 47 cities of 50,000 to 100,000 population shows that only seven have as many as two Jews in elected office; two-thirds of them have none. Jewish participation is somewhat larger in appointed office. Generally, the larger the city, the more likely Jews are to hold public office.

A number of elements enter into this low level of participation. The likelihood is that Jews find it to their economic interest not to participate in partisan causes. Nor do they have any great tradition of politics as an occupation. The anti-Semitic factor, however, is not to be discounted in the party councils that select candidates. Only when the Jewish population becomes large enough are these anti-Semitic tendencies outweighed by practical considerations.

But if its political role is minor, Jewish participation in civic affairs and community services keeps growing. In part, this reflects the rising Jewish economic position, a fact which is given due recognition by the old line leadership of community organizations and causes. Jews participate on the boards of community chests in a majority of communities of all size levels, even where the Jewish population is less than one percent. Communities that score low on social acceptability of Jews, score high on Jewish participation in community affairs. This works almost in inverse ratio—the more that Jews are excluded from socially elite organizations and residential areas, the more they seem to be in positions of civic and social service leadership.

Jews of Middletown are more likely to be "joiners." A study of an upstate New York city shows that 90 percent belong to some organization and that half belong to organizations of a general community nature. Contacts between Jews and Gentile occur in "lodge" organizations and in civic, charitable and business groups. On the whole, these contacts are pleasant and comfortable, only occasionally disturbed by feelings of social distance or anti-Semitism.

Jews are more sensitive on this score. Among those belonging to mixed organizations, 39 percent said that Gentiles felt "differently" toward them than toward their own group. Only 9 percent of the non-Jews said that this was really so. One in twelve among the Jews said that he knew of instances in which Jewish members had been treated differently from others. Yet, this has not prevented the Jews from participating widely in this city's organized community life—except for the socially elite groups and the political, labor and church organizations.

Intimate social friendships, however, are on a very restrictive basis. Most Jews in Middletown, U. S. A. seem to have all-Jewish social circles. In the special sampling, this was true for eighty-five out of one hundred and fifty families. Only eight families participated in a predominantly Gentile social group and for ten others the Gentile participating in Jewish circles was the spouse of a Jew.

What are the factors in this pattern of exclusiveness? About 15 percent of the Gentiles who have an all-Gentile social group say they would not like Jews becoming part of it. But two-thirds say it would make no difference. In part, the perpetuation of the exclusively Jewish social group is caused by the way the social machinery works. Of seventy men, only twelve belonged exclusively to Jewish organizations. But thirty-four among their wives maintained this exclusion. And it is normally the wife who sets the social pattern.

Underlying many of these processes is the strong Jewish taboo on intermarriage. Over one-half of this town's Jews said they would "find it distasteful to have a Gentile marry someone in their family."

Nevertheless, this is not the whole picture. When asked about socializing with their closest Gentile contacts, over half of the Jews in the special study said that they "visited back and forth in each others' homes fairly regularly." Another 22 percent said they had "done something social together outside the home." Thus, about three-fourths of the Jewish community did *some* socializing with at least close Gentile contacts. The most fruitful friendships were those made in organizational life. Neighborhood contacts seem to be at least productive of social mixing.

About 20 percent of the Gentiles, when asked how they feel about mixing socially with Jews, said they would not like it. But the general impression was that many persons, when given an opportunity, interact in a friendly way despite articulated attitudes of anti-Semitism. The more prejudiced a person is and the closer the relationship with a Jew, the more psychological pressure there seems to be for the Gentile to exempt his friend from his anti-Jewish prejudices.

It is the absence of contact opportunities between Gentiles and Jews more than anti-Semitic prejudice that places a serious limitation on the formation of mixed friendships. Jews who socialize with Gentiles express more friendly feelings toward them, but avoidance patterns tend to develop when there are rebuffs which make a Jew feel ill at ease.

Social insulation appears to intensify social pressures within the Jewish community. Public opinion is rapidly mobilized on Jewish community affairs. It operates as a strong pressure to conform. And strict sanctions operate to maximize financial contributions to Jewish causes.

Another result of the encompassing primary relationships within the Jewish community is the emotional impact of ideological positions about such issues as Zionism or the assimilation of the Jews that are in direct conflict with one's own position. It is disturbing to be in conflict on deeply held values with close friends. But because of the strong need for interpersonal harmony in keeping the Jewish community functioning smoothly, these ideological differences tend to be repressed in favor of an apparent unanimity even though such unanimity does not exist.

There is, of course, no single way in which the Jews of Middletown, U. S. A. react to the sociological and economic conditions of their existence as a readily defined minority group in a Gentile community. It comes down to the individual and what is important to him; how he relates himself to other Jews and to the majority of non-Jews; how he meets the disabilities and the advantages of his Jewishness. Dr. John P. Dean, in analyzing the researches of the Cornell group, attempted to delineate a number of images of Jews in terms of their psychological adjustment to life in Middletown. Among the more comfortable forms of adjustment he found these:

> The Jew who doesn't care what Gentiles think of him. He is sustained by the life of the Jewish community and has a strong attachment to Jewish traditions.

> The Jew who desires status in both the Gentile and Jewish groups and feels that he has won the respect of both. He participates in the life of the larger community. Any socializing he does with Gentiles is largely selective to protect him from direct encounters with anti-Semitism.

> The Jew who is not concerned with what the Jewish community thinks of him, since he has disassociated himself from it. He doesn't necessarily deny being Jewish but it is not likely to come up since he has found the Gentile group

where he is accepted. His participation in the Gentile group also tends to be selective.

The Jew whose self-esteem is based not on what the Gentile and Jewish groups think of him but on something else, such as a career in the arts, in science, or an ideological cause or occupation that places him in a group where he need not be confronted with decisions on "Jewishness."

Among the less comfortable forms of adjustment, Dr. Dean found these:

The Jew who wants to be accepted by both Gentile and Jew, but for some reason feels rejected by the Jewish community. Perhaps he feels guilty about having deserted the Jewish community. If the psychological stress about this is considerable, he may pass for Gentile to keep Jews from activating his guilt.

The Jew who wants to be accepted by both groups and has succeeded in gaining the respect of the Jewish community. He participates in the community-at-large, but because of rebuffs he feels looked down on by Gentiles. He is bitter about restrictive practices.

The Jew who cares only for status in the Jewish community but has been rejected, perhaps because of an ill-becoming expression of his Jewishness that alienates other Jews.

The Jew who wants acceptance from both groups and feels rejected by both. He is the most marginal of any of the types and is probably in the most difficult psychological situation. He is deeply ambivalent about having left the fold, but has not found acceptance among Gentiles.

But in the final analysis, the average Jew in Middletown finds that he has only one and not four forms of "comfortable" adjustment as an individual—granting that he doesn't want to isolate himself. He cannot "adjust" if he hasn't the acceptance of his fellow Jews. Nor can he be comfortable if he has not learned to cope with anti-Semitic reactions he might meet among non-Jews. He can live happily only if he learns to become a "comfortable participator" in both the Jewish and general community.

CHAPTER FIFTEEN

ANTI-SEMITISM TODAY:
AN EPILOGUE

by BENJAMIN R. EPSTEIN

Times and patterns change in the United States, even for so unyielding a phenomenon as anti-Semitism.

Twenty years ago, anti-Semitism was reaching a peak of intensity in America. Goaded by the successes of the Nazis under Hitler, Christian Fronters, Bundists and others were quite capable of abusing and beating Jews in the largest cities of the country. Those were frightening years; even the most unprejudiced of people often seemed hesitant to fight the tide. The halls of Congress, too, heard their share of anti-Semitic vituperation. The Jews, so the usual charge went, were enemies of the Republic—after all, they were trying to get us into the war to save the skins of their brethren abroad.

Ten years later, the picture had changed considerably. The immediate postwar years brought a renewed dedication to the principle of equality for all men. The impact and meaning of genocide, the wartime spirit of unity, a generally higher level of sophistication on the matter of "race" helped bring this about. The late 1940's saw the formation of human-relations councils and "unity" groups throughout the country. They were the years of the launching of vast human-relations education projects, of the passage of effective civil rights legislation in many states. The nation's mass media, too, communicated the feeling—Hollywood, for example, turned out a whole cycle of films fighting prejudice, such as *Gentleman's Agreement, Lost Boundaries* and *Crossfire.*

316

The picture today once more is different. Now there is little overt anti-Semitism and few cases of the violence that occurred twenty years ago. But much of the brave-new-world spirit of ten years ago is gone, too. Today, anti-Semitism flows a quiet course, hidden, subtle and pervasive, just as harmful—and even harder to fight.

It could have been much worse. Sustained high production and employment have weakened the economic basis for the scapegoating of Jews. The tensions of the cold war could, conceivably, have had serious effects on the status of the Jew in the United States; the effort to label all Jews as Communists or Communist sympathizers was, potentially, a real danger to their security. Strangely, despite the furious drive of professional anti-Semites, the equation never seemed to stick.

Anti-Semitism today is harder to cope with because, in a sense, it has gone underground. Civil-rights laws and educational campaigns have done their work; they take a toll of overt manifestations of anti-Semitism, but they have a long way to go before they affect basic attitudes as well as behavior. Anti-Semitism may be, to some extent, out of fashion publicly, but it is still practiced. Those who practice it may be defensive or guilt-ridden, their acts more devious.

This is evident in the methods used to maintain policies of exclusion described in detail elsewhere. That all these practices of discrimination take heavy toll, our studies make abundantly clear—particularly now, when social and economic status seem to have a closer relationship in American life than in previous eras. We are constantly reminded that this is the age of big business, big industry and the organization man. Personnel selection for big business has become a science of sorts. New tests scrutinize far more than just the routine job qualifications of an executive. Now they probe into a man's golf and drinking scores —as well as those of his wife. An employee's relationships with his parents, his athletic aptitudes in school, his table manners, dress and clubs are all matters of concern. For better or worse, this calls for a type of conformity or at least adjustment, to the prevailing ways of a community. If you are denied membership in the social organism because you are Jewish, you are apt to be denied a job which demands such membership as a pre-requisite.

The Organization Man and many other Americans have taken to life in the suburbs. There is little basic change in people's intergroup attitudes just because they travel on the New York Central instead of the IRT; social discrimination is becoming a matter of pressing concern in many areas of suburban life. Unchecked, it can conceivably bring about a new type of segregation—marked by sycamore-laned ghettos and "For Christians only" communities, without even the nodding relationships Jewish and Christian neighbors once had when meeting in their apartment-house elevator.

These are some of the dimensions and specifics of the problem of combating anti-Semitism today. The problems are often elusive, but to say merely that there is hope for their solution would be unfair to all American experience. Our capacity for social development is unlimited. Barring some major world catastrophe, American anti-Semitism will continue to decrease. You can tell it in the attitudes of our cultural, religious and political leaders. You can tell it in the great growth of community organization in the United States, the process of people banding together on behalf of many democratic causes. You can tell it in the development of modern education in the United States, which, with human-relations education as its base, is capable of producing a generation of Americans emotionally rich and fulfilled, incapable of joining a hate movement or even tolerating one.

But the phenomenon of anti-Semitism is deep-rooted; it will not die in our time. And before it does it will claim many more victims.